Vedic Hymns

Vedic Hymns

Prayers for Divine Blessings

Devarshi Sharma

MLBD PUBLICATIONS

Motilal Banarsidass Publications

MOTILAL BANARSIDASS
PUBLICATIONS
4741/23, Ansari Road, Daryaganj, New Delhi - 110002 (India)
Email: *mlbd@mlbd.com* | *sales@mlbd.com* | *exports@mlbd.com*
Website: *www.mlbd.com*

Vedic Hymns
by
Devarshi Sharma

First Edition Published in 2023

Published in India by Motilal Banarsidass Publications

ISBN : 978-93-91759-61-2 (PB)

Printed and bound in India

ॐ गं गणपतये नमो नमः

नमो व्रातपतये नमो गणपतये नमः प्रमथपतये नमस्तेऽस्तु
लम्बोदरायैकदन्ताय विघ्नविनाशिने शिवसुताय श्रीवरदमूर्तये नमो नमः ॥

[कृ० यजुर्वेदीय गणपत्यथर्वशीर्ष १०]

Our Gracious Shri Gurudev

परमपूज्य बाबा श्री नीब करौरी जी महाराज

MOST REVERED BABA NEEB KARORI JI MAHARAJ

ध्यानमूलं गुरोर्मूर्ति पूजा मूलं गुरोर्पदम् ।
मंत्र मूलं गुरोर्वाक्यं मोक्षमूलं गुरोर्कृपा ॥

ॐ पूर्णमदः पूर्णमिदं पूर्णात्पूर्णमुदच्यते।
पूर्णस्य पूर्णमादाय पूर्णमेवावशिष्यते॥

वेदमूर्ति तपोनिष्ठ
आचार्य प्रवर पं० तपेश्वरी प्रसाद "वाणी भूषण"
Embodiment of Vedic-scriptures
Ācārya Pt. Tapeśwarī Prasād "Vāṇībhūṣaṇ"

This book is dedicated to
MY HIGHLY REVERENTIAL FATHER,
MY CHIEF INSPIRATION.

ॐ सहनाववतु । सह नौ भुनक्तु । सह वीर्यं करवावहै
तेजस्विनावधीतमस्तु मा विद्विषावहै ॥
!! ॐ शान्तिः शान्तिः शान्तिः !!

मातु श्री

श्रीमती राजरानी देवी

My Reverential Mother

ŚRĪMATĪ RĀJRĀNI DEVĪ

Introduction

Since time immemorial a lot has been penned down on the Vedas by the most venerable, great and divine Ācāryās; one cannot fathom its depth. Though all that is superb, yet human mind goes on, ceaselessly, and never stops at any point of time; and I also strongly felt an urge to venture on it and do something differently. This work is nothing else other than the grace of my "Āradhya", the blessings of "Gurudev" and that of my revered father, who was a renowned scholar of the Vedas and, especially, the Upaniṣads. I know well I am nobody even to add an iota from my own side, as I know little Sanskrit, and more so, the Vedic one.

In some very special given personal conditions, I was seeking solace in our scriptures. My conviction has always been that our ancient scriptures alone have power to comfort an aching soul. I was, therefore, surfing across in the midst of a wide selection of books available in my son-in-law's home in the USA. And, fortunately, I happened to come across a book on the Vedic prayers. Reading it engrossed my mind, fetching peace for me. And this, in turn, motivated me to take up this humble task of rendering it into English, which may help readers who are unable to understand the original Sanskrit Text. This is the most invaluable treasure of the Vedas, as this is SANATAN (eternal) and true for all times.

Vedas and Sanatan Dharm are inseparable from each other. Vedic knowledge is the most ancient and precious knowledge in the entire universe. Its vastness is unfathomable and greatness cannot be measured. Vedic Hymns are Sanskrit oblations to various Gods; each God is the master or controller of His or Her assigned department and is under the vigilance of the Supreme Brahman, who pervades everything, animate or inanimate. Since the Supreme Brahman is Omnipotent, Omniscient and Omnipresent, He can be Impersonal Brahman (Nirākār-Nirguṇ Parbrahm

Parmātmā) and at the same time He can manifest in person as Sākār-Saguṇ Bhagwan (like Bhagwān Ram and Bhagwān Kṛṣṇa). When the Nirguṇ Brahman takes the Sākār-Saguṇ form, His appearance and actions are all Divine with full potency of Brahman, but some ignorant and foolish people think that He is just an ordinary human being with some special powers. This special attribute of being personal and impersonal according to His desire is what makes Him God Parabrahman Parmātmā. Vedic Hymns not only impart peace, prosperity, righteousness and auspiciousness, but give liberation as well. The main goal of human life is to attain Mokśa (liberation from the cycle of birth and rebirth).

In this age of materialism and technology, people do not even have time for their spiritual needs and growth. They are either busy in pursuing their material needs and greed, merry-making or indulging in sense-gratification. Only a few people want to work towards the upliftment of their soul. They know that we are not this body, we are soul. The nature of the soul, like that of Brahman, is sat-chid-ānand (Sat means Existence or the Truth, Chid is the Consciousness, and Ānand is the Bliss). Since the soul is a minute part of the Brahman, its original nature is pure; and it wants to reach its origin, Brahman, just as the rivers eagerly flow towards the mighty ocean and become one with the ocean. In order to achieve this goal, we have to overcome illusionary forces (Māyā) through self-realization. Vedic Hymns if chanted with purity of mind and heart can give inconceivable benefits not just for body, but for soul too. It is my humble request to the people- be sincere while performing the Vedic Hymns because these are not merely for ritualistic use or personal benefit, but are powerhouse for entire humanity to charge and elevate their soul to the next level until it reaches its destination.

Of course, I have taken up wide assistance of some most authentic works, the Hindi translation of some thoroughly Sanātanī ācāryās. And this has been my prime concern as to ascertain that the mantrās are taken up in their true and nearest right perspective.

Vedas are **THE ROOTS OF ALL RIGHTEOUSNESS "VEDOKHILO DHARMA MŪLAM"**. Bhagvān Manu regards the Vedas as the foremost basic support of all SANĀTANĪ scriptures, be it Dharma-śastrās, Smritīs, Upaniṣads, Ďarśan or Purāṇās etc. The Vedas are eternal (SANĀTAN), not the creation of any human being. They are revelations to the great Ṛṣīs (sages) and are known as **APAURUṢEYA**; the direct communication of the divine truth to the great sages and seers by the **IMPERSONAL SUPREME** Himself. Vedas are the quintessence of all knowledge. They have no beginning or end as is the PARAMĀTMĀ Himself. And when there is implosion as per His will or **MĀYĀ**, the Vedas also disappear and reappear again with the rest of the creation or evolution. **"KALPĀDAU VIŚRIJĀMYAHAM"**. As the sages are the seers of this celestial wisdom, they are called **MANTRA DRAŚTA**. Lord Indra tells ṛṣi Bharadwāj that the Vedas are numberless, not the four ones alone as known to the world. And apart from other subjects, the Vedas have three main disciplines, enunciated vividly-- the **KARMAKĀND**, the **UPĀSANĀKĀND**, and the **GYĀNKĀND**, i.e., Karma, Devotion and Knowledge. These are the paths to realizing salvation. The Rigveda leads to acquiring knowledge, the Yajurveda to karmā or action, and the Sāmveda is given to achieving devotion (Bhakti). The most coveted goal of all the three is achieving liberation from transmigration of soul.

Another important salient feature for us to understand is to get acquainted with the three key terms, i.e., **Samhitā**, **Brāhmaṇās**, and **Āraṇyakās** in the Vedas. Samhitās are simply the mantras used in performing yajñās (fire-sacrifices). Brāhmaṇās go to explain what the samhitās are all about and how they should be used in sacrifices. Together they are known as **Karmakāṇd**. Whereas, the Āraṇyakās are known as **Gyānkānd** comprising mainly the **Upaniṣads**, the vast treasure house of divine knowledge.

In a nutshell, it can be said that the Vedas are like a wish-fulfilling Cow, KĀMDHENU. One may achieve **Dharma** (righteousness), **Artha** (prosperity), **Kāma** (fulfilment of desires and peace) and also **Mokśa** (liberation from cycle of birth and rebirth). These are also known as the four achievable (**Puruṣārth Catuśtaya**) in life.

The mantras selected in this book are commonly recited by the learned Āćāryās of Sanatān Dharm all over the world and would be of tremendous help, especially, to our Indian diaspora and others also in understanding the meaning and purpose of these mantras. They bring peace, prosperity, wellness and welfare to the entire humanity. As this presentation is free from bearing the unnecessary burden of commentary and purport, I believe, this will bring out the simple meaning out of this nectar of Vedic Mantras. This is my humble presentation reaching all of you in the form of this publication.

—**AUTHOR**

Acknowledgement

I would like to express my gratitude towards everyone who assisted me in any manner in completing this work. Most importantly to my revered father, who in many a way left a lasting and indelible impression on my life. My obsessively strong admiration for the Vedas and Vedic literature is a very special gift of my father to me. His recitations and chanting of Ved mantrās in unison with other Āćāryās in Kāśī-tradition were resounding and most fascinating, not only for me, but for the audiences too. Though very late, yet I believe, this humble work is, ultimately, a culmination of the inspiration and blessings from my father. Hence, my first obeisance naturally goes to my learned father, Āćāryā Pandit Tapeshwari Prasad "Vāṇībhūṣaṇ". Similarly, I am indebted to my pious, traditional, and simple mother Śrīmatī Rajrani Devi. I will always be indebted to my gracious and diligent wife, late Śrīmatī Saraswati Sharma, who always stood by me in my material and spiritual endeavour. I also want to acknowledge the influence of my father-in-law. Pt. Vidyadharji, who dedicated his life promoting and protecting Vedic Dharm.

Although this has been a tough exercise, yet the grace of the great Sanātanī Āćāryās, their masterly works, their assistance helped tremendously in comprehending these Vedic treatises, and rendering them in English nearly in their right perspective. I am grateful to Geetapress, Gorakhpur for their monumental services in publishing an extensive quantity of literature on Sanātan Dharm which is only possible with the Divine grace of Paramātmā Himself, and upholding the cause of Sanatan Dharm, for the welfare of the entire humanity, indiscriminately. My nephew, Maitreya Sharma, diligently accomplished the enormous task of organizing, formatting, and typing all hymns into text form. My brother Patanjali Sharma was always there to assist as needed. I also acknowledge affectionately, my grandson,

Suchit Upadhyay's expression of interest in my endeavour and his hard work in designing the book cover. And I would like to appreciate heartily the remarkable assistance of my daughter, Śrīmatī Chārū Upādhyāy in discussing the ambiguities of even the most authentic Hindi translation of the mantrās, and in fixing them as required, as well as in proof-reading also. I am very thankful to all of them for their invaluable contributions. I am grateful for the kind support and hard work by the entire team from Motilal Banarsidass Publishers.

Thank you all, once again, for all your support and hard work which made the publishing of **Vedic Hymns: Prayers for Divine Blessings** possible.

Devarshi Sharma

माघ शुक्ल पंचमी (वसंत पंचमी)
वि० सं० २०७९
Māgh śukla pancamī (Vasant pancamī)
V. Samvat 2079
26th of Jaunary, 2023

Contents

Transliteration-Key

अ	आ	इ	ई	उ	ऊ	ए	ऐ
a	ā	i	ī	u	ū	e	ae
ओ	औ	अं	अः	ऋ	ॠ	ऌ	
o	au	ṁ	ḥ	ṛ	ṝ	ḷ	
क	ख	ग	घ	ङ	च	छ	ज
ka	kha	ga	gha	ṅa	ca	cha	ja
झ	ञ	ट	ठ	ड	ढ	ण	त
jha	ña	ṭa	ṭha	ḍa	ḍha	ṇa	ta
थ	द	ध	न	प	फ	ब	भ
tha	da	dha	na	pa	pha	ba	bha
म	य	र	ल	व	स	ष	श
ma	ya	ra	la	va	sa	ṣa	śa
ह	क्ष	त्र	ज्ञ			ꣳ	
ha	kśa	tra	jña	gvung (as rhymes as young)			

Welfare Hymns
(स्वस्तिवाचन)

'Swastivācan' is a kind of compendium of vedic-mantrās, in order to pray for the welfare of mankind. It is a given practice in the vedic-culture to have recitation of 'swastivācan', a concise selection of mantrās, especially, concerned with the general welfare. This is performed in the beginning of an auspicious occasion, may it be a religious or a family event. It comprises twelve mantrās. In vedic language, a mantra is called a 'ṛcā'. ṛṣī Gautam is the seer of these mantrās, meaning these 'ṛcās' got manifested to ṛṣī Gautam. Indra, (Fire) Agni, Varuṇ and some others are the Gods of these mantrās. These Gods, together, are known as 'Viśvedev' (विश्वेदेव).

Maharshi Gautam invokes the Gods, in these mantrās of 'swastivācan' to ward off the possible impediments, if any, likely to arise during the course of these auspicious events, and prays for the well-being of all. Two of the twelve mantrās enunciated here are the peace-recitals, at the end.

May all the Gods be propitious to us and may we have:

आ नो भद्राः क्रतवो यन्तु विश्वतोऽदब्धासो अपरीतास उद्भिदः ।
देवा नो यथा सदमिद् वृधे असन्नप्रायुवो रक्षितारो दिवे दिवे ॥ १ ॥

ā no bhadrā: kratavo yantu viśvato'dabdhāso aparītāsa udbhida: |
devā no yathā sadamid vṛdhe asannaprāyuvo rakṣitāro dive dive || 1 ||

O Visvedev! (All the Gods, together) though, self-unmanifested, yet manifesting beneficent sacrifices, may we receive these beneficent sacrifices from all sides, uninterrupted. May the Gods, protecting us day per day, actively, shedding all sluggishness, be effortful for our progress and our welfare. (1)

❍ ❍ ❍

देवानां भद्रा सुमतिर्ऋजूयतां देवानाꣳ रातिरभि नो निवर्तताम् ।
देवानाꣳ सख्यमुपसेदिमा वयं देवा न आयुः प्रतिरन्तु जीवसे ॥२॥

devānāṃ bhadrā sumatirṛjūyatāṃ devānāꣳ rātirabhi no nivartatām |

devānāꣳ sakhyamupasedimā vayaṃ devā na āyu: pratirantu jīvase || 2 ||

May the Gods, desiring to have patrons (यजमान), have propitious and noble intellect for us. May They be keen on doing good unto us. Let us have the charity of Gods, alongwith their amity. May the Gods enhance our life-span, making it a worthful living.

❍ ❍ ❍

तान्पूर्वया निविदा हूमहे वयं भगं मित्रमदितिं दक्षमस्त्रिधम् ।
अर्यमणं वरुणꣳ सोममश्विना सरस्वती
नः सुभगा मयस्करत् ॥ ३ ॥

tānpūrvayā nividā hūmahe vayaṃ bhagaṃ mitramaditiṃ dakṣamasridham |
aryamaṇaṃ varuṇaꣳ somamaśvinā sarasvatī na: subhagā mayaskarat || 3 ||

With the vedic eternal voices (mantrās), we invoke the unbudging Sun, Mitra (the presiding God of Day and life-breath), Aditi (mother of Gods, Devmatā), Prajāpati (Brahmā, the creator), Aryamā (the presiding God of Eyes, & the solar-sphere), Varuṇa (the presiding deity of night, one of the life-winds, the releasing wind), the Moon and Aświnī kumaras (the twin sons of Aświnī, the wife of the Sun, who concealed herself in the form of a mare), and the

Great-Voice of opulent Saraswatī with celestial brilliance, to provide us with bliss. (3)

❍ ❍ ❍

तन्नो वातो मयोभु वातु भेषजं तन्माता पृथिवी तत्पिता द्यौः ।
तद् ग्रावाणः सोमसुतो मयोभुवस्तदश्विना श्रृणुतं धिष्ण्या युवम् ॥ ४ ॥

tanno vāto mayobhu vātu bheṣajaṃ tanmātā pṛthivī tatpitā dyau: |
tad grāvāṇa: somasuto mayobhuvastadaśvinā śrṛṇutaṃ dhiṣṇyā yuvam ||4||

May God of Winds make us available pleasant medicinal herbs, mother earth and fatherly heaven, make available for us, pleasant medicinal herbs, and may the pleasant (Grava-stone)* manifest the unseen provider of the pleasant medicinal herbs. O Aswinikumārās! Thou art the chief supporting base of all, kindly listen to our prayer. (4)

* pressing out Soma-juice

❍ ❍ ❍

तमीशानं जगतस्तस्थुषस्पतिं धियञ्जिन्वमवसे हूमहे वयम् ।
पूषा नो यथा वेदसामसद् वृधे रक्षिता पायुरदब्धः स्वस्तये ॥ ५ ॥

tamīśānaṃ jagatastasthuṣaspatiṃ dhiyañjinvamavase hūmahe vayam |
pūṣā no yathā vedasāmasad vṛdhe rakṣitā pāyuradabdha: svastaye || 5 ||

We invite the Lord of both the animate and the inanimate, who provides solace to the intellect, Lord Rudra, to protect us. The imperishable nourisher Lord, who safeguards the vedic-knowledge, wealth and sons, May He be the source of our growth and be propitious. (5)

❍ ❍ ❍

स्वस्ति न इन्द्रो वृद्धश्रवाः स्वस्ति नः पूषा विश्ववेदाः ।
स्वस्ति नस्ताक्ष्र्यो अरिष्टनेमिः स्वस्ति नो बृहस्पतिर्दधातु ॥ ६ ॥

svasti na indro vṛddhaśravā: svasti na: pūṣā viśvavedā: |
svasti nastārkṣyo ariṣṭanemi: svasti no
bṛhaspatirdadhātu || 6 ||

O highly renowned Indra (the king of Gods)! Be propitious to us. O Omniscient Sun! Be propitious to us. O Garuḍa (Eagle)! The dissipater of all bad omens, Be propitious to us; and O Brihaspati! The God of wisdom, kindly be propitious to us. (6)

❍ ❍ ❍

पृषदश्वा मरुतः पृश्निमातरः शुभं यावानो विदथेषु जग्मयः ।
अग्निजिह्वा मनवः सूरचक्षसो विश्वे नो देवा अवसागमन्निह ॥ ७ ॥

pṛṣadaśvā maruta: pṛśnimātara: śubhaṃ yāvāno
vidatheṣu jagmaya: |
agnijihvā manava: sūracakṣaso viśve no devā
avasāgamanniha || 7 ||

O Mārut (The God of Wind), having spotted horses, born of mother Aditi, benevolent to all, visitor of sacrificial spots (yajnāśālā), having fire-like tongue, omniscient, with Sun like eyes, alongwith the hosts and other Gods*, come to our sacrificial ceremony in order to receive sacrificial offerings of oblations of grains (7).

* Viśvedeva, the presiding deities in different spheres.

❍ ❍ ❍

भद्रं कर्णेभिः श्रृणुयाम देवा भद्रं पश्येमाक्षभिर्यजत्राः।
स्थिरैरङ्गैस्तुष्टुवाꣳसस्तनूभिर्व्यशेमहि देवहितं यदायुः ॥ ८ ॥

bhadraṃ karṇebhi:śṛṇuyāma devā bhadraṃ
paśyemākṣabhiryajatrā:|
sthirairaṅagaistuṣṭuvāꣳ sastanūbhirvyaśemahi
devahitaṃ yadāyu: || 8 ||

O Gods! (The chief-deities in various spheres) Let our ears hear auspicious and beneficial thoughts, (devoid of any censure, calumny and insinuations against any one); and let us be fixed in our worship services and prayers. Let our eyes also see all good and auspicious, and with our stout body and sound limbs with son etc., may we keep on listening with our ears the beneficial talks. May we see auspicious things with our eyes and may we enjoy such an age which is dedicated to worshipping Gods. (8)

❍ ❍ ❍

शतमिन्नु शरदो अन्ति देवा यत्रा नश्चक्रा जरसं तनूनाम् ।
पुत्रासो यत्र पितरो भवन्ति मा नो मध्या रीरिषतायुर्गन्तोः ॥ ९ ॥

śataminnu śarado anti devā yatrā naścakrā jarasaṃ tanūnām |
putrāso yatra pitaro bhavanti mā no madhyā rīriṣatāyurganto: || 9 ||

O Gods! (All the deities) Be Thou near us unto the age of a hundred years. At an age, when our body becomes old, and our sons become fathers, and they have their sons, let our dynamic bodies continue to live, let it not be broken* till then. (9)

* uninterrupted life-span

❍ ❍ ❍

अदितिद्यौरदितिरन्तरिक्षमदितिर्माता स पिता स पुत्रः ।
विश्वे देवा अदितिः पञ्च जना अदितिर्जातमदितिर्जनित्वम् ॥ १० ॥

aditidyauraditirantarikṣamaditirmātā sa pitā sa putra: |
viśve devā aditi: pañca janā aditirjātamaditirjanitvam ||10||

The uninterrupted Supreme energy is the heaven, (the abode of God), so is the form of space, and the same Supreme energy is the mother, father and son. All the Gods are the forms of the Supreme-energy, other four of the varṇās (classes) alongwith the fifth 'antyaj', the most lowly ones, are all pervaded by the same Supreme-energy, and those who were born earlier, or would be born later, in future, are all forms of the same Supreme-energy. (10)

❍ ❍ ❍

द्यौः शान्तिरन्तरिक्षꣳ शान्तिः पृथिवी शान्तिरापः शान्तिरोषधयः शान्तिः ।
वनस्पतयः शान्तिर्विश्वे देवाः शान्तिर्ब्रह्म शान्तिः सर्वꣳ शान्तिः शान्तिरेव शान्तिः सा मा शान्तिरेधि ॥ ११ ॥

dyau: śāntirantarikṣaꣳ śānti: pṛthivī śāntirāpa: śāntiroṣadhaya: śānti: |
vanaspataya: śāntirviśve devā: śāntirbrahma śānti: sarvaꣳ śānti: śāntireva śānti: sā mā śāntiredhi || 11 ||

The tranquility in heaven, the tranquility in space (the physical universe beyond the earth's atmosphere), the tranquility on earth, the tranquility in oceans (water, as an element), the tranquility in herbs (with their efficacy) and that in vegetation, the tranquility in Gods (overseeing the entire world), the tranquility in Brahm (the causal Supreme-energy), the tranquility in the entire universe, and the natural tranquility pervading the world, O Paramātmā (Oversoul)! Let Thy grace bestow upon me that tranquility. (11)

❍ ❍ ❍

यतो यतः समीहसे ततो नो अभयं कुरु ।
शं नः कुरु प्रजाभ्योऽभयं नः पशुभ्यः ॥ १२ ॥

[शु० यजुर्वेद]

yato yata: samīhase tato no abhayaṃ kuru |
śaṃ na: kuru prajābhyo'bhayaṃ na: paśubhya: || 12 ||
[śu. yajurveda]

O Paramātmā (Oversoul)! The way Thou art maintaining our well-being, make us fearless the same way. Grace our progeny with their well-being, and let our animals be also fearless. (12)

❍ ❍ ❍

Vedic-Accolades of Lord Gaṇeś
(वैदिक गणेश-स्तवन)

गणानां त्वा गणपतिꣳ हवामहे प्रियाणां त्वा प्रियपतिꣳ
हवामहे निधीनां त्वा निधिपतिꣳ हवामहे वसो मम ।
आहमजानि गर्भधमा त्वमजासि गर्भधम् ॥
[शु॰यजु॰ २३। १९]

gaṇānāṃ tvā gaṇapatiꣳ havāmahe priyāṇāṃ tvā priyapatiꣳ
havāmahe nidhīnāṃ tvā nidhipatiꣳ havāmahe vaso mama |
āhamajāni garbhadhamā tvamajāsi garbhadham ||
[śu.yaju. 23| 19]

O Supreme God Gaṇeś! The chief commander of the entire groups (troops of attendants), the protector of matter and beings and the Lord of the reservoir of the entire opulences of happiness! We invoketh Thee Lord. Thou art the begetter of the creation, the bearer of the Brahma*. Nature that bears the universe in itself. Thou art the Lord of the nature too. May we appropriately know Thee.

* हिरण्यगर्भ

❍ ❍ ❍

नि षु सीद गणपते गणेषु त्वामाहुर्विप्रतमं कवीनाम् ।
न ऋते त्वत्क्रियते किं चनारे महामर्कं मघवञ्चित्रमर्च ॥
[ऋक्॰ १०। ११२। ९]

ni ṣu sīda gaṇapate gaṇeṣu tvāmāhurvipratamaṃ kavīnām |
na ṛte tvatkriyate kiṃ canāre mahāmarkaṃ maghavañcitramarca ||
[ṛv. 10|112|9]

O Lord of the Groups! (गणपते) May Thou be seated amongst us, entreating Thee. Thou art known as extremely wise and Omniscient in the midst of called poets, perceiving beyond physical senses (क्रान्त दर्शी). No activity, either auspicious or inauspicious, begins without worshipping Thee. Therefore, O Lord, munificent! The Overlord of the opulences (ऋद्धि) and the supernatural accomplishments (सिद्धि), accept our worshipful prayers.

❍ ❍ ❍

गणानां त्वा गणपतिं हवामहे कविं कवीनामुपम-श्रवस्तमम् ।
ज्येष्ठराजं ब्रह्मणां ब्रह्मणस्पत आ नः शृण्वन्नूतिभिः सीद
सादनम् ॥
[ऋक्० २। २३। १]

gaṇānāṃ tvā gaṇapatiṃ havāmahe kaviṃ
kavīnāmupama-śravastamam |
jyeṣṭharājaṃ brahmaṇāṃ brahmaṇaspata ā
na:śṛṇvannūtibhi: sīda sādanam ||
[ṛv. 2| 23| 1]

O Overlord of Thy groups (गणों)! Poet of pre-eminence among poets, perceiving beyond (क्रान्तदर्शियों के मध्य) physical senses, the loving elder son of Lord Śiva-Goddess Śivā, provider of opulences in abundence and happiness! We invoke Thee. O Lord! Be seated as a nourisher and protector in our dwelling, hearing our accolades.

❍ ❍ ❍

नमो गणेभ्यो गणपतिभ्यश्च वो नमो नमो
व्रातेभ्यो व्रातपतिभ्यश्च वो नमो नमो
गृत्सेभ्यो गृत्सपतिभ्यश्च वो नमो नमो
विरूपेभ्यो विश्वरूपेभ्यश्च वो नमः ॥
[शुक्लयजु० १६। २५]

namo gaṇebhyo gaṇapatibhyaśca vo namo namo vrātebhyo vrātapatibhyaśca vo namo namo gṛtsebhyo gṛtsapatibhyaśca vo namo namo virūpebhyo viśvarūpebhyaśca vo nama: ||
[śuklayaju. 16| 25]

Salutations
Salutations to the special troops, serving the Gods, chiefs of various troops of different chairs like that of Lord Mahākāleśwar, Viśwanāth (Lord of the Universe and God of death), organizations, organization-chiefs, intellectuals, masters in support of robeless who are highly renounced (परमहंस), unattached, the fourth period in life (ascetics) Sanyāsī or ascetic, and all the realised-souls (आत्मविद्).

❍ ❍ ❍

ॐ तत्कराटाय विद्महे हस्तिमुखाय धीमहि ।
तन्नो दन्ती प्रचोदयात् ॥
[कृ॰ यजुर्वेदीय मैत्रायणी॰ २ । ९ । १ । ६]

oṃ tatkarāṭāya vidmahe hastimukhāya dhīmahi |
tanno dantī pracodayāt ||
[kṛ. yajurvedīya maitrāyaṇī. 2 | 9 | 1 | 6]

That God with moving trunk, God GAṆAPATI, that we know and we meditate on His elephant-face, May that God who has one tusk, encourage us to tread on the righteous path.

❍ ❍ ❍

नमो व्रातपतये नमो गणपतये नमः प्रमथपतये नमस्तेऽस्तु लम्बोदरायैकदन्ताय विघ्ननाशिने शिवसुताय श्रीवरदमूर्तये नमः ॥
[कृ॰ यजुर्वेदीय गणपत्यथर्वशीर्ष १०]

namo vrātapataye namo gaṇapataye nama: pramathapataye namaste'stu lambodarāyaikadantāya vighnanāśine śivasutāya śrīvaradamūrtaye nama: ||
[kṛ. yajurvedīya gaṇapatyatharvaśīrṣa 10]

Salutations to the Overlord of groups, salutations to the First-Chief, salutations to the Big-bellied, having a single tusk, the averter of obstacles, son of Lord Śiva, and revered Fulfiller of wishes, the boon-granter.

❍ ❍ ❍

Nectar of Nectars

The boat of truth takes the righteous across.
(Ṛg. 9|73|1)

❍ ❍ ❍

O Paramātmā! May we tread on the path of welfare (rigteousness). **(Ṛg. 5|51|15)**

❍ ❍ ❍

Munificents attain immortal-state. **(Ṛg. 1|125|6)**

❍ ❍ ❍

O Paramātmā Oversoul! Bless us with propitious mind, propitious Karmās and propitious energy.
(Ṛg. 10|25|1)

❍ ❍ ❍

Brahmaṇaspati Hymns
(श्री गणपति सूक्त)

The vedic God Gaṇeś, the averter of obstacles, is also known as Brahmaṇaspati. He is the overseer of the treasure of entire knowledge and literature (consisting of words, spiritual 'śāstrās' and other works). There is a reference, made by an ancient renowned scholar, revered Skand Swāmī, the authority on the Vedas, of Brahmaṇaspati. In the beginning of his commentary on the "Rigveda'. He writes:

विघ्नेश विधिमार्तण्डचन्द्रेन्द्रोपेन्द्र वन्दित ।
नमो गणपते तुभ्यं ब्रह्मणां ब्रह्मणस्पते ॥

O averter of obstacles, Gaṇapati revered by The Brahmā, sun, moon, Indra and Viśṇu, the master of the mantrās, salutation unto Thee.

The Mudgal Purāṇ also mentions:

सिद्धि बुद्धिपतिं वन्दे ब्रह्मणस्पतिसंज्ञितम् ।
माङ्गल्येशं सर्वपूज्यं विघ्नानां नायकं परम् ॥ (8.49.17)

O master of auspiciousness, venerable of all, the leader of obstacles, renowned as Brahmaṇaspati, I bow unto Thee. There are many other mantrās of 'Brahmaṇaspati'. The fortieth mantra of the first part of the Rigveda is 'Brahmaṇaspati Sūktam'. It's seer is 'Kaṇva Ghor'. This is being presented here: This comprises 8 mantrās.

उत्तिष्ठ ब्रह्मणस्पते देवयन्तस्त्वेमहे ।
उप प्र यन्तु मरुत सुदानव इन्द्र प्राशूर्भवा सचा ॥ १ ॥

uttiṣṭha brahmaṇaspate devayantastvemahe |
upa pra yantu maruta sudānava indra
prāśūrbhavā sacā || 1 ||

O master of wisdom! Rise, desirous of godliness, we entreat Thee. Come over alongwith the great bestower, powerful Mārut (God of wind). O Indra (King of gods)! Together with all others, imbibe soma-juice*. (1)

• Juice of soma plant makes one immortal.

❍ ❍ ❍

त्वामिद्धि सहसस्पुत्र मर्त्य उपब्रूते धने हिते ।
सुवीर्यं मरुत आ स्वश्व्यं दधीत यो व आचके ॥ २ ॥

tvāmiddhi sahasasputra martya upabūrate dhane hite |
suvīryaṃ maruta ā svaśvyaṃ dadhīta yo va ācake || 2 ||

O Brave! Born with strength and courage, men summon Thee for support, when engaged in war. O Mārut! Those, who eulogise Thee, they achieve highly trained horses and wealth of great bravery. (2)

❍ ❍ ❍

प्रैतु ब्रह्मणस्पतिः प्र देव्येतु सूनृता ।
अच्छा वीरं नर्यं पङ्क्तिराधसं देवा यज्ञं नयन्तु नः ॥ ३ ॥

praitu brahmaṇaspati: pra devyetu sūnṛtā |
acchā vīraṃ naryaṃ paṅktirādhasaṃ devā yajñaṃ nayantu na: || 3 ||

May the wise Brahmaṇaspati reach us. May the embodiment of Truth, Goddess also reach us. May all the Gods, propitious to mankind, bring alongwith them some highly venerable, well and brave Yajna performers. (3)

❍ ❍ ❍

यो वाघते ददाति सूनरं वसु स धत्ते अक्षिति श्रवः ।
तस्मा इळां सुवीरामा यजामहे सुप्रतूर्तिमनेहसम् ॥ ४ ॥

yo vāghate dadāti sūnaraṃ vasu sa dhatte akṣiti śrava: |
tasmā ilāṃ suvīrāmā yajāmahe supratūrtimanehasam || 4 ||

If one gives donation to the Yajna performer from one's honestly earned income, one is blessed with indestructible fame. We pray in his favour for an invincible motherland which has great warriors, and power of vanquishing its enemies. (4)

❍ ❍ ❍

प्र नूनं ब्रह्मणस्पतिर्मन्त्रं वदत्युक्थ्यम् ।
यस्मिन्निन्द्रो वरुणो मित्रो अर्यमा देवा ओकांसि चक्रिरे ॥ ५ ॥

pra nūnaṃ brahmaṇaspatirmantraṃ vadatyukthyam |
yasminnindro varuṇo mitro aryamā devā okāṃsi cakrire || 5 ||

Brahmaṇaspati chants the mantrās specifically where, Indra (King of Gods), Varuṇa (presiding God of night and passing-wind) (अपान वायु), Mitra (presiding God of Day and life-breath (प्राणवायु) and Aryamā, (The chief God of Eyes and solar-sphere) and other deities have built their dwellings. (5)

❍ ❍ ❍

तमिद् वोचेमा विदथेषु शंभुवं मन्त्रं देवा अनेहसम् ।
इमां च वाचं प्रतिहर्यथा नरो विश्वेद् वामा वो अश्नवत् ॥ ६ ॥

tamid vocemā vidatheṣu śaṃbhuvaṃ mantraṃ devā anehasam |
imāṃ ca vācaṃ pratiharyathā naro viśved vāmā vo aśnavat || 6 ||

O Gods! We recite that pleasing, indestructible mantra in the fire sacrifices (यज्ञ). O Leaders! If you praise that speech in the form of mantra, blessed Ye will be with all the happiness. (6)

❍ ❍ ❍

को देवयन्तमश्नवज् जनं को वृक्तबर्हिषम् ।
प्रप्र दाश्वान् पस्त्याभिरस्थिताऽन्तर्वावत् क्षयं दधे ॥ ७ ॥

ko devayantamaśnavaj janaṃ ko vṛktabarhiṣam |
prapra dāśvān pastyābhirasthitā'ntarvāvat kṣayaṃ dadhe || 7 ||

Who else, other than Brahmaṇaspati, shall take care of men, who are desirous of godliness. Who else, other than the Brahamaṇaspati shall come to the worshipper, spreading over his sanctified cloth in order to worship Him. With the blessings of the Brahamaṇaspati the bestower advances and prospers with his subjects, and the house-holders alongwith their children are under the shelter of His divine grace. (7)

❍ ❍ ❍

उप क्षत्रं पृञ्चीत हन्ति राजभिर्भये चित् सुक्षितिं दधे ।
नास्य वर्ता न तरुता महाधने नार्भे अस्ति वज्रिणः ॥ ८ ॥
(ऋक० १ । ४०)

upa kṣatraṃ pṛñcīta hanti rājabhirbhaye cit sukṣitiṃ dadhe |
nāsya vartā na tarutā mahādhane nārbhe asti vajriṇa: || 8 ||
(ṛka. 1 | 40)

Brahmanaspati accumulates the power of the warriors (Kśatriyās, the fighting class of the four classifications of varṇās). The enemies are eliminated with the support of the kings. Even under the most petrifying conditions, the Brahmaṇaspati remains calm and patient. There is none to defeat this bearer of Vajra weapon in the big wars, and none can defeat Him in the small wars. (8)

Goddess Lakśmī, Goddess of Prosperity, Bliss, Wealth and Welfare

Śrī Lakśmī Hymns
(श्री सूक्त)

In Sanskrit, 'Śrī' has a number of connotations. 'Śrī' stands for prosperity, lusture, lovliness, splendour, beauty, decoration, majesty, dignity, bliss, wealth, welfare, goddess of beauty, goddess of welfare, Lakśamī, wisdom, the three Vedas and an honorific prefix also.

The seers (Ṛṣī-sages) of this, 'Śrī-mantrās', are Ānand Kardam, Ciklīt and Jātveda. The God of the the mantrās is 'Śrī and the metres are 'anuṣtup' and 'triśtup' (systematically arranged and measured rhythm is metre). In the worship of a goddess, 'Śrī Sūkta' is highly regarded and accepted. Especially, in worshipping goddess Lakśamī, recitation of 'Śrī Sūkta', i.e., Lakśamī-Hymns is most important. Telling of these mantrās of 'Śrī Sūkta', wishing lustre and prosperity and performing 'yajña' (fire sacrifice) is most fructifying. This Sūkta is recited in the Rig-appendix (supplement of Rigveda). The mantrās are being presented here:

ॐ हिरण्यवर्णां हरिणीं सुवर्णरजतस्त्रजाम् ।
चन्द्रां हिरण्मयीं लक्ष्मीं जातवेदो म आ वह ॥ १ ॥

oṃ hiraṇyavarṇāṃ hariṇīṃ suvarṇarajatasrajām |
candrāṃ hiraṇmayīṃ lakṣmīṃ jātavedo ma ā vaha || 1 ||

O Omniscient Jātveda (God of Fire), invoke for me, Goddess Lakśamī who is blissful as glittering moonlight, having golden complexion with greenish tinge, adorning gold and silver necklaces. (1)

❍ ❍ ❍

तां म आ वह जातवेदो लक्ष्मीमनपगामिनीम् ।
यस्यां हिरण्यं विन्देयं गामश्वं पुरुषानहम् ॥ २ ॥

tāṃ ma ā vaha jātavedo lakṣmīmanapagāminīm |
yasyāṃ hiraṇyaṃ vindeyaṃ gāmaśvaṃ puruṣānaham || 2 ||

O God of Fire (Agni)! Invoke for me Goddess Lakśamī, who is imperishable, whose arrival shall bring in for me gold, cows, steed and sons. (2)

❍ ❍ ❍

अश्वपूर्वां रथमध्यां हस्तिनादप्रमोदिनीम् ।
श्रियं देवीमुप ह्वये श्रीर्मा देवी जुषताम् ॥ ३ ॥

aśvapūrvāṃ rathamadhyāṃ hastinādapramodinīm |
śriyaṃ devīmupa hvaye śrīrmā devī juṣatām || 3 ||

Seated in the midst of a chariot driven by horses, the Goddess rejoices, hearing trumpeting of elephants, That Goddess, I invoke. May I have the grace of That Goddess Lakśamī. (3)

❍ ❍ ❍

कां सोस्मितां हिरण्यप्राकारामार्द्रां
ज्वलन्तीं तृप्तां तर्पयन्तीम् ।
पद्मेस्थितां पद्मवर्णां
तामिहोप ह्वये श्रियम् ॥ ४ ॥

kāṃ sosmitāṃ hiraṇyaprākārāmārdrāṃ
jvalantīṃ tṛptāṃ tarpayantīm |
padmesthitāṃ padmavarṇāṃ
tāmihopa hvaye śriyam || 4 ||

The divine mother Goddess Lakśamī, who is in reality Brahm (Absolute Bliss), pleasing, smiling, lustrous as gold, compassionate, splendorous, fully perfect, favourable and kind unto devotees*, seated on the lotus, and having lotus complexion, That Goddess Lakśamī, I invoke. (4)

• Fulfilling their wishes

❍ ❍ ❍

चन्द्रां प्रभासां यशसा ज्वलन्तीं
श्रियं लोके देवजुष्टामुदाराम् ।
तां पद्मिनीमीं शरणं प्र पद्ये
अलक्ष्मीर्मे नश्यतां त्वां वृणे ॥ ५ ॥

candrāṃ prabhāsāṃ yaśasā jvalantīṃ
śriyaṃ loke devajuṣṭāmudārām |
tāṃ padminīmīṃ śaraṇaṃ pra padye
alakṣmīrme naśyatāṃ tvāṃ vṛṇe || 5 ||

I take the shelter of the lotus-handed Goddess Lakśamī having radiant loveliness as that of the moonlight, lustre, glowing glory and generosity, who is worshipped even by the Gods in heaven. O Goddess! Let my penury be eliminated. I surrender unto Thee as my shelter. (5)

❍ ❍ ❍

आदित्यवर्णे तपसोऽधि जातो
वनस्पतिस्तव वृक्षोऽथ बिल्वः ।
तस्य फलानि तपसा नुदन्तु
या अन्तरा याश्च बाह्या अलक्ष्मीः ॥ ६ ॥

ādityavarṇe tapaso'dhi jāto
vanaspatistava vṛkṣo'tha bilva: |
tasya phalāni tapasā nudantu
yā antarā yāśca bāhyā alakṣmī: || 6 ||

O Goddess Lakśamī, having the sun like brilliant complexion! Thy undergone penances caused auspicious and great wood apple* (बिल्वफल) to fructify in the trees. Let the fruits of that tree eliminate our inner and outer penury**. (6)

* Bilva tree

** inner weaknesses, ignorance and outer of the senses

❍ ❍ ❍

उपैतु मां देवसखः
कीर्तिश्च मणिना सह ।
प्रादुर्भूतोऽस्मि राष्ट्रेऽस्मिन्
कीर्तिमृद्धिं ददातु मे ॥ ७ ॥

upaitu māṃ devasakha:
kīrtiśca maṇinā saha |
prādurbhūto'smi rāṣṭre'smin
kīrtimṛddhiṃ dadātu me || 7 |||

O Goddess! Let me be blessed to have the friend of the Gods, Kuber (the God of riches) (meaning thereby His riches), and his friend, Maṇibhadra and the daughter of Dakśa-Prajāpati* (meaning thereby glory). I am born in this nation, bless me, O Goddess! to have riches (prosperity) (वृद्धि) and glory (यश-public praise and fame). (7)

• Kīrti (कीर्ति) (having material and spiritual richness)

❍ ❍ ❍

क्षुत्पिपासामलां ज्येष्ठामलक्ष्मीं नाशयाम्यहम् ।
अभूतिमसमृद्धिं च सर्वां निर्णुद मे गृहात् ॥ ८ ॥

kṣutpipāsāmalāṃ jyeṣṭhāmalakṣmīṃ nāśayāmyaham |
abhūtimasamṛddhiṃ ca sarvāṃ nirṇuda me gṛhāt || 8 ||

The elder sister of Goddess Lakśamī, A-LAKŚAMĪ, who is the presiding deity of wretchedness (appearing mean, miserable and contemptible*, hunger and thirst, making her body skinny) I desire her elimination. O Goddess! Let penury and inauspiciousness be driven far away from my dwelling. (8)

• distressed with

❍ ❍ ❍

गन्धद्वारां दुराधर्षां नित्यपुष्टां करीषिणीम् ।
ईश्वरीं सर्वभूतानां तामिहोप ह्वये श्रियम् ॥ ९ ॥

gandhadvārāṃ durādharṣāṃ nityapuṣṭāṃ karīṣiṇīm |
īśvarīṃ sarvabhūtānāṃ tāmihopa hvaye śriyam || 9 ||

The Supreme controller of all the elements, comprising entirely the whole of creation*, whose entrace is fragrant, unconquerable and ever thriving, uninterruptedly, and who resides in the midst of cows' dry-dung, that Goddess Lakśamī, I invoke in my abode. (the cows being sacred, so is their refuse also). (9)

• human, divine or even inanimate.

❍ ❍ ❍

मनसः काममाकूतिं वाचः सत्यमशीमहि ।
पशूनां रूपमन्नस्य मयि श्रीः श्रयतां यशः ॥ १० ॥

manasa: kāmamākūtiṃ vāca: satyamaśīmahi |
paśūnāṃ rūpamannasya mayi śrī: śrayatāṃ yaśa: || 10 ||

Ardently desiring Goddess Lakśamī to grace my household by Her arrival, May I achieve all the desires arising in mind and their accomplishment by mere wish and may I achieve the veracity of speech. May I achieve alongwith cows and other cattle, different grains and consumables in abundance. May the Goddess Lakśamī arrive in my home in the form of glory. (10)

❍ ❍ ❍

कर्दमेन प्रजा भूता मयि सम्भव कर्दम ।
श्रियं वासय मे कुले मातरं पद्ममालिनीम् ॥ ११ ॥

kardamena prajā bhūtā mayi sambhava kardama |
śriyaṃ vāsaya me kule mātaraṃ padmamālinīm || 11 ||

We are descendants of sage Kardam, son of Goddess Lakśamī. O sage Kardam! May Thou be born in our ancestral* household and we pray Thee to consecrate mother Goddess Lakśamī, wearing lotus-garland, in our clan.

* lineage

❍ ❍ ❍

आपः सृजन्तु स्निग्धानि चिक्लीत वस मे गृहे ।
नि च देवीं मातरं श्रियं वासय मे कुले ॥ १२ ॥

āpa: sṛjantu snigdhāni ciklīta vasa me gṛhe |
ni ca devīṃ mātaraṃ śriyaṃ vāsaya me kule || 12 ||

May Goddess Lakśamī produce sweet and tender articles and water. O son of Goddess Lakśamī, Chiklīt kindly grace our home by residing here and make Divine mother, Goddess Lakśamī also to dwell alongwith, in our clan (lineage).

❍ ❍ ❍

आर्द्रां पुष्करिणीं पुष्टिं पिङ्गलां पद्ममालिनीम् ।
चन्द्रां हिरण्मयीं लक्ष्मीं जातवेदो म आ वह ॥ १३ ॥

ārdrāṃ puṣkariṇīṃ puṣṭiṃ piḍglāṃ padmamālinīm |
candrāṃ hiraṇmayīṃ lakṣmīṃ jātavedo ma ā vaha || 13 ||

O God of Fire, Jātveda! Invoke Goddess Lakśamī to dwell in our home, who is blissful as the blooming moonlight, cool-natured, lotus-handed, has a thriving-form, is gold-complexioned, and adorns a lotus-garland. (13)

❍ ❍ ❍

आर्द्रां यः करिणीं यष्टिं सुवर्णां हेममालिनीम् ।
सूर्यां हिरण्मयीं लक्ष्मीं जातवेदो म आ वह ॥ १४ ॥

ārdrāṃ ya: kariṇīṃ yaṣṭiṃ suvarṇāṃ hemamālinīm |
sūryāṃ hiraṇmayīṃ lakṣmīṃ jātavedo ma ā vaha || 14 ||

O Jātveda (God of Fire)! Invoke Goddess Lakśamī (for me), who despite wielding restrain on the wicked, is of gentle disposition and loving-nature, providing auspiciousness and support, like a stick (**दण्ड**), having charming complexion, adorning gold-necklaces and is also sun like and like glittering-gold. Kindly invoke that Goddess Lakśamī for me. (14)

❍ ❍ ❍

तां म आ वह जातवेदो लक्ष्मीमनपगामिनीम् ।
यस्यां हिरण्यं प्रभूतं गावो दास्योऽश्वान् विन्देयं पुरुषानहम् ॥ १५ ॥

**tāṃ ma ā vaha jātavedo lakṣmīmanapagāminīm |
yasyāṃ hiraṇyaṃ prabhūtaṃ gāvo dāsyo'śvān
vindeyaṃ puruṣānaham || 15 ||**

O Jātveda (God of Fire)! Invoke for me that unfailing Goddess Lakśamī, whose arrival brings in for us plenty of wealth, abundant number of cows, maid servants, steeds and sons. (15)

❍ ❍ ❍

यः शुचिः प्रयतो भूत्वा जुहुयादाज्यमन्वहम् ।
सूक्तं पञ्चदशर्चं च श्रीकामः सततं जपेत् ॥ १६ ॥

**ya: śuci: prayato bhūtvā juhuyādājyamanvaham |
sūktaṃ pañcadarścaṃ ca śrīkāma: satataṃ japet || 16 ||**

Let one, desirous of wealth, observe restraints and offer oblations of purified-butter (Ghee) in sacrificial-fire, alongwith recitation of these fifteen-mantrās of (hymns) 'Śrī Sūktam', regularly, everyday.

❍ ❍ ❍

पद्मानने पद्मविपद्मपत्रे पद्मप्रिये पद्मदलायताक्षि ।
विश्वप्रिये विष्णुमनोऽनुकूले त्वत्पादपद्मं मयि सं नि धत्स्व ॥ १७ ॥

**padmānane padmavipadmapatre padmapriye
padmadalāyatākṣi |
viśvapriye viṣṇumano'nukūle tvatpādapadmaṃ mayi
saṃ ni dhatsva || 17 ||**

O lotus-faced! Placer of lotus-feet on lotus-leaf! Lotus-lover! Large-lotus-eyed! Loved-one of the world! Harmonious to Lord Vishnu's heart! Let Thy lotus-feet be installed in my heart. (17)

❍ ❍ ❍

पद्मानने पद्मऊरू पद्माक्षि पद्मसम्भवे ।
तन्मे भजसि पद्माक्षि येन सौख्यं लभाम्यहम् ॥ १८ ॥

padmānane padmūrū padmākṣi padmasambhave |
tanme bhajasi padmākṣi yena saukhyaṃ labhāmyaham || 18 ||

O Lotus like glowing-faced! O Lotus-breasted! O Lotus-eyed! One who appears from a lotus! O Lotus-eyed Goddess Lakśamī! Kindly nourish and bring me up in a manner, which provides me happiness. (18)

❍ ❍ ❍

अश्वदायि गोदायि धनदायि महाधने ।
धनं मे जुषतां देवि सर्वकामांश्च देहि मे ॥ १९ ॥

aśvadāyi godāyi dhanadāyi mahādhane |
dhanaṃ me juṣatāṃ devi sarvakāmāṃśca dehi me || 19 ||

❍ ❍ ❍

O Goddess, embodiment of abundant-wealth, provider of steeds, cows and abundance of valuable material possessions, let me be provided with (profuse amount of) wealth and all desirable material objects (for ever). (19)

पुत्रपौत्रधनं धान्यं हस्त्यश्वाश्वतरी रथम् ।
प्रजानां भवसि माता आयुष्मन्तं करोतु मे ॥ २० ॥

putrapautradhanaṃ dhānyaṃ hastyaśvāśvatarī ratham |
prajānāṃ bhavasi mātā āyuṣmantaṃ karotu me || 20 ||

(O Goddess!) Thou art mother of all beings. Bless my sons, grandsons with wealth, valuable material possessions, elephants, steeds, mules and chariots, and bless them with long, lasting life. (20)

❍ ❍ ❍

धनमग्निर्धनं वायुर्धनं सूर्यो धनं वसुः ।
धनमिन्द्रो बृहस्पतिर्वरुणो धनमश्विना ॥ २१ ॥

dhanamagnirdhanaṃ vāyurdhanaṃ sūryo dhanaṃ vasu: |
dhanamindro bṛhaspatirvaruṇo dhanamaśvinā || 21 ||

Fire, wind, sun, class of deities (8 in number, Kubera, Śiva, Agni, tank, tie of a yoke, ray of light, sun, light) 'Vasugaṇa', Indra, Brihaspati, Varuṇ and Aswini-Kumars, These are all embodiments of (unimaginable) opulences. (21)

❍ ❍ ❍

वैनतेय सोमं पिब सोमं पिबतु वृत्रहा ।
सोमं धनस्य सोमिनो मह्यं ददातु सोमिनः ॥ २२ ॥

vainateya somaṃ piba somaṃ pibatu vṛtrahā |
somaṃ dhanasya somino mahyaṃ dadātu somina: || 22 ||

O Vainteya (Garud, king of birds [Eagle])! Kindly drink the soma- juice (a plant, its juice makes the drinker immortal - R.V. IX - Book, devoted to the glorification of soma, moon), O Indra! The eliminator of Vrittāsur, kindly drink soma-juice. Let Garuda (Eagle) and Indra provide that soma, cherished mostly by the prosperous, to me, as I ardently desire that soma juice. (22)

❍ ❍ ❍

न क्रोधो न च मात्सर्यं न लोभो नाशुभा मतिः ।
भवन्ति कृतपुण्यानां भक्त्या श्रीसूक्तजापिनाम् ॥ २३ ॥

na krodho na ca mātsaryaṃ na lobho nāśubhā mati: |
bhavanti kṛtapuṇyānāṃ bhaktyā śrīsūktajāpinām || 23 ||

When people morally, religiously and meritoriously perform 'Śrīsūkta' 'Japa' (repeatedly chanting matra) with devotion, they neither have anger, malice and greed nor their mind and intelligence ever gets polluted. (23)

❍ ❍ ❍

सरसिजनिलये सरोजहस्ते
धवलतरांशुकगन्धमाल्यशोभे ।
भगवति हरिवल्लभे मनोज्ञे
त्रिभुवनभूतिकरि प्र सीद मह्यम् ॥ २४ ॥

sarasijanilaye sarojahaste
dhavalatarāṃśukagandhamālyaśobhe |
bhagavati harivallabhe manojñe
tribhuvanabhūtikari pra sīda mahyam || 24 ||

O Goddess! Inhabitant of lotus, holding lotus in hand, adorning ultra-white robes, fresh with anointment of scented fragrance of beautifying flower-garland, dear to Lord Viṣṇu, all attractive and giver of opulences of the three worlds, be favourable and happy on me. (24)

❍ ❍ ❍

विष्णुपत्नीं क्षमां देवीं माधवीं माधवप्रियाम् ।
लक्ष्मीं प्रियसखीं भूमिं नमाम्यच्युतवल्लभाम् ॥ २५ ॥

viṣṇupatnīṃ kṣamāṃ devīṃ mādhavīṃ
mādhavapriyām |
lakṣmīṃ priyasakhīṃ bhūmiṃ
namāmyacyutavallabhām || 25 ||

My salutations to Goddess Lakśamī who is consort of Lord Viṣṇu, embodiment of forgiveness in the form of mother Earth, loving to Kṛṣṇa, dear friend and beloved of the imperishable Brahm-Viṣṇu, I offer my obeisances to Goddess Lakśamī.

❍ ❍ ❍

महालक्ष्म्यै च विद्महे विष्णुपत्न्यै च धीमहि ।
तन्नो लक्ष्मीः प्र चोदयात् ॥ २६ ॥

mahālakṣmyai ca vidmahe viṣṇupatnyai ca dhīmahi |
tanno lakṣmī: pra codayāt || 26 ||

We know the Supreme Goddess Lakśamī, the consort of Lord Viṣṇu and meditate on Her. O that Supreme Goddess! Exhort us to tread on the righteous path (in life).

* This is form of a Lakśamī-Gāyatrī.

❍ ❍ ❍

आनन्दः कर्दमः श्रीदश्चिक्लीत इति विश्रुताः ।
ऋषयः श्रियः पुत्राश्च श्रीर्देवीर्देवता मताः ॥ २७ ॥

ānanda: kardama: śrīdaściklīta iti viśrutā: |
ṛṣaya: śriya: putrāśca śrīrdevīrdevatā matā: || 27 ||

In the yester-epoch, there were four renowned sages, known as Ānanda, Kardam, Śrīda and Ćiktit. In the next to this epoch, all of them became Goddess Lakśamī's sons; later on with these sons, the Great Lakśamī became divinely resplendent, and the Gods were also blessed by the generosity of the same Supreme Goddess Lakśamī. (27)

❍ ❍ ❍

ऋणरोगादिदारिद्र्यपापक्षुदपमृत्यवः
भयशोकमनस्तापा नश्यन्तु मम सर्वदा ॥ २८ ॥

ṛṇarogādidāridryapāpakṣudapamṛtyava:
bhayaśokamanastāpā naśyantu mama sarvadā || 28 ||

Bless me Goddess Lakśamī by perishing and removing impediments of indebtedness, disease, penury, sins, hunger, untimely death, fear, grief and mental worry. (28)

❍ ❍ ❍

श्रीर्वर्चस्वमायुष्यमारोग्यमाविधाच्छोभमानं महीयते ।
धनं धान्यं पशुं बहुपुत्रलाभं शतसंवत्सरं दीर्घमायुः ॥ २९ ॥
[ऋक् परिशिष्ट]

śrīrvarcasvamāyuṣyamārogyamāvidhācchobhamānaṃ mahīyate |
dhanaṃ dhānyaṃ paśuṃ bahuputralābhaṃ śatasaṃvatsaraṃ dīrghamāyu: || 29 ||
[ṛk pariśiṣṭa]

Great Goddess Lakśamī, arrange and bless us (mankind) with vital strength, long life, good health, wealth and prosperity, cattle and sons in good number, and a long life for a hundred years, and bedecked by these, may the men get glory and honour. (29)

Puruṣa Hymns (A)
[पुरुष सूक्त (क)]

The Vedic Hymn on the Supreme Being 'पुरुष सूक्त' 'Puruṣa Sūkta' carries paramount importance amongst available Vedic-Sutrās. Puruṣa is 'Supreme' of the Vedic-Gods. This sūtra occurs in all the four Vedas, of course, with slight variations in the Sāma Veda and the Atharva Veda. The 90th Sūkta in the 10th part (Mandal) of the Rig Veda is 'Puruṣa Sūkta'. The 31st chapter in the Yajurveda is this Sūkta, and the 6th Sūkta in the 19th part of the Atharvaveda is also 'Puruṣa Sūkta'. The Taittriya Āraṇyaka of the Krișṇa Yajurveda is the Sāma Veda. In it occurs this Sūkta with some modifications. Vedavyāsa calls it as the essence of all the Śrutīs, since this Sūkta occurs in all the Vedas. Puruṣa Sūkta is also available in the Mudgal Upaniṣad with additional two hymns (mantrās). This sūtra comprises sixteen hymns (mantrās). Nārāyan is the sage, and 'Puruṣa', Lord Viśṇu, is the Supreme Being.

Puruṣa Sūkta refers to the Puruṣottam (Supreme Being), the supreme cause of all causes. He is the chief source of creation of the manifested universe. The visible creation is but a fourth part only of the Virāta Puruṣa. The rest remains unmanifested*. Virāt is all pervasive.

'तदन्तरस्य सर्वस्य तदसर्वस्यास्य बाह्यतः'।

(Īśā Upaniṣad)

The all pervasive (Paramapuruṣa) is inside each and every animate and inanimate being and matter, respectively. (Īśā Upaniṣad). The 'Puruṣa Sūkta' enunciates worshipping of 'Yajña Puruṣa' (the Supreme Being) through oblations in

* The rest of the three-fourth comprises Vaikuntha (the divine Vaikuntha, the abode of Viśṇu, Kailās, the divine abode of Lord Śiva and Sāketa, Goloka.

fire-sacrifice, chanting the Sūkta mantrās. These mantrās are being translated hereunder, although it is a difficult text to explain. Its language being archaic, it does not lend itself to interpretations. Nonetheless, Puruṣa Sūkta is in essence the vedantic philosophy, the vedic tradition as well as that of the Bhagvat Gītā and Śrīmad Bhāgvat Purāṇ. It incorporates the principles of meditation (upāsanā), knowledge (jñana), and devotion (bhakti) alongwith rituals and duties (dharma and karma). It is, therefore, recited in almost all vedic rituals and ceremonies. The mantrās (hymns) follow:

ॐ सहस्त्रशीर्षा पुरुषः सहस्त्राक्षः सहस्त्रपात् ।
स भूमिꣳ सर्वत स्पृत्वाऽत्यतिष्ठद्दशाङ्गुलम् ॥ १ ॥

oṃ sahasraśīrṣā puruṣa: sahasrākṣa: sahasrapāt |
sa bhūmiꣳ sarvata spṛtvā'tyatiṣṭhaddaśāṅgulam || 1 ||

Om, The Puruṣa (the Supreme Being) has thousands* of fore-heads, thousands of eyes, thousands of feet. He has enveloped this world entirely from all sides and has transcended it even by ten angulās (fingers). He is still infinitely above the entire creation.

The mantra (hymn), simply, depicts that the Oversoul (Puruṣa) is Omnipresent, Omniscient and Omnipotent. He is all pervasive.

* means numberless

❍ ❍ ❍

पुरुष एवेदꣳ सर्वं यद्भूतं यच्च भाव्यम् ।
उतामृतत्वस्येशानो यदन्नेनातिरोहति ॥ २ ॥

puruṣa evedaꣳ sarvaṃ yadbhūtaṃ yacca bhāvyam |
utāmṛtatvasyeśāno yadannenātirohati || 2 ||

Om The Puruṣa is verily all this. (All this creation, i.e., manifestation as the universe is the Puruṣa). All that which existed in the past, and all that which will come into existence in the future is also the Puruṣa. In essence, the Puruṣa is the Lord of Devatās and of those who sustain their life by eating grains. The Puruṣa is the Supreme ruler of all.

❍ ❍ ❍

एतावानस्य महिमातो ज्यायाँश्च पूरुषः ।
पादोऽस्य विश्वा भूतानि त्रिपादस्यामृतं दिवि ॥ ३ ॥

etāvānasya mahimāto jyāyāṁśca pūruṣa: |
pādo'sya viśvā bhūtāni tripādasyāmṛtaṃ divi || 3 ||

So immense is His greatness. The Puruṣa, however, is (even) greater than this. The entire (visible) universe is but only one quarter of the Puruṣa, and His three parts exist, enternally, in the spiritual domain. (The eternal spiritual domain comprises Vaikuntha, Goloka, Sāketa, Śivaloka, etc.) (3)

❍ ❍ ❍

त्रिपादूर्ध्व उदैत्पुरुषः पादोऽस्येहाभवत् पुनः ।
ततो विष्वङ् व्यक्रामत्साशनानशने अभि ॥ ४ ॥

tripādūrdhva udaitpuruṣa: pādo'syehābhavat puna: |
tato viṣvaṅ vyakrāmatsāśanānaśane abhi || 4 ||

The three quarters (parts) of the Puruṣa (His Energy) ascended above (in Transcendental Realm), and His one quarter of Energy manifests itself as (material) creation time and again. And He pervades the entire creation comprising both the animate being and inanimate matter. (4)

❍ ❍ ❍

ततो विराडजायत विराजो अधि पूरुषः ।
स जातो अत्यरिच्यत पश्चाद्भूमिमथो पुरः ॥ ५ ॥

tato virāḍajāyata virājo adhi pūruṣa: |
sa jāto atyaricyata paścādbhūmimatho pura: || 5 ||

From Him (The Ādipuruṣa – The Supreme Being) was born the Virāt (the immeasurable universe in form). The Virāt, being the substratum, another Puruṣa – being Brahmā emanated, greatly illuminated. Later, He created the earth, manifesting from His own Being and then, the bodies (of the living beings). (Gods, men and Tiryak – in a slanting direction, etc.) (5)

❍ ❍ ❍

तस्माद्यज्ञात्सर्वहुतः सम्भृतं पृषदाज्यम् ।
पशूँस्ताँश्चक्रे वायव्यानारण्या ग्राम्याश्च ये ॥ ६ ॥

tasmādyajñātsarvahuta: sambhṛtaṃ pṛṣadājyam |
paśūṁstāṁścakera vāyavyānāraṇyā grāmyāśca ye || 6 ||

From that sacrificial Fire where in, all (The Puruṣa) has been offered as oblation, from that (sacrificial Puruṣa), He, Himself emanated curd, purified butter (Dahi-Ghee) etc., and beings survivable in the air (birds, etc.), in the forests, wild animals and reptiles etc. and in the inhabitable villages, domesticated animals and other beings. (6)

❍ ❍ ❍

तस्माद्यज्ञात्सर्वहुत ऋचः सामानि जज्ञिरे ।
छन्दाꣳसि जज्ञिरे तस्माद्यजुस्तस्मादजायत ॥ ७ ॥

tasmādyajñātsarvahuta ṛca: sāmāni jajñire |
chandāꣳsi jajñire tasmādyajustasmādajāyata || 7 ||

From that yajna (sacrife) where in the Cosmic Being (i.e., Viārt) was Himself the oblation, were born the riks (the Rig Veda) and the samans (the Sāma Veda) mantrās, the chandās (vedic metres, as Gayatrī, Anuṣṭup etc.) and the Yajur Veda. (7)

❍ ❍ ❍

तस्मादश्वा अजायन्त ये के चोभयादतः ।
गावो ह जज्ञिरे तस्मात्तस्माज्जाता अजावयः ॥ ८ ॥

tasmādaśvā ajāyanta ye ke cobhayādata: |
gāvo ha jajñire tasmāttasmājjātā ajāvaya: || 8 ||

From that (i.e. Virāt) were born horses, and also animals like donkeys and mules, having two rows of teeth (in both jaws). And from That were born cows and goats and sheep. (8)

❍ ❍ ❍

तं यज्ञं बर्हिषि प्रौक्षन् पुरुषं जातमग्रतः ।
तेन देवा अयजन्त साध्या ऋषयश्च ये ॥ ९ ॥

taṃ yajñaṃ barhiṣi praukṣan puruṣaṃ jātamagrata: |
tena devā ayajanta sādhyā ṛṣayaśca ye || 9 ||

The first Divine creation, the Devās, the Sadhyās, and the ṛisīs consecrated the Puruṣa, sprinkling water with the Kuśa Grass (barhiśi) on Him and performed sacrifice by the same (the Puruṣa had born (already) in the beginning, i.e. appeared the shining Viṛāt).

❍ ❍ ❍

यत्पुरुषं व्यदधुः कतिधा व्यकल्पयन् ।
मुखं किमस्यासीत् किं बाहू किमूरू पादा उच्येते ॥ १० ॥

yatpuruṣaṃ vyadadhu: katidhā vyakalpayan |
mukhaṃ kimasyāsīt kiṃ bāhū kimūrū pādā ucyete || 10 ||

As the Devās (Gods), mentally imagined performing the sacrifice of the Puruṣa (the Cosmic Being) in order to have further creation, they had their inquisitiveness about Him. What became of His mouth? What were His two arms, and that of His two thighs? And what were, His feet, known as? (10)

❍ ❍ ❍

ब्राह्मणोऽस्य मुखमासीद्बाहू राजन्यः कृतः ।
ऊरू तदस्य यद्वैश्यः पद्भ्याꣳ शूद्रो अजायत ॥ ११ ॥

brāhmaṇo'sya mukhamāsīdbāhū rājanya: kṛta: |
ūrū tadasya yadvaiśya: padbhyāꣳ śūdro ajāyata || 11 ||

The Brāhmaṇās came from His Mouth, the kśatriyās came

from His Ārms, the Vaiśyās came from His thighs, and the śūdrās came from His Feet. (This is the one Virāt (Cosmic Being), comprising all the four Varṇās). (11)

* came from meaning – were born

❍ ❍ ❍

चन्द्रमा मनसो जातश्चक्षोः सूर्यो अजायत ।
श्रोत्राद्वायुश्च प्राणश्च मुखादग्निरजायत ॥ १२ ॥

candramā manaso jātaścakṣo: sūryo ajāyata |
śrotrādvāyuśca prāṇaśca mukhādagnirajāyata || 12 ||

From His (Puruṣa) mind was born the moon, from His eyes was born the sun, from His ears were born air and breath, and from His mouth was born Agni. (12)

❍ ❍ ❍

नाभ्या आसीदन्तरिक्षꣳ शीर्ष्णो द्यौः समवर्तत ।
पद्भ्यां भूमिर्दिशः श्रोत्रात्तथा लोकाँ अकल्पयन् ॥ १३ ॥

nābhyā āsīdantarikṣaꣳ śīrṣṇo dyau: samavartata |
padbhyāṃ bhūmirdiśa: śrotrāttathā
lokāṁ akalpayan || 13 ||

The antarikśha* evolved out of His navel. Dyuloka (heaven) came out from His head. The bhūmi (earth) came into existence from the feet of the Puruṣa, and diśa (the directions, ten in number) were produced from His ears. Thus, the entire worlds were imagined to exist in the Puruṣa, Himself. (13)

* The wide spread space around in the universe.

❍ ❍ ❍

यत्पुरुषेण हविषा देवा यज्ञमतन्वत ।
वसन्तोऽस्यासीदाज्यं ग्रीष्म इध्मः शरद्धविः ॥ १४ ॥

yatpuruṣeṇa haviṣā devā yajñamatanvata |
vasanto'syāsīdājyaṃ grīṣma idhma: śaraddhavi: || 14 ||

When the Gods performed the yajña (the sacrificial Fire) with the Puruṣa as haviṣa (the oblation material), the vasanta (spring) became the clarified butter (Ghee) for the yajña, the summer (Gṛiṣma) transformed itself as samidhā (the fuel of wood), and the autumn (śarad) was there to serve as havi (purodāś, i.e., ground rice, rounded as a cake to offer as oblation into the sacrificial fire). (14)

❍ ❍ ❍

सप्तास्यासन् परिधयस्त्रिः सप्त समिधः कृताः ।
देवा यद्यज्ञं तन्वाना अबध्नन् पुरुषं पशुम् ॥ १५ ॥

saptāsyāsan paridhayastri: sapta samidha: kṛtā: |
devā yadyajñaṃ tanvānā abadhnan
puruṣaṃ paśum || 15 ||

(In performing this yajña) The Devās fastened the paśu (sacrificial animal)* and there were seven paridhis (enclosures of fuel sticks as the seven seas). And twenty one kinds of chandās (metres, three metres, Gāyatri, Atijagatī and Kriti, and each one in seven ways) as samidhā (sacrificial fuel sticks). (15)

* as the Puruṣa-form.

❍ ❍ ❍

यज्ञेन यज्ञमयजन्त देवास्तानि धर्माणि प्रथमान्यासन् ।
ते ह नाकं महिमानः सचन्त यत्र पूर्वे साध्याः सन्ति देवाः ॥ १६ ॥
[शु॰ यजु॰ ३१ । १-१६]

yajñena yajñamayajanta devāstāni dharmāṇi
prathamānyāsan |
te ha nākaṃ mahimāna: sacanta yatra pūrve sādhyā:
santi devā: || 16 ||
[śu. yaju. 31 | 1-16]

The Devās performed the yajña (sacrificial ceremony) contemplating on the Cosmic Being (Puruṣa), worshipping

Him in the yajña-form. The rituals used in it, became primary dharma, and, thus firstly, dharma came into existence. Observing those dharmās, the Devās becoming highly reverent, enjoy pleasures of heaven, where ancient sādhyās live.

(We, therefore, pray with our folded hands to the all-pervading inanimate-animate Virāt, the Cosmic Puruṣa.) (16)

❍ ❍ ❍

Puruṣa Hymns (B)

[पुरुष सूक्त (ख)]

As the 'Puruṣa Sūkta' carries paramount importance in the entire vedic literature, this Sūkta (hymn) is available in all the four Vedas. In the Mudgal-Upaniṣad, the Rig Veda, there are two additional mantrās (Hymns), and the other sixteen are as much the same as with some variations in their order.

According to the Mudgal Upaniṣad, the first four mantrās (Hymns) enunciate the four-rounded God-forms of Vāsudeva, Sankarṣaṇa, Pradyumna and Aniruddha. The first mantrā "Om Sahasra śīrṣā Puruṣah...", sheds light on Lord Vāsudeva, the all pervading and even transcendent, the infinite. It is His divine and brilliant glow that illumines the inmost hearts of all beings, and yet, He remains unalloyed from all of these. And this is the Super-Conscious-form of Lord Vāsudeva.

In the second mantrā, "Om Puruṣa Evedam...", the Sankarṣaṇa form of the Supreme is being described. This form is the divine Life-force. The entire world gets manifested in the past, the present, and the future through this alone, and this Sankarṣaṇa form is manifestation of His Lordship and Sovereignty. And this is the Supreme God's Omnipresent, Omniscient and Omnipotent form.

In the third mantrā of the Sūkta, "Om Etāvānasya Mahimāto...", the Spreme Lord's splenderous form as Pradyumna is depicted. Pradyumna is the Lord's compact-beauty form, His divine Kāma (love) and contemplatively, approachable personality. The Supreme Being, in this unimaginable opulence of the Divine compact-beauty personified manifests Himself in the eternal-lokās (worlds). The Upaniṣad thus clarifies the real significance of śruti.

The fourth mantrā depicts the Supreme Lord's, Aniruddha

form, having the power to ward off what is most difficult, or hard to get rid of. This form of the Lord is endowed with the illusionary-power, i.e., the Yogamayā. That is the universe, or the basic cause of 'creation', and this is the Lord's fourth Super human opulence (divine energy) of His Lotus Feet.

The two additional mantrās, the 16th and the 17th are not available in the known copies of the Rigveda, but in separately published editions of 'Puruṣa Sūkta', the mantrās are there. In the original Upaniṣads also, they are indicated. These mantrās appear in 'Paramātmikopaniṣad', 'Mahāvākyopaniṣad' and 'cityupaniṣad'. The 17th mantrā is found in 'Taittiriya Āraṇyaka' also.

The mantrās are being translated hereunder:

ॐ सहस्त्रशीर्षा पुरुषः सहस्त्राक्षः सहस्त्रपात् ।
स भूमिं विश्व तो वृत्वा त्यतिष्ठद्दशाङ्गुलम् ॥ १ ॥

oṃ sahasraśīrṣā puruṣa: sahasrākṣa: sahasrapāt |
sa bhūmiṃ viśva to vṛtvā tyatiṣṭhaddaśāgdbhalam || 1 ||

Om, The Puruṣa (the Supreme Being) has thousands* of fore-heads, thousands of eyes, thousands of feet. He has enveloped this world entirely from all sides and has transcended it even by ten angulās (fingers). He is still infinitely above the entire creation.
The mantra (hymn), simply, depicts that the Oversoul (Puruṣa) is Omnipresent, Omniscient and Omnipotent. He is all pervasive.

* meaning numberless

❍ ❍ ❍

ॐ पुरुष एवेदं सर्वं यद्भूतं यच्च भव्यम् ।
उतामृतत्वस्येशानो यदन्नेनातिरोहति ॥ २ ॥

oṃ puruṣa evedaṃ sarvaṃ yadbhūtam yacca bhavyam |
utāmṛtatvasyeśāno yadannenātirohati || 2 ||

Om! The Puruṣa is verily all this. (All this creation, i.e., manifestation as the universe is the Puruṣa). All that which existed in the past, and all that which will come into existence in the future is also the Puruṣa. In essence, the Puruṣa is the Lord of Devatās and of those who sustain their life by eating grains. The Puruṣa is the Supreme ruler of all.

❍ ❍ ❍

ॐ एतावानस्य महिमातो ज्यायांश्च पूरुषः ।
पादोऽस्य विश्वा भूतानि त्रिपादस्यामृतं दिवि ॥ ३ ॥

oṃ etāvānasya mahimāto jyāyāṁśca pūruṣa: |
pādo'sya viśvā bhūtāni tripādasyāmṛtaṃ divi || 3 ||

Om! The entire COSMOS, past, future, and present is the opulence of the Supreme Lord. He is even greater than His ever expanding material Supreme form. The visible Universe situated is only in one quarter of the Supreme Lord. The eternal spiritual realms (Vaikunth, Golok, Sāket Lok, Śivlok, etc.) are established in the remaining three quarters of the Supreme Lord. (3)

❍ ❍ ❍

ॐ त्रिपादूर्ध्व उदैत् पुरुषः पादोऽस्येहाभवत्पुनः ।
ततो विष्वङ् व्यक्रामत् साशनानशने अभि ॥ ४ ॥

oṃ tripādūrdhva udait puruṣa: pādo'syehābhavatpuna: |
tato viṣvaṅ vyakrāmat sāśanānaśane abhi || 4 ||

Om! This mantrā describes the opulence of the Supreme Being and explains as to how one can attain Mokśa (Liberation). That Supreme Lord with His inconceivable inner form illumines in the three quarters of His spiritual domain which is beyond this illusionary universe (His devine form is eternally effulgent, since there is no existence of Māyā (Illusion) in that spiritual realm. His one part exists as this creation, and He is the creation Himself. Therefore the Supreme Puruṣa pervades the entire animate and inanimate creation. (4)

❍ ❍ ❍

ॐ तस्माद् विराळजायत विराजो अधि पूरुषः ।
स जातो अत्यरिच्यत पश्चाद् भूमिमथो पुरः ॥ ५ ॥

oṃ tasmād virāḻajāyata virājo adhi pūruṣa: |
sa jāto atyaricyata paścād bhūmimatho pura: || 5 ||

Om! From that original Supreme being (Ādi Puruṣa) emanated this entire inconceivable universe. That Supreme Puruṣa became the chief presiding God known as Hiraṇyagarbh (The Golden Womb), that Hiraṇyagarbh after emerging became extremely effulgent. Later on the Hiraṇyagarbh produced the earth and other planets, and physical bodies of (Devtās, men and Tiryak, etc.)

This mantrā describes, how Lord Viśṇu manifests Māyā, the illusory energy of His Supreme Self and the Jīv or the living being. (5)

❍ ❍ ❍

ॐ यत्पुरुषेण हविषा देवा यज्ञमतन्वत ।
वसन्तो अस्यासीदाज्यं ग्रीष्म इध्मः शरद्धविः ॥ ६ ॥

oṃ yatpuruṣeṇa haviṣā devā yajñamatanvata |
vasanto asyāsīdājyaṃ grīṣma idhma: śaraddhavi: || 6 ||

Om! The gods contemplating to offer obtations to the Puruṣa, performed yajña on the body of Puruṣa. In this yajña, the Vasanta (spring) became the clarified Butter (Ghee), the Summer (Griśma) transformed itself as the fuel of wood (Samidhā), and the Autumn (Śarad) was there to serve as a special offering (Purodaś, i.e., ground rice, rounded as cake to offer as oblation into the sacrificial fire). In other words, the Gods offered oblations by contemplating in their minds. (This mantrā describes the 'cosmos creation yajña', unlike the yajña performed with grains, clarified butter and other special ingredients). (6)

❍ ❍ ❍

ॐ तं यज्ञं बर्हिषि प्रौक्षन् पुरुषं जातमग्रतः ।
तेन देवा अयजन्त साध्या ऋषयश्च ये ॥ ७ ॥

oṃ taṃ yajñaṃ barhiṣi praukṣan puruṣaṃ jātamagrata: |
tena devā ayajanta sādhyā ṛṣayaśca ye || 7 ||

Om! First of all the gods, seekers, and the sages, contemplated on performing yajña in their minds by considering the Puruṣa as the sacrificial animal and then purifying Him by sprinkling water over Him with Kuśa Grass. (7)

❍ ❍ ❍

ॐ तस्माद्यज्ञात्सर्वहुतः सम्भृतं पृषदाज्यम् ।
पशून् ताँश्चक्रे वायव्यानारण्यान् ग्राम्याश्च ये ॥ ८ ॥

oṃ tasmādyajñātsarvahuta: sambhṛtaṃ pṛṣadājyam |
paśūn tāṁścakera vāyavyānāraṇyān grāmyāśca ye || 8 ||

Om! In that yajña, wherein everything was offered, the Cosmos Puruṣa Himself was the oblation, that yajña produced clarified Butter (Ghee), milk, etc. That Yajña Puruṣa produced birds who live in the air, people living in the villages and animals living in the forest (the result of the yajña was the creation of all the creatures inhabiting the Sky, Earth and Water). (8)

❍ ❍ ❍

ॐ तस्माद्यज्ञात्सर्वहुत ऋचः सामानि जज्ञिरे ।
छन्दांसि जज्ञिरे तस्माद् यजुस्तस्मादजायत ॥ ९ ॥

oṃ tasmādyajñātsarvahuta ṛca: sāmāni jajñire |
chandāṃsi jajñire tasmād yajustasmādajāyata || 9 ||

Om! The yajña, wherein everything was offered from that Yajña Puruṣa, appeared the Rig Ved and the Sāma Ved. From that Puruṣa appeared the Gāyatrī Mantra and the Rhythmic metres and Yajurved also appeared from the Yajña Puruṣa. (9)

❍ ❍ ❍

ॐ तस्मादश्वा अजायन्त ये के चोभयादतः ।
गावो ह जज्ञिरे तस्मात्तस्माज्जाता अजावयः ॥ १० ॥

oṃ tasmādaśvā ajāyanta ye ke cobhayādata: |
gāvo ha jajñire tasmāttasmājjātā ajāvaya: || 10 ||

Om! The Yajña Puruṣa produced the horses, animals having two rows of teeth (Donkeys and Mules), cattle, goats and sheep were also born of the Yajña Puruṣa. (10)

❍ ❍ ❍

ॐ यत्पुरुषं व्यदधुः कतिधा व्यकल्पयन् ।
मुखं किमस्य कौ बाहू का ऊरु पादा उच्येते ॥ ११ ॥

oṃ yatpuruṣaṃ vyadadhu: katidhā vyakalpayan |
mukhaṃ kimasya kau bāhū kā ūru pādā ucyete || 11 ||

Om! The Yajña Puruṣa on whom the Gods contemplated upon was being imagined as having various attributes. In order to expand the creation of Gods, seekers and sages questioned and imagined as to who was the mouth of the Yajña Puruṣa? Who were the arms? Who were the thighs? And who became the feet? All this has been mentioned. (11)

❍ ❍ ❍

ॐ ब्राह्मणोऽस्य मुखमासीद्बाहू राजन्यः कृतः ।
ऊरू तदस्य यद् वैश्यः पद्भ्यां शूद्रो अजायत ॥ १२ ॥

oṃ brāhmaṇo'sya mukhamāsīdbāhū rājanya: kṛta: |
ūrū tadasya yad vaiśya: padbhyāṃ śūdro ajāyata || 12 ||

Om! Brāhmaṇ was the mouth of the Yajña Puruṣa and therefore Brāhmaṇs were born out of the mouth of the Yajña Puruṣa. Kśatriyās became both the arms, therefore the Kśatriyas were born out of both arms of the Yajña Puruṣa. Vaiśyās became both the thighs of the Yajña Puruṣa. The Śūdrās were born out of the feet of the Yajña Puruṣa. (12)

❍ ❍ ❍

ॐ चन्द्रमा मनसो जातश्चक्षोः सूर्यो अजायत ।
मुखादिन्द्रश्चाग्निश्च प्राणाद् वायुरजायत ॥ १३ ॥

oṃ candramā manaso jātaścakṣo: sūryo ajāyata |
mukhādindraścāgniśca prāṇād vāyurajāyata || 13 ||

Om! Moon was born out of the mind of Yajña Puruṣa. Sun was born out of His eyes. Indra and Agni were born out of His mouth and Vāyu was born out of the vital breath of the Yajña Puruṣa. (13)

❍ ❍ ❍

ॐ नाभ्या आसीदन्तरिक्षं शीर्ष्णो द्यौः समवर्तत ।
पद्भ्यां भूमिर्दिशः श्रोत्रात्तथा लोकाँ अकल्पयन् ॥ १४ ॥

oṃ nābhyā āsīdantarikṣaṃ śīrṣṇo dyau: samavartata |
padbhyāṃ bhūmirdiśa: śrotrāttathā lokāṁ
akalpayan || 14 ||

Om! Out of the navel of the Yajña Puruṣa emanated the entire space (Antarikśa). Heaven appeared out of His forehead, Earth appear from His feet and all the directions came into existence from the ears of the Yajña Puruṣa. In this way the entire universe was imagined to have come into existence within Him. (14)

❍ ❍ ❍

ॐ सप्तास्यासन् परिधयस्त्रिः सप्त समिधः कृताः ।
देवा यद्यज्ञं तन्वाना अबध्नन् पुरुषं पशुम् ॥ १५ ॥

oṃ saptāsyāsan paridhayastri: sapta samidha: kṛtā: |
devā yadyajñaṃ tanvānā abadhnan
puruṣaṃ paśum || 15 ||

Om! (In performing this yajña) The Devās fastened the Paśu (sacrificial animal) who is the Yajña Puruṣa Himself and there were seven Paridhis (enclosures of fuel sticks as the seven seas). Twenty one kinds of chandās (metres, three metres, Gayatrī, Atijagatī and Kriti and each one forming in seven ways) as Samidhā (sacrificial fuel sticks). (15)

❍ ❍ ❍

ॐ वेदाहमेतं पुरुषं महान्त-
मादित्यवर्णं तमसस्तु पारे ।
सर्वाणि रूपाणि विचित्य धीरो
नामानि कृत्वाभिवदन् यदास्ते ॥ १६ ॥

oṃ vedāhametaṃ puruṣaṃ mahānta-
mādityavarṇaṃ tamasastu pāre |
sarvāṇi rūpāṇi vicitya dhīro
nāmāni kṛtvābhivadan yadāste || 16 ||

Om!
I have known that Supreme Being (Puruṣa), who is, brilliantly shining like the Sun, and is beyond the darkness (of ignorance, i.e. Tamas). That Supreme Being, who sports within the intelligence of all beings, created all kinds of forms with their nomenclature, in the very beginning of creation; and dwells everywhere dealing with those names. (This mantrā describes the all pervading divine opulence of the Supreme Lord.) (16)

❍ ❍ ❍

ॐ धाता पुरस्ताद्यमुदाजहार
शक्रः प्रविद्वान् प्रदिशश्चतस्त्रः ।
तमेवं विद्वानमृत इह भवति
नान्यः पन्था विद्यते अयनाय ॥ १७ ॥

oṃ dhātā purastādyamudājahāra
śakra: pravidvān pradiśaścatasra: |
tamevaṃ vidvānamṛta iha bhavati
nānya: panthā vidyate ayanāya || 17 ||

Om! Brahmā, the Prajāpati eulogises Him in the ancient times, Indra (the King of the Gods) had known Him, pervading in all the four directions; and anyone who knows Him (pervading in all forms), thus becomes immortal in this life (itself). In order to attain liberation (from transmigration), there is no path other than this (merging with the Supreme-Self or the Abode of the Great Lord, Puruṣa). (17)

❍ ❍ ❍

ॐ यज्ञेन यज्ञमयजन्त देवा-
स्तानि धर्माणि प्रथमान्यासन् ।
ते ह नाकं महिमानः सचन्त
यत्र पूर्वे साध्याः सन्ति देवाः ॥ १८ ॥
[ऋग्वेद, मुद्गलोपनिषद्]

oṃ yajñena yajñamayajanta devā-
stāni dharmāṇi prathamānyāsan |
te ha nākaṃ mahimāna: sacanta
yatra pūrve sādhyā: santi devā:[+] || 18 ||
[ṛgveda, mudgalopaniṣad]

\+ a particular class of celestial beings.
This is the 16th mantrā in the Puruṣa Sūkta (A) Part.

Om! The Upaniṣad indicates in this mantrā for the attainment of liberation from this mortal world. And for this most aspired for goal in life, this śruti is interpreted as follows:

The Devtās worship the Yajña form of the Supreme Puruṣa, through performing Yajña, as a result, all the Dharma (righteousness) comes into existence. The devtās, by following those righteous deeds, become pious and glorious, and attain Heaven, where the ancient Sādhya Devās dwell.

❍ ❍ ❍

Viṣṇu Hymns (A)
[विष्णु सूक्त (क)]

The seer of this sūkta is sage 'Dīrghātmā'. The Supreme Lord Viṣṇu holds varied forms and karmās (actions). He is known as 'Mahā Viṣṇu' in His unparalleled, The Supreme Lord's form. The yajña and the (water-producing) Sun are also His forms. (The Sun causes waters in the oceans and other places to evaporate and rain again, hence the chief source of water). He is the ancient most, creator of the universe, ever new and, inexhaustibly, beautiful. The attraction of the world, Goddess Lakśamī is His consort. The chanting of His name and His dallying acts (His playful acts, i.e. Līlā) enables one to achieve liberation (Paramapada-मोक्ष), which is the highest goal in a man's life.

If one looks at Him (with expectation), The Lord, too reciprocates, obliging the devotee by fulfilling his aspirations. The text is presented with translation, hereunder:

इदं विष्णुर्वि चक्रमे त्रेधा नि दधे पदम् ।
समूढमस्य पाꣳसुरे स्वाहा ॥ १ ॥

idaṃ viṣṇurvi cakrame tredhā ni dadhe padam |
samūḍhamasya pāꣳsure svāhā || 1 ||

The all pervading, Supreme Lord, Viṣṇu is bearing this universe, and in three steps of His feet, He places one step over earth, the other over in space, and the third step over the heaven. It, simply, means that He is Omnipresent, in every nook and corner. In Lord Viṣṇu lies the enitre creation (universe). And we offer oblation in His name. (1)

❍ ❍ ❍

Lord Viṣṇu on Sheshshaiya

इरावती धेनुमती हि भूतꣳसूयवसिनी मनवे दशस्या ।
व्यस्कभ्ना रोदसी विष्णवेते दाधर्थ
पृथिवीमभितो मयूखैः स्वाहा ॥ २ ॥

**irāvatī dhenumatī hi bhūtaꣳsūyavasinī
manave daśasyā |
vyaskabhnā rodasī viṣṇavete dādhartha
pṛthivīmabhito mayūkhai: svāhā || 2 ||**

The earth gives grains, cows, edibles as the favourable means for the welfare of all beings. O Lord Viṣṇu! Thy radiant energy is all pervasive, holding the earth from all sides. We offer oblation unto Thy Supreme form. (2)

❍ ❍ ❍

देवश्रुतौ देवेष्वा घोषतं प्राची प्रेतमध्वरं
कल्पयन्ती ऊर्ध्वं यज्ञं नयतं मा जिह्वरतम् ।
स्वं गोष्ठमा वदतं देवी दुर्ये
आयुर्मा निर्वादिष्टं प्रजां मा
निर्वादिष्टमत्र रमेथां वर्ष्मन् पृथिव्याः ॥ ३ ॥

**devaśrutau deveṣvā ghoṣataṃ prācī pretamadhvaraṃ
kalpayantī ūrdhvaṃ yajñaṃ nayataṃ mā jihvaratam |
svaṃ goṣṭhamā vadataṃ devī durye
āyurmā nirvādiṣṭaṃ prajāṃ mā
nirvādiṣṭamatra ramethāṃ varṣman pṛthivyā: || 3 ||**

(O Lord!) Thou shalt speak in the midst of the renowned scholars, to go towards the east and make the yajña (sacrificial-fire) elevated, (not letting it down) supporting fire sacrifice. Let the residents of sanctums go to the cowsheds to reside there and bless them with wealth, as long as they live, be favourable to their progeny, and may Thee always reside, in this happy place. (3)

❍ ❍ ❍

विष्णोर्नुकं वीर्याणि प्र वोचं यः
पार्थिवानि विममे रजाꣳसि।
यो अस्कभायदुत्तर ꣳ सधस्थं विचक्रमाण-
स्त्रेधोरुगायो विष्णवे त्वा ॥ ४ ॥

viṣṇornukaṃ vīryāṇi pra vocaṃ ya:
pārthivāni vimame rajāꣳsi|
yo askabhāyaduttara ꣳ sadhasthaṃ vicakramāṇa-
stredhorugāyo viṣṇave tvā || 4 ||

That all pervading Oversoul Viṣṇu, who created the universe, the space and the heaven by His power and capacity, is applauded in the three worlds, for His prowess, holding the highest position, lending it elegance. How can one eulogise the glories of that Omnipresent Supreme Lord Viṣṇu! (4)

❍ ❍ ❍

दिवो वा विष्ण उत वा पृथिव्या
महो वा विष्ण उरोरन्तरिक्षात् ।
उभा हि हस्ता वसुना पृणस्वा
प्र यच्छ दक्षिणादोत सव्याद्विष्णवे त्वा ॥ ५ ॥

divo vā viṣṇa uta vā pṛthivyā
maho vā viṣṇa urorantarikṣāt |
ubhā hi hastā vasunā pṛṇasvā
pra yaccha dakṣiṇādota savyādviṣṇave tvā || 5 ||

O Lord Viṣṇu! With Thy generosity, kindly provide the entire world with happiness, and ensure provisions of the produces of the earth and happiness with properties from the space. O Omniscient Lord! O provider of all happiness, who provides with both of Thy hands, we worship Thee as the Supreme. (5)

❍ ❍ ❍

प्र तद्विष्णु स्तवते वीर्येण
मृगो न भीमः कुचरो गिरिष्ठाः।
यस्योरुषु त्रिषु विक्रमणेष्व-
धिक्षियन्ति भुवनानि विश्वा ॥ ६ ॥

pra tadviṣṇu stavate vīryeṇa
mṛgo na bhīma: kucaro giriṣṭhā:|
yasyoruṣu triṣu vikramaṇeṣva-
dhikṣiyanti bhuvanāni viśvā || 6 ||

O all-pervading Lord Viṣṇu! Like a ferocious lion roaming around in the mountains, Thou art worthy of being extolled for Thy unparalleled strength. All the beings live in the three worlds of the all-pervasive Lord Viṣṇu. (6)

❍ ❍ ❍

विष्णो रराटमसि विष्णोः श्नप्त्रे स्थो विष्णोः
स्यूरसि विष्णोर्ध्रुवोऽसि । वैष्णवमसि विष्णवे त्वा ॥ ७ ॥
[शु० यजु० ५ । १५-२१]

viṣṇo rarāṭamasi viṣṇo: śnaptre stho viṣṇo:
syūrasi viṣṇodhruvo'si | vaiṣṇavamasi viṣṇave tvā || 7 ||
[śu. yaju. 5 | 15-21]

The (divine, brilliant) light of the all-pervasive Lord Viṣṇu is spreading, continually, all over the universe. He is the cause of its stability, and He is the cause of the expansion of Universe from Him; and the Lord Supreme exists in each atom, each particle. O the Creator of the universe Lord! We worship Thee. (7)

(Śukla Yajurveda 5/15-21)

Viṣṇu Hymns (B)

[विष्णु सूक्त (ख)]

Many other versions of 'Viṣṇu Sūkta' are also available in the Vedas. The 100th Sūkta in the Rigveda is also Viṣṇu Sūkta. It comprises prayers to Lord Viṣṇu to bless us with wealth and prosperity and pure intellect. This sūkta describes the pastimes (Līlā) of Lord Vāman. The sage of the sūkta is Maitrāvaruṇi Vasiṣth, the metre is 'Triṣtup', and the God is Viṣṇu. The text is given hereunder with translation:

नू मर्तो दयते सनिष्यन् यो विष्णव उरुगायाय दाशत् ।
प्र यः सत्राचा मनसा यजात एतावन्तं नर्यमाविवासात् ॥ १ ॥

nū marto dayate saniṣyan yo viṣṇava urugāyāya dāśat |
pra ya: satrācā manasā yajāta etāvantaṃ
naryamāvivāsāt || 1 ||

That man alone gets wealth soon, who desiring it keenly, performs elegant worship of the most revered of all, Lord Viṣṇu, by offering oblations of superior order, chanting mantrās, and also serves Him (The One, who is the greatest well-wisher of man) with salutations. (1)

❍ ❍ ❍

त्वं विष्णो सुमतिं विश्वजन्यामप्रयुतामेवयावो मतिं दाः।
पर्चो यथा नः सुवितस्य भूरेरश्वावतः पुरुश्चन्द्रस्य रायः ॥ २ ॥

tvaṃ viṣṇo sumatiṃ viśvajanyāmaprayutāmevayāvo
matiṃ dā:|
parco yathā na: suvitasya bhūreraśvāvata:
paruścandrasya rāya: || 2 ||

The maker of the dreams of the worshippers come true, O Lord Viṣṇu! Bless us with a pure and faultless intellect which would enable us to own abundant number of horses and wealth, which pleases many.

❍ ❍ ❍

त्रिर्देवः पृथिवीमेष एतां वि चक्रमे शतर्चसं महित्वा ।
प्र विष्णुरस्तु तवसस्तवीयान् त्वेषं ह्यस्य स्थविरस्य नाम ॥ ३ ॥

trirdeva: pṛthivīmeṣa etāṃ vi cakrame śatarcasaṃ mahitvā |
pra viṣṇurastu tavasastavīyān tveṣaṃ hyasya sthavirasya nāma || 3 ||

Adorned with these qualities of charity etc., Lord Viṣṇu, in His incarnation as Vāman, seized this earth, which was lighted with numberless rays with His great three foot-steps. May That ancient than the most ancient Viṣṇu be our Master. Being this much ancient (स्थविर), the name Viṣṇu and His form is illumined. (3)

वि चक्रमे पृथिवीमेष एतां क्षेत्राय विष्णुर्मनुषे दशस्यन् ।
ध्रुवासो अस्य कीरयो जनास उरुक्षितिं सुजनिमा चकार ॥ ४ ॥

vi cakrame pṛthivīmeṣa etāṃ kṣetrāya viṣṇurmanuṣe daśasyan |
dhruvāso asya kīrayo janāsa urukṣitiṃ sujanimā cakāra || 4 ||

Lord Viṣṇu covered up the three worlds with His three steps, superceding the three worlds from the demons in order to provide inhabitation to the Gods. The Gods eulogising (स्तुतिकर्ता प्रशंसक)Lord Viṣṇu are unfaltering (in this world and the other world). Viṣṇu, the Lord of beautiful incarnations, built an expansive inhabitation for His worshippers. (4)

❍ ❍ ❍

प्र तत् ते अद्य शिपिविष्ट नामाऽर्यः शंसामि वयुनानि विद्वान् ।
तं त्वा गृणामि तवसमतव्यान् क्षयन्तमस्य रजसः पराके ॥ ५ ॥

pra tat te adya śipiviṣṭa nāmā'rya: śaṃsāmi vayunāni vidvān |
taṃ tvā gṛṇāmi tavasamatavyān kṣayantamasya rajasa: parāke || 5 ||

O Lord Viṣṇu, effulgent with excessive rays! O Revered (Ārya)! We, quite young ones, shall eulogise Thine (that) very ancient name Viṣṇu, despite being well aware of other knowable subjects, because Thou art residing away from this world of passion. (5)

❍ ❍ ❍

किमित् ते विष्णो परिचक्ष्यं भूत् प्र यद् ववक्षे शिपिविष्टो अस्मि।
मा वर्पो अस्मदप गूह एतद् यदन्यरूपः समिथे बभूथ ॥ ६ ॥

kimit te viṣṇo paricakṣyaṃ bhūt pra yad vavakṣe śipiviṣṭo asmi|
mā varpo asmadapa gūha etad yadanyarūpa: samithe babhūtha || 6 ||

O Lord Viṣṇu! As Thou sayest of Thyself, 'I am śipiviṣṭa (pervaded by rays)', is it, then, justified for Thee to conceal that form? Do not conceal Thy form from us. It is another form that Thou had adorned during war. (6)

❍ ❍ ❍

वषट्ते विष्णवास आ कृणोमि तन्मे जुषस्व शिपिविष्ट हव्यम् ।
वर्धन्तु त्वा सुष्टुतयो गिरो मे यूयं पात स्वस्तिभिः सदा नः ॥ ७ ॥
[ऋग्वेद ७ । १००]

vaṣaṭte viṣṇavāsa ā kṛṇomi tanme juṣasva śipiviṣṭa havyam |
vardhantu tvā suṣṭutayo giro me yūyaṃ pāta svastibhi: sadā na: || 7 ||
[ṛgveda 7 | 100]

O Lord Viṣṇu! For Thee, I make an oblation to the deity Fire, orally, (vaṣatkār वषट्कार- means an exclamation of making oblation – may the God of Fire bear it.) O Lord, pervaded by rays, oblige me by accepting that oblation. May Thee flourish by our eulogies, and Thou shalt kindly bless us forever by nourishing us. (7)

(Rigveda 7/100)

❍ ❍ ❍

One, observing oneness of the mind, speech and action, is a great-soul, i.e., Mahātmā; behaving otherwise than this, one is nothing else but a wicked-soul, i.e., Durātmā.

❍ ❍ ❍

May brothers bear no ill intention with each other, sisters bear no hatred with one another, with uniform speed and uniformity in rules, may they speak auspiciously. **(Ath. Veda 3|30|3)**

❍ ❍ ❍

Lead me from the unreal to the Real.
Lead me from darkness to Light.
Lead me from death to Immortality.

(Brihada. Upaniṣad)

असतो मा सद्गमय ।
तमसो मा ज्योतिर्गमय ।
मृत्योर्मा अमृतम् गमय ।

❍ ❍ ❍

Nārāyaṇa Hymns
(नारायण सूक्त)

The sage of this sūkta is Nārāyaṇa, the God is Āditya-Puruṣa, and metres are Bhūrigārṣī Triṣtup, Nicyṛdārṣī Triṣtup and Ārṣyanuṣtup. This sūkta consits of six mantrās. Apart from the sixteen mantrās of Puruṣa-sūkta (Śuklayajurveda), these six mantrās are additional to those sixteen. This is also known as later Nārāyaṇa sūkta. This sūkta points out about the knowledge of a man's duty alongside evolving creation, and it also brings to light the glory of Lord Viṣṇu (the Cosmic-Puruṣa). The special feature of it is, that all the Gods come under the influence of the scholar of these mantrās. The sūkta goes as under:

अद्‌भ्यः सम्भृतः पृथिव्यै रसाच्च विश्वकर्मणः समवर्तताग्रे ।
तस्य त्वष्टा विदधद्रूपमेति तन्मर्त्यस्य देवत्वमाजानमग्रे ॥ १ ॥

adbhya: sambhṛta: pṛthivyai rasācca viśvakarmaṇa: samavartatāgera |
tasya tvaṣṭā vidadhadrūpameti tanmartyasya devatvamājānamagre || 1 ||

Expanding out of His (The Parampuruṣa) generosity, the Virātapuruṣa manifested Himself out of the all spread over water in order to cause the element of earth to come into existence. The Sun appears as His form in the act of creation, who is the chief God for the mankind. (This is how the expansion of creation begins.)

Aditi's son is Sun (सूर्य), they are six to twelve in number, comprising Varuṇ, Mitra, Aryamān, Bhaga, Dakśa, and Anśa; when their number was twelve, they were interpreted as personifications of the Sun, as the Sun appears in different aspects during the succeeding months of the year.

❍ ❍ ❍

वेदाहमेतं पुरुषं महान्तमादित्यवर्णं तमसः परस्तात् ।
तमेव विदित्वाति मृत्युमेति नान्यः पन्था विद्यतेऽयनाय ॥ २ ॥

vedāhametaṃ puruṣaṃ mahāntamādityavarṇaṃ tamasa: parastāt |
tameva viditvāti mṛtyumeti nānya: panthā vidyate'yanāya || 2 ||

I have known the Supreme Being (Puruṣa), who is brilliantly shining like the Sun, and is beyond the darkness of 'Tamas', i.e. ignorance. Liberation from death is possible only on attaining knowledge of the Supreme Being. There is no path other than this, i.e. His shelter. (2)

❍ ❍ ❍

प्रजापतिश्चरति गर्भे अन्तरजायमानो बहुधा वि जायते ।
तस्य योनिं परि पश्यन्ति धीरास्तस्मिन् ह तस्थुर्भुवनानि विश्वा ॥ ३ ॥

prajāpatiścarati garbhe antarajāyamāno bahudhā vi jāyate |
tasya yoniṃ pari paśyanti dhīrāstasmin ha tasthurbhuvanāni viśvā || 3 ||

That Oversoul moves inside the cosmic womb of creation. Though unborn, He takes birth in different forms. Only a self-disciplined man attains His real sight. And in Him lies the entire creation. (3)

❍ ❍ ❍

यो देवेभ्य आतपति यो देवानां पुरोहितः ।
पूर्वो यो देवेभ्यो जातो नमो रुचाय ब्राह्मये ॥ ४ ॥

yo devebhya ātapati yo devānāṃ purohita: |
pūrvo yo devebhyo jāto namo rucāya brāhmaye || 4 ||

Salutations to the Self-illumining Brahm, who shines like the Sun for the Gods, helping in fulfilling their assignments, and Who appears even before the Gods (Themselves).

❍ ❍ ❍

रुचं ब्राह्मं जनयन्तो देवा अग्रे तदब्रुवन् ।
यस्त्वैवं ब्राह्मणो विद्यात्तस्य देवा असन् वशे ॥ ५ ॥

rucaṃ brāhmaṃ janayanto devā agre tadabruvan |
yastvaivaṃ brāhmaṇo vidyāttasya devā asan vaśe || 5 ||

After the manifestation of the illumined Brahm, in the beginning of creation, the Gods exhorted, 'That brāhmaṇa who realizes Thee in this real form, the Gods will be under his control.' (5)

❍ ❍ ❍

श्रीश्च ते लक्ष्मीश्च पत्न्यावहोरात्रे पार्श्वे
नक्षत्राणि रूपमश्विनौ व्यात्तम् ।
इष्णन्निषाणामुं म इषाण
सर्वलोकं म इषाण ॥ ६ ॥
[शु० यजुर्वेद]

śrīśca te lakṣmīśca patnyāvahorātre pārśve
nakṣatrāṇi rūpamaśvinau vyāttam |
iṣṇannisāṇāmuṃ ma iṣāṇa
sarvalokaṃ ma iṣāṇa || 6 ||
[śu. yajurveda]

O Cosmic-Being (Puruṣa)! The goddesses of prosperity and lusture (Lakśmī) are Thy consorts. Day and night are Thy lateral parts. The numberless stars are Thy forms. The heaven and earth are Thy widely opened mouth. Desire for transcendental-world (Parloka), when desiring. 'May I become all pervasive' (By attaining Brahmatva) – have this desire, have this desire. (6)

(Śukla Yajurveda)

❍ ❍ ❍

Lord Rudra, Most Munificent (Karuṇāvaruṇālay Paramātmā)

Rudra Hymns
(रुद्र सूक्त)

The recitation of 'Rudra Sūkta' carries special importance, in order to please the creator of the universe, an ever blissful, Lord Śiva. In adoration of Lord Śiva, the stream of water is dear most to Him. There is, therefore, a tradition of performing 'Rudrābhiṣekam' in His worship. This sūkta, if repeated eleven times, while reciting the eight-chapter Rudra Hymns, the 'Abhiṣekam' is considered complete. It is very fructifying from the point of view of eradication of 'Tritāpās', the three categories of human suffereings, the physical (Daihik)[1], also known as (Ādhyātmik), the natural calamities (Daivik)[2] and the mundane (Bhautik)[3]. The Abhiṣekam (stream of water or milk, or some other substance on the 'Śiva-Linga' alongwith recitation of the eight chapter Rudra Hymns is Abhiṣeka-ceremony) emancipates the devotee from the 'Tritāpās'.

The 'Rudra Sūkta' comprises mantrās (hymns) eulogising Lord Śiva, the cosmic energy for destruction. This energy is manifested through the thunder and lightning in the sky, to man-made wars, and some desirable termination of life in our old age, and under other prolonged sufferings. And the text goes as under:

ॐ नमस्ते रुद्र मन्यव उतो त इषवे नमः ।
बाहुभ्यामुत ते नमः ॥ १ ॥

---

1 'Daihik' (Physical) sufferings are visible and invisible ones, we undergo in life, like many physical diseases and accidents and desires and lustful thoughts, anger, greed, envy and hatred.

2 Daivik (Natural) sufferings like earthquakes, tsunami, hurricanes and floods, sometimes, epidemics.

3 Bhautik (worldly causes) sufferings are man-made ones, like personal enemies, warring nations, belligerent neighbours, etc.

Om namaste rudra manyava uto ta iṣave nama: |
bāhubhyāmuta te nama: || 1 ||

Om, O Rudra! The eliminator of sufferings (or the one who enlightens), salutations to Thy ire, and also to Thy arrows and arms. (1)

❍ ❍ ❍

या ते रुद्र शिवा तनूरघोराऽपापकाशिनी ।
तया नस्तन्वा शन्तमया गिरिशन्ताभि चाकशीहि ॥ २ ॥

yā te rudra śivā tanūraghorā'pāpakāśinī |
tayā nastanvā śantamayā giriśantābhi cākaśīhi || 2 ||

O Giriśānta! (Inhabiting mount Kailās engaged in welfare of the world, or confering happiness to the people getting engaged in speech, or existing in rains providing pleasure to the people) O Rudra! Behold by Thy auspicious, gentle, and (only) righteousness-emitting body, with that body of immeasurable pleasure protect us. (2)

❍ ❍ ❍

यामिषुं गिरिशन्त हस्ते बिभर्ष्यस्तवे ।
शिवां गिरित्र तां कुरु मा हिꣳसीः पुरुषं जगत् ॥ ३ ॥

yāmiṣuṃ giriśanta haste bibharṣyastave |
śivāṃ giritra tāṃ kuru mā hiꣳsī: puruṣaṃ jagat || 3 ||

O Omniscient Lord Rudra! Who dwells on mount Kailās, engaged in welfare of the world, and existing in rains, protects the universe. May the arrow, Thou art holding in Thy hand to eliminate the ememies, be auspicious; and Thou shalt not destroy my sons, grandsons, cows and horses. (3)

❍ ❍ ❍

शिवेन वचसा त्वा गिरिशाच्छा वदामसि ।
यथा नः सर्वमिज्जगदयक्ष्मꣳ सुमना असत् ॥ ४ ॥

śivena vacasā tvā giriśācchā vadāmasi |
yathā na: sarvamijjagadayakṣmaꣳ sumanā asat || 4 ||

O Lord of mount Kailās (reposing there)! We pray with our auspicious hymns to attain Thee. We beseech Thee to make our world free from sufferings, illness and discord, and our mind fully purged of evils. (4)

❍ ❍ ❍

अध्यवोचदधिवक्ता प्रथमो दैव्यो भिषक् ।
अहींश्च सर्वाञ्जम्भयन्त्सर्वाश्च
यातुधान्योऽधराचीः परा सुव ॥ ५ ॥

adhyavocadadhivaktā prathamo daivyo bhiṣav |
ahīṃśca sarvāñjambhayantsarvāśca
yātudhānyo'dharācī: parā suva || 5 ||

Lord Rudra! O Highly venerable, chief amongst all the Gods, favourable to Gods, and eradicator of diseases, speak mostly to me, enable me to become superb. O Rudra! Annihilate all violent creatures, as snakes, tigers, etc. and drive away also the lowly moving evil spirits and (female) demons. (5)

❍ ❍ ❍

असौ यस्ताम्रो अरुण उत बभ्रुः सुमङ्गलः ।
ये चैनꣳ रुद्रा अभितो दिक्षु श्रिताः
सहस्रशोऽवैषाꣳ हेड ईमहे ॥ ६ ॥

asau yastāmro aruṇa uta babhru: sumaṅgala: |
ye cainaꣳ rudrā abhito dikṣu śritā:
sahasraśo'vaiṣāꣳ heḍa īmahe || 6 ||

This Sun, who is copper-red when rising, golden-yellow when setting, and yellowish all other times, this, highly, auspicious and beneficent one is, verily, Rudra. In the form of rays, thousands of Rudras are surrounding the Sun in all directions, may I ward off their ire by my devotional worship. (6)

❍ ❍ ❍

असौ योऽवसर्पति नीलग्रीवो विलोहितः ।
उतैनं गोपा अदृश्रन्नदृश्रन्नुदहार्यः स दृष्टो मृडयाति नः ॥ ७ ॥

**asau yo'vasarpati nīlagrīvo vilohita: |
utainaṃ gopā adṛśrannadṛśrannudahārya: sa dṛṣṭo mṛḍayāti na: || 7 ||**

The blue-throated Rudra, because of bearing poison, existing in the Sun-sphere in the form of the Sun, who shines reddish, when rising or setting and whom even innocent cowherd and water-carrying maids can also behold; Let Him make us happy. (7)

❍ ❍ ❍

नमोऽस्तु नीलग्रीवाय सहस्राक्षाय मीढुषे ।
अथो ये अस्य सत्वानोऽहं तेभ्योऽकरं नमः ॥ ८ ॥

Let my salutations be to Lord Rudra, who is blue-throated and has a thousand eyes, and who brings rains in the form of Indra. I offer my obeisances to His followers also. (8)

❍ ❍ ❍

प्रमुञ्च धन्वनस्त्वमुभयोरार्त्न्योर्ज्याम् ।
याश्च ते हस्त इषवः परा ता भगवो वप ॥ ९ ॥

**pramuñca dhanvanastvamubhayorārtnyorjyām |
yāśca te hasta iṣava: parā tā bhagavo vapa || 9 ||**

O Lord Rudra! Let loose the string from the middle of both ends of Thy bow and throw away the arrows from Thy hand (meaning be graceful unto us). (9)

❍ ❍ ❍

विज्यं धनुः कपर्दिनो विशल्यो बाणवाँ२ उत ।
अनेशन्नस्य या इषव आभुरस्य निषङ्गधिः ॥ १० ॥

**vijyaṃ dhanu: kapardino viśalyo bāṇavāṁ2 uta |
aneśannasya yā iṣava ābhurasya niṣaṅgadhi: || 10 ||**

Let the bow of Kapardin (having matted locks and twisted hair) Lord Rudra be without string, and the arrows in Thy quiver be pointless and get destroyed (become incapable to strike), and also Thy sheath becomes empty of swords, meaning thereby, Rudra be, wholly, kind unto us. (10)

❍ ❍ ❍

या ते हेतिर्मीढुष्टम हस्ते बभूव ते धनुः ।
तयाऽस्मान्विश्वतस्त्वमयक्ष्मया परि भुज ॥ ११ ॥

yā te hetirmīḍhuṣṭama haste babhūva te dhanu: |
tayā'smānviśvatastvamayakṣmayā pari bhuja || 11 ||

O Rudra! The provider of abudant rains, having the weapon of bow in Thy hand, with that strong bow, protect us from all sides.

❍ ❍ ❍

परि ते धन्वनो हेतिरस्मान्वृणक्तु विश्वतः ।
अथो य इषुधिस्तवारे अस्मन्नि धेहि तम् ॥ १२ ॥

pari te dhanvano hetirasmānvṛṇaktu viśvata: |
atho ya iṣudhistavāre asmanni dhehi tam || 12 ||

O Rudra! Let us be spared by Thy arrow from all sides, and keep Thy quiver of arrows far away from us. (12)

❍ ❍ ❍

अवतत्य धनुष्ट्वꣳ सहस्राक्ष शतेषुधे ।
निशीर्य शल्यानां मुखा शिवो नः सुमना भव ॥ १३ ॥

avatatya dhanuṣṭvaꣳ sahasrākṣa śateṣudhe |
niśīrya śalyānāṃ mukhā śivo na: sumanā bhava || 13 ||

O Rudra! Having a thousand eyes, and bearing a hundred quivers, setting aside the string of the bow and making the front edges of arrows blunt, (kindly) bestow upon us your tranquil and joyous form. (13)

❍ ❍ ❍

नमस्त आयुधायानातताय धृष्णवे ।
उभाभ्यामुत ते नमो बाहुभ्यां तव धन्वने ॥ १४ ॥

namasta āyudhāyānātatāya dhṛṣṇave |
ubhābhyāmuta te namo bāhubhyāṃ tava dhanvane || 14 ||

O Rudra! Our salutations to Thee for Thy skill and boldness in killing enemies and to Thy unloaded arrows, and also salutations to Thy both arms and bow.

❍ ❍ ❍

मा नो महान्तमुत मा नो
अर्भकं मा न उक्षन्तमुत मा न उक्षितम् ।
मा नो वधीः पितरं मोत मातरं
मा नः प्रियास्तन्वो रुद्र रीरिषः ॥ १५ ॥

mā no mahāntamuta mā no
arbhakaṃ mā na ukṣantamuta mā na ukṣitam |
mā no vadhī: pitaraṃ mota mātaraṃ
mā na: priyāstanvo rudra rīriṣa: || 15 ||

O Rudra! Do not kill our preceptor, elderly male relations (paternal uncles, etc.), children and youth, babies in the womb, our parents and our dear sons and grandsons etc.(15)

❍ ❍ ❍

मा नस्तोके तनये मा न आयुषि
मा नो गोषु मा नो अश्वेषु रीरिषः ।
मा नो वीरान् रुद्र भामिनो वधी-
र्हविष्मन्तः सदमित् त्वा हवामहे ॥ १६ ॥

mā nastoke tanaye mā na āyuṣi
mā no goṣu mā no aśveṣu rīriṣa: |
mā no vīrān rudra bhāmino vadhī-
rhaviṣmanta: sadamit tvā havāmahe || 16 ||

O Rudra! Do not destroy our descendants, our longivity of

age, our cows and horses, and our ferocious braves. We invoke Thee always with our oblations. (16)

❍ ❍ ❍

नमो हिरण्यबाहवे सेनान्ये दिशां च पतये नमो
नमो वृक्षेभ्यो हरिकेशेभ्य: पशूनां पतये नमो नम:
शष्पिञ्जराय त्विषीमते पथीनां पतये नमो नमो
हरिकेशायोपवीतिने पुष्टानां पतये नम: ॥ १७ ॥

namo hiraṇyabāhave senānye diśāṃ ca pataye namo
namo vṛkṣebhyo harikeśebhya: paśūnāṃ pataye namo nama:
śaṣpiñjarāya tviṣīmate pathīnāṃ pataye namo namo
harikeśāyopavītine puṣṭānāṃ pataye nama: || 17 ||

Salutations to Lord Rudra, the chief of hosts, bearing gold on arms, salutations to Lord Rudra, tendng directions, salutations to the green haired Rudras in the form of trees fully laden with green branches and leaves; salutations to Lord, who maintains all beings, salutations to the Lord radiant like the yellow off-shoot of grass; salutations to the maintainer of pathways; salutations to the blue-haired Lord, wearing auspicious sacred-thread (yajñopavīta); and to the Lord of mankind, filled with qualities. (17)

❍ ❍ ❍

नमो बभ्लुशाय व्याधिने ऽन्नानां पतये नमो
नमो भवस्य हेत्यै जगतां पतये नमो
नमो रुद्रायाततायिने क्षेत्राणां पतये नमो
नम: सूतायाहन्त्यै वनानां पतये नम: ॥ १८ ॥

namo babhluśāya vyādhine 'nnānāṃ pataye namo
namo bhavasya hetyai jagatāṃ pataye namo
namo rudrāyātatāyine kṣetrāṇāṃ pataye namo
nama: sūtāyāhantyai vanānāṃ pataye nama: || 18 ||

Salutations to Lord Rudra, having Kapil's complexion or

who rides on the bull and has power to pierce the enemies; salutation to the Lord, who is the preserver of grains; salutation to Rudra, the instrument of annihilation of the world*; salutation to Him who maintains the world; salutation to Rudra who protects the physical bodies; salutation to Rudra, the charioteer who does not kill; salutations to Lord Rudra, who protects fields (and sacred places) and forest.(18)

* or destroyer of miseries

❍ ❍ ❍

नमो रोहिताय स्थपतये वृक्षाणां पतये नमो
नमो भुवन्तये वारिवस्कृतायौषधीनां पतये नमो
नमो मन्त्रिणे वाणिजाय कक्षाणां पतये नमो
नम उच्चैर्घोषायाक्रन्दयते पत्तीनां पतये नमः ॥ १९ ॥

namo rohitāya sthapataye vṛkṣāṇāṃ pataye namo
namo bhuvantaya vārivaskṛtāyauṣadhīnāṃ pataye namo
namo mantriṇe vāṇijāya kakṣāṇāṃ pataye namo
nama uccairghoṣāyākrandayate pattīnāṃ
pataye nama: || 19 ||

Salutations to the red-complexioned Lord Rudra in the form of divine builder of houses etc., Viśwakarmā and to the protector of trees; salutations to Him, who expands the creation and brings prosperity; salutations to Rudra the saver of medicinal vegetation; salutations to the Lord, apt in criticism in the form of trader, to the Lord protector of vine (that grows around and over) and trees in forests; salutations to Lord Rudra, who utters fearsome cry, and makes enemies shed tears, and salutations to the Lord Rudra, who protects the marching soldiers (on elephant, horses, chariots and on foot). (19)

❍ ❍ ❍

नमः कृत्स्नायतया धावते सत्वनां पतये नमो नमः
सहमानाय निव्याधिन आव्याधिनीनां पतये नमो
नमो निषङ्गिणे ककुभाय स्तेनानां पतये नमो
नमो निचेरवे परिचरायारण्यानां पतये नमः ॥ २० ॥

nama: kṛtsnāyatayā dhāvate satvanāṃ pataye namo nama:
sahamānāya nivyādhina āvyādhinīnāṃ pataye namo namo niṣaṅigaṇe kakubhāya stenānāṃ pataye namo namo nicerave paricarāyāraṇyānāṃ pataye nama: || 20 ||

Salutations to Rudra who pulls the string of the bow up to His ear, running swift in battle or who gives full advantage (to one, seeking it); salutation to Rudra, the protector of those who come to His shelter; salutatins to the Lord, who sets aside the enemies and pierces them; salutations to Rudra, the protector of brave armed forces, striking vehemently and who wields the sword, effectively; salutations to the Lord, the saver of hidden thieves, and protecting who move around in market-places etc., intending to steal and carry away goods, and salutations to Rudra, the protector of forests. (20)

❍ ❍ ❍

नमो वञ्चते परिवञ्चते स्तायूनां पतये नमो नमो
निषङ्गिण इषुधिमते तस्कराणां पतये नमो नमः
सृकायिभ्यो जिघाꣳसद्भ्यो मुष्णतां पतये नमो
नमोऽसिमद्भ्यो नक्तञ्चरद्भ्यो विकृन्तानां पतये नमः ॥ २१ ॥

namo vañcate parivañcate stāyūnāṃ pataye namo namo niṣaṅigaṇa iṣudhimate taskarāṇāṃ pataye namo nama: sṛkāyibhyo jighāꣳsadbhyo muṣṇatāṃ pataye namo namo'simadbhyo nattañcaradbhyo vikṛntānāṃ pataye nama: || 21 ||

Salutations to Rudra, who, deceptively, robs the master, breaching his trust and who protects the stealer of concealed wealth; salutations to Rudra, who bears quiver and arrows and protects those who steal openly. Salutations to the bearer of thunderbolt, who intends to kill enemies, and protects one, who intends to steal grains in fields; Salutations to Rudra, bearing sword, moving around during night to attack beings; and He protects those who kill others to rob their wealth. (21)

❍ ❍ ❍

नम उष्णीषिणे गिरिचराय कुलुञ्चानां पतये
नमो नम इषुमद्भ्यो धन्वायिभ्यश्च वो नमो
नम आतन्वानेभ्यः प्रतिदधानेभ्यश्च वो नमो
नम आयच्छद्भ्यो ऽस्यद्भ्यश्च वो नमः ॥ २२ ॥

nama uṣṇīṣiṇe giricarāya kuluñcānāṃ pataye
namo nama iṣumadbhyo dhanvāyibhyaśca vo namo
nama ātanvānebhya: pratidadhānebhyaśca vo namo
nama āyacchadbhyo 'syadbhyaśca vo nama: || 22 ||

Salutations to Rudra, who wears a turban and moves around the mountains on different places; salutations to Rudra, the protector of deceitful robbers of others' fields and houses; salutations to Rudras who bear bow and arrows to scare people; salutations to Rudras, who attach the string on bow, to Rudras, who shoot arrows on the bow; salutations to Rudras, who pull, aptly, Their bows, and let the arrows fly off well. (22)

❍ ❍ ❍

नमो विसृजद्भ्यो विध्यद्भ्यश्च वो नमो
नमः स्वपद्भ्यो जाग्रद्भ्यश्च वो नमो
नमः शयानेभ्य आसीनेभ्यश्च वो नमो नम-
स्तिष्ठद्भ्यो धावद्भ्यश्च वो नमः ॥ २३ ॥

namo visṛjadbhyo vidhyadbhyaśca vo namo
nama: svapadbhyo jāgradbhyaśca vo namo
nama: śayānebhya āsīnebhyaśca vo namo nama-
stiṣṭhadbhyo dhāvadbhyaśca vo nama: || 23 ||

Salutations to Rudras who shoot arrows to overpower the sinners, to Rudras who pierce the enemies; salutations to Rudras who experience the stages of dream, the stages of awakening and those of asleep; salutations to Rudras in sitting forms, in standing and dynamic forms in great speed. (23)

❍ ❍ ❍

नमः सभाभ्यः सभापतिभ्यश्च वो नमो
नमोऽश्वेभ्यो ऽश्वपतिभ्यश्च वो नमो नम
आव्याधिनीभ्यो विविध्यन्तीभ्यश्च वो नमो
नम उगणाभ्यस्तृꣳहतीभ्यश्च वो नमः ॥ २४ ॥

nama: sabhābhya: sabhāpatibhyaśca vo namo
namo'śvebhyo 'śvapatibhyaśca vo namo nama
āvyādhinībhyo vividhyantībhyaśca vo namo
nama ugaṇābhyastṛꣳhatībhyaśca vo nama: || 24 ||

Salutations to Rudras who are in the form of members of assemblies, and those presiding over them; salutations to Rudras in the form of horses and those who ride to command them; to Rudras who pierce in every manner in the form of Gods' army, to Rudras piercing in a speical way as Gods' squad, salutations; salutations to Rudras having forms of mother-Goddesses of superior order in groups to nourish as Brāhmī, and to Rudras, in the form of competent (in killing) mother Goddess Durga and others. (24)

❍ ❍ ❍

नमो गणेभ्यो गणपतिभ्यश्च वो नमो नमो
व्रातेभ्यो व्रातपतिभ्यश्च वो नमो नमो
गृत्सेभ्यो गृत्सपतिभ्यश्च वो नमो नमो
विरूपेभ्यो विश्वरूपेभ्यश्च वो नमः ॥ २५ ॥

namo gaṇebhyo gaṇapatibhyaśca vo namo namo
vrātebhyo vrātapatibhyaśca vo namo namo
gṛtsebhyo gṛtsapatibhyaśca vo namo namo
virūpebhyo viśvarūpebhyaśca vo nama: || 25 ||

Salutations to Rudras in the form of Gaṇās in attendence (assemblage of beings*), and to their lords; salutations to Rudras in the form of groups of diverse sections (castes and classes), and to the Rudras in the form of lords of these

* grotesque and monstrous

sections; salutations to Rudras assuming forms of intelligent seekers of the Supreme (Brahmn), and to the lords of these seekers; salutations to Rudras having forms of low and despicable appearance; salutations to Rudras assuming various diverse forms in world. (25)

❍ ❍ ❍

नमः सेनाभ्यः सेनानिभ्यश्च वो नमो
नमो रथिभ्यो अरथेभ्यश्च वो नमो नमः
क्षतृभ्यः संग्रहीतृभ्यश्च वो नमो नमो
महद्भ्यो अर्भकेभ्यश्च वो नमः ॥ २६ ॥

nama: senābhya: senānibhyaśca vo namo
namo rathibhyo arathebhyaśca vo namo nama:
kṣatṛbhya: saṃgrahītṛbhyaśca vo namo namo
mahadbhyo arbhakebhyaśca vo nama: || 26 ||

Salutations to Rudras in the form of armies and the chiefs of such armies; salutations to Thee who art in the form of owners of chariots, and who art without chariots; salutations to Rudras as chiefs of chariots, and those who are as charioteers (drivers); salutations to Rudras who are in the form of beings of elevated class and enlightened (in the field), and to those who are deficient in skills. (26)

❍ ❍ ❍

नमस्तक्षभ्यो रथकारेभ्यश्च वो नमो
नमः कुलालेभ्यः कर्मारेभ्यश्च वो नमो
नमो निषादेभ्यः पुञ्जिष्ठेभ्यश्च वो नमो नमः
श्वनिभ्यो मृगयुभ्यश्च वो नमः ॥ २७ ॥

namastakṣabhyo rathakārebhyaśca vo namo
nama: kulālebhya: karmārebhyaśca vo namo
namo niṣādebhya: puñjiṣṭhebhyaśca vo namo nama:
śvanibhyo mṛgayubhyaśca vo nama: || 27 ||

Salutations to Rudras in the form of artisans; salutations to those Rudras having forms of architects of chariots; salutations to those Rudras as potters, as blacksmiths; salutations to Rudras moving around in forest and mountains as niśādās (tribes as hunters and mountaineers), to those as fowlers who net birds; salutations to Rudras as leashes on dogs' necks, and as hunters desiring hunting deers.

❍ ❍ ❍

नमः श्वभ्यः श्वपतिभ्यश्च वो नमो
नमो भवाय च रुद्राय च नमः
शर्वाय च पशुपतये च नमो नील-
ग्रीवाय च शितिकण्ठाय च ॥ २८ ॥

nama: śvabhya: śvapatibhyaśca vo namo
namo bhavāya ca rudrāya ca nama:
śarvāya ca paśupataye ca namo nīla-
grīvāya ca śitikaṇṭhāya ca || 28 ||

Salutations to Rudras assuming forms of dogs, and to Rudras in the form of their masters; salutations to Rudra who is the cause of creation of beings; salutations to Rudra who eliminates sufferings and wipes away the sins; salutations to Rudra who protects beings in bondage; salutation to Rudra whose throat is blue as He drank deadly poison; and to Rudra who has white throat, salutations. (28)

❍ ❍ ❍

नमः कपर्दिने च व्युप्तकेशाय च
नमः सहस्राक्षाय च शतधन्वने च
नमो गिरिशयाय च शिपिविष्टाय च
नमो मीढुष्टमाय चेषुमते च ॥ २९ ॥

nama: kapardine ca vyuptakeśāya ca
nama: sahasrākṣāya ca śatadhanvane ca
namo giriśayāya ca śipiviṣṭāya ca
namo mīḍhuṣṭamāya ceṣumate ca || 29 ||

Salutations to Rudra having matted locks, salutations to Rudra who is clean-shaven; salutations to Rudra in the form of Indra with thousands of eyes and bearing hundreds of bows; salutations to Rudra who dwells on Kailās mountain, slumbering there; salutations to Rudra as Lord Viṣṇu, pervading inside all beings; salutations to Rudra in the form of clouds, showering, abundantly, and salutations to Rudra bearing arrows. (29)

❍ ❍ ❍

नमो ह्रस्वाय च वामनाय च
नमो बृहते च वर्षीयसे च
नमो वृद्धाय च सवृधे च
नमोऽग्न्याय च प्रथमाय च ॥ ३० ॥

namo hrasvāya ca vāmanāya ca
namo bṛhate ca varṣīyase ca
namo vṛddhāya ca savṛdhe ca
namo'gnyāya ca prathamāya ca || 30 ||

Salutations to Rudra, assuming a small size, who adopts the form of a dwarf; salutations to Rudra with a huge body; salutations to Rudra, having very old age, salutations to Him as an ancient one; salutations to Rudra adorned with the attributes of learnings and humility in the form of scholars' companion; salutations to Him who was before all other things and foremost; and salutations to Rudra who is the chief, everywhere at all times. (30)

❍ ❍ ❍

नम आशवे चाजिराय च नमः
शीघ्र्याय च शीभ्याय च
नम ऊर्म्याय चावस्वन्याय च नमो
नादेयाय च द्वीप्याय च ॥ ३१ ॥

nama āśave cājirāya ca nama:
śīghryāya ca śībhyāya ca
nama ūrmyāya cāvasvanyāya ca naṁo
nādeyāya ca dvīpyāya ca || 31 ||

Salutations to universally pervading Rudra; salutations to Rudra who is dynamic; salutation to Rudra, present in all swiftly moving articles; salutations to the self-praising Rudra, present in the current of waters; salutations to Rudra present in the waves and in still-water form; salutations to Rudra, pervading rivers, pervading islands. (31)

❍ ❍ ❍

नमो ज्येष्ठाय च कनिष्ठाय च नमः
पूर्वजाय चापरजाय च
नमो मध्यमाय चापगल्भाय च
नमो जघन्याय च बुध्न्याय च ॥ ३२ ॥

namo jyeṣṭhāya ca kaniṣṭhāya ca nama:
pūrvajāya cāparajāya ca
namo madhyamāya cāpagalbhāya ca
namo jaghanyāya ca budhnyāya ca || 32 ||

Salutations to much eulogised senior Lord Rudra; salutations to Rudra who is so much young or junior; salutations to Rudra, born first of all, as Hiraṇyagarbh (the gold-egg) in the universe; and to Him, assuming form of engulfing fire at the time of universal dissolution, salutations; salutation to Rudra, in the form of offspring of celestial beings and animal creation (Tiryagādi), in the middle of creation and complete annihilation (Pralaya); salutations to Rudra in the primitive form or to His modest form; Salutations to Rudra born of the hinderpart* (of animals, as cow etc.); and salutation to Rudra existing underneath (in the roots of the trees, etc.) (32)

* hips, buttocks etc. of a woman (pudendum)

❍ ❍ ❍

नमः सोभ्याय च प्रतिसर्याय च
नमो याम्याय च क्षेम्याय च
नमः श्लोक्याय चावसान्याय च
नम उर्वर्याय च खल्याय च ॥ ३३ ॥

nama: sobhyāya ca pratisaryāya ca
namo yāmyāya ca kṣemyāya ca
nama: ślokyāya cāvasānyāya ca
nama urvaryāya ca khalyāya ca || 33 ||

Salutation to Rudra born in the midst of celestial musicians, Gandharvās or in a mixed world of pious and sinful men; salutations to Rudra who is in the acts of Yama* (or existing in the safety threads in hand during marriage); salutations to Rudra being there in efficient deeds; salutation to Rudra evolving during recitation of vedic mantrās; salutations to Him who is expounded as the meaningful gist of the Vedantic philosophy (Upaniṣadās); salutations to Rudra in the form of wealth of bounties of grains in fields, and salutations to Him appearing in threshing lands. (33)

* punishing sinners agonising them in hell

❍ ❍ ❍

नमो वन्याय च कक्ष्याय च नमः
श्रवाय च प्रतिश्रवाय च नम
आशुषेणाय चाशुरथाय च नमः
शूराय चावभेदिने च ॥ ३४ ॥

namo vanyāya ca kakṣyāya ca nama:
śravāya ca pratiśravāya ca nama
āśuṣeṇāya cāśurathāya ca nama:
śūrāya cāvabhedine ca || 34 ||

Salutations to Rudras in the form of trees and creepers in the forests or in the form of Varuṇa; salutations to Rudra exisiting in dry grass or cluster of trees; salutations to Him in the form of sound and its echo; salutations to Rudra whose armies march swiftly, and salutations to Him where chariots move on swiftly; salutations to Rudra who manifests bravery in war, and salutations to Rudra who pierces enemies. (34)

❍ ❍ ❍

नमो बिल्मिने च कवचिने च नमो
वर्मिणे च वरूथिने च
नमः श्रुताय च श्रुतसेनाय च नमो
दुन्दुभ्याय चाहनन्याय च ॥ ३५ ॥

namo bilmine ca kavacine ca namo
varmiṇe ca varūthine ca
nama: śrutāya ca śrutasenāya ca namo
dundubhyāya cāhananyāya ca || 35 ||

Salutations to Rudra who wears helmet; salutations to Him who wears a cotton robe, protecting body; salutations to Rudra who wears iron-plated breast-cover; salutations to Him whose chariot has a top dome; salutations to Rudra who is renowned in the world, and whose army is also renowned; salutations to Rudra who is present in kettle-drum (दुन्दुभी); salutations to Him who is there in the drum sticks and other musical instruments. (35)

❍ ❍ ❍

नमो धृष्णवे च प्रमृशाय च
नमो निषङ्गिणे चेषुधिमते च नमस्ती-
क्ष्णेषवे चायुधिने च नमः स्वा-
युधाय च सुधन्वने च ॥ ३६ ॥

namo dhṛṣṇave ca pramṛśāya ca
namo niṣaṅigaṇe ceṣudhimate ca namastī-
kṣṇeṣave cāyudhine ca nama: svā-
yudhāya ca sudhanvane ca || 36 ||

Salutations to Rudra who is wise and bold; salutations to Him who has discriminating wisdom to differentiate between truth and untruth; salutations to Rudra, bearing sword; salutations to Him who possesses quiver alongwith pointed arrows; salutations to Rudra who has many other weapons; salutations to Him, who wields excellent trident and splendid pināk bow. (36)

❍ ❍ ❍

नमः स्रुत्याय च पथ्याय च नमः
काट्याय च नीप्याय च नमः कुल्याय
च सरस्याय च नमो नादे-
याय च वैशन्ताय च ॥ ३७ ॥

nama: srutyāya ca pathyāya ca nama:
kāṭyāya ca nīpyāya ca nama: kulyāya
ca sarasyāya ca namo nāde-
yāya ca vaiśantāya ca || 37 ||

Salutations to Rudra who is present in the narrow paths; salutations to Rudra who is there in the broad ways, suitable for chariots, elephants and horses; salutations to Rudra being there in different paths; salutations to Him who is there in places of waterfalls, in plains and valleys of mountains; salutations to Rudra who is there in canal ways and the one who is Omniscient, and being there as concealed, resides in all the beings' inner-self* (अन्तर्यामी); salutations to Rudra, being born in ponds; salutations to Him existing in rivers as water-form, and salutations to Rudra who is there (even) in small ponds. (37)

* in bodies

❍ ❍ ❍

नमः कूप्याय चावट्याय च
नमो वीध्र्याय चातप्याय च
नमो मेघ्याय च विद्युत्याय च
नमो वर्ष्याय चावर्ष्याय च ॥ ३८ ॥

nama: kūpyāya cāvaṭyāya ca
namo vīdhryāya cātapyāya ca
namo meghyāya ca vidyutyāya ca
namo varṣyāya cāvarṣyāya ca || 38 ||

Salutations to Rudra who is present in wells; salutations to Him residing there in the pits; salutations to Rudra who has pious nature, and is present in the clouds of winter season or in the midst of the lunar asterisms; salutations to Him who appears in the sunshine; salutations to Rudra who is in the clouds and in the lightning; salutations to Him, being there in the rains or in the condition of no rains. (38)

❍ ❍ ❍

नमो वात्याय च रेष्म्याय च
नमो वास्तव्याय च वास्तुपाय च
नमः सोमाय च रुद्राय च
नमस्ताम्राय चारुणाय च ॥ ३९ ॥

namo vātyāya ca reṣmyāya ca
namo vāstavyāya ca vāstupāya ca
nama: somāya ca rudrāya ca
namastāmrāya cāruṇāya ca || 39 ||

Salutation to Rudra, being there in the winds; salutations to Rudra, present during the period of annihilation; salutation to Rudra, present there in household, land and inhabiting all bodies; salutations to Rudra in the form of guardian of the household; salutations to all auspicious Rudra seated alongwith His highly potent consort, Umā in the moon, who is the Supreme-knowledge; salutations to Rudra, the destroyer of unwished calamity by all means; salutations to copper-complexioned, the rising Sun like Rudra, and salutations to Rudra who has a reddish complexion, similar to the hue after sun rise. (39)

❍ ❍ ❍

नमः शङ्गवे च पशुपतये च नम
उग्राय च भीमाय च नमोऽग्रेवधाय
च दूरेवधाय च नमो हन्त्रे च हनीयसे
च नमो वृक्षेभ्यो हरिकेशेभ्यो नमस्ताराय ॥ ४० ॥

nama: śaṅgave ca paśupataye ca nama
ugrāya ca bhīmāya ca namo'grevadhāya
ca dūrevadhāya ca namo hantre ca hanīyase
ca namo vṛkṣebhyo harikeśebhyo namastārāya || 40 ||

Salutations to Rudra who provides happiness to devotees, and salutations to Him as the Lord of the creatures; salutations to the vehement, fierce form of Rudra during the period of annihilation; salutations to Him who throws a scare at sight to enemies; salutations to Rudra who kills by standing in front, and salutations to Rudra who causes destruction, remaining afar; salutations to Rudra the slayer, in the form of killer of all, during complete destruction (pralaya); salutations to Rudra, having leaf like green-complexioned locks of hair in the form of Kalpa-tree, and salutations to Rudra who liberates the deserving ones by His knowledgeable discourses. (40)

❍ ❍ ❍

नमः शम्भवाय च मयोभवाय च नमः शङ्कराय
च मयस्कराय च नमः शिवाय च शिवतराय च ॥ ४१ ॥

nama: śambhavāya ca mayobhavāya ca nama: śaṅkarāya
ca mayaskarāya ca nama: śivāya ca śivatarāya ca || 41 ||

Salutations to Rudra, the begetter of happiness; salutations to Rudra, who provides enjoyments (wordly pleasures) and liberation; salutation to Rudra who is, inherently, of the nature of conferring mundane pleasure; salutations to Him who Himself is the form of monotheism as per vedantic philosophy; salutations to the sinless auspicious Rudra, and to Rudra who turns His devotees auspicious and sinless. (41)

❍ ❍ ❍

नमः पार्याय चावार्याय च नमः
प्रतरणाय चोत्तरणाय च नमस्तीर्थ्याय
च कूल्याय च नमः शष्प्याय च फेन्याय च ॥ ४२ ॥

nama: pāryāya cāvāryāya ca nama:
prataraṇāya cottaraṇāya ca namastīrthyāya
ca kūlyāya ca nama: śaṣpyāya ca phenyāya ca || 42 ||

Salutations to Rudra as existing, on the shore beyond the sea of the world or as above the world in the form of liberated Viṣṇu; salutations to Rudra, pervading the entire world; salutations to Rudra who draws off men, well beyond the sea of sins and sufferings of the world; salutations to Rudra, who by imparting highest knowledge of the Supreme, liberates men from the mundane life; salutations to Him who is consecrated in holy places; salutations to Rudra, present on the banks of the rivers, like the Ganges, etc.; salutations to Rudra, appearing as Kuśā-grass and as tender blades of grass on the banks of the rivers, as the Ganges etc.; salutations to Rudra appearing in the form of foam as a result of polluted water. (42)

❍ ❍ ❍

नमः सिकत्याय च प्रवाह्याय च नमः
किꣳशिलाय च क्षयणाय च नमः कपर्दिने
च पुलस्तये च नम इरिण्याय च प्रपथ्याय च ॥ ४३ ॥

nama: sikatyāya ca pravāhyāya ca nama:
kiꣳśilāya ca kṣayaṇāya ca nama: kapardine
ca pulastaye ca nama iriṇyāya ca prapathyāya ca || 43 ||

Salutations to Rudra in the form of sand in rivers; salutations to Him being there in the current of waters; salutations to Rudra present in the petty rocky areas and present in fully still waters; salutations to Rudra who wears the crown of matted locks (of hair); salutations to Him who always stands before His devotees for their welfare; salutations to the

Omniscient Lord; salutations to Rudra in the form of barren lands, and salutations to Him for being there in trodden paths by men. (43)

❍ ❍ ❍

नमो व्रज्याय च गोष्ठ्याय च नम-
स्तल्प्याय च गेह्याय च नमो हृदय्याय च
निवेष्प्याय च नमः काट्याय च गह्वरेष्ठाय च ॥ ४४ ॥

namo vrajyāya ca goṣṭhyāya ca nama-
stalpyāya ca gehyāya ca namo hṛdayyāya ca
niveṣpyāya ca nama: kāṭyāya ca gahvareṣṭhāya ca || 44 ||

Salutations to Rudra for being there in the herd of cows or salutations to Him as Lord Gopeśwar, dwelling in Vraja; salutations to Rudra being there in the form of cow-shed; salutations to Him, reclining on bed; salutations to Rudra being present in homes; salutations to Rudra who is enshrined in our hearts in the form of 'Jīva' (imparting to it life, motion and sensation); salutations to Him in the whirling waters; salutations to Rudra who is there in impassable dense forests, and salutations to Him being there in inaccessible mountain caves etc. or in deep waters. (44)

❍ ❍ ❍

नमः शुष्क्याय च हरित्याय च नमः
पाꣳसव्याय च रजस्याय च नमो लोप्याय
चोलप्याय च नम ऊर्व्याय च सूर्व्याय च ॥ ४५ ॥

nama: śuṣkyāya ca harityāya ca nama:
pāꣳsavyāya ca rajasyāya ca namo lopyāya
colapyāya ca nama ūrvyāya ca sūrvyāya ca || 45 ||

Salutations to Rudra for being present in things like dry wood etc. seated as a Supreme Being; salutations to Rudra in the form of earth covered or smeared with dust; salutations to Him in the form of Rajoguṇa (the second of the three

Guṇās), (the quality causing great passion, predominating in men) or to Him as pollen (in flowers); salutations to Rudra who remains awakened when all the senses are quiet (not active), and salutations to Him who stays as a witness during annihilation of the world (Pralaya Kala); salutations to Him who is in the form of special kind of grass* in the midst of its other kinds; salutations to Rudra in the form of fire (electricity present in waters – Hydro electric**), and salutations to Him who exists (even) in the fire of complete destruction (Pralayāgni).

* Utapya – kind of grass
** Badavānal

❍ ❍ ❍

नमः पर्णाय च पर्णशदाय च नम उद्गुरमाणाय
चाभिघ्नते च नम आखिदते च प्रखिदते
च नम इषुकृद्भ्यो धनुष्कृद्भ्यश्च वो नमो नमो
वः किरिकेभ्यो देवानाᳬं हृदयेभ्यो नमो विचिन्वत्केभ्यो
नामे विक्षिणत्केभ्यो नम आनिर्हतेभ्यः ॥ ४६ ॥

nama: parṇāya ca parṇaśadāya ca nama udguramāṇāya
cābhighnate ca nama ākhidate ca prakhidate
ca nama iṣukṛdbhyo dhanuṣkṛdbhyaśca vo namo namo
va: kirikebhyo devānāᳬ hṛdayebhyo namo
vicinvatkebhyo nāme vikṣiṇatkebhyo nama
ānirhatebhya: || 46 ||

Salutations to Rudra as green leaves of trees; salutations to Him who exists in withered leaves (during this period) – later in the form of spring season; salutations to Rudra who exists in men, solely, dedicated in achieving the four desirables puruṣārtha of human life; salutations to Rudra engaged in the killing spree of enemies all around; salutations to Him who makes the non-devotees suffer and wretched in all ways; salutations to Rudra who gets moved with pity to see his devotees unhappy and suffering; salutations to Rudras engaged in manufacturing arrows and bows; salutations to

Rudras who are as heart of the Gods, i.e., Fire, Wind and Sun etc. who sustain the world by rains etc.; salutations to Rudras like God of Fire etc., who discriminate between righteous and sinners; salutations to the Rudras as God of fire etc.; salutations to Rudra in the form of God of fire, for removing the sins, diseases and inauspiciousness of the devotees and standing as a witness to their sins and pious deeds; and salutations to Rudras like Fire, Wind, Sun, etc., who go forth mainly, from these worlds in the very bignning of the creation. (46)

❍ ❍ ❍

द्रापे अन्धसस्पते दरिद्र नीललोहित ।
आसां प्रजानामेषां पशूनां मा भेर्मा
रोङ्मो च नः किंचनाममत् ॥ ४७ ॥

drāpe andhasaspate daridra nīlalohita |
āsāṃ prajānāmeṣāṃ paśūnāṃ mā bhermā
roḍmo ca na: kiṃcanāmamat || 47 ||

O Drāpe! (epithet of Śiva) (who lets sinners lead contemptible lives), O Andhasaspate! (an epithet of Śiva), O Daridra! (pauper), O Nīlalohit! Do not frighten our progenies and our cattle (cow etc.), let them not perish or get ill (suffer from diseases). अन्धसस्पते (Nourisher of Soma) (सोमपालक). (47)

❍ ❍ ❍

इमा रुद्राय तवसे कपर्दिने क्षयद्वीराय प्र भरामहे
मतीः। यथा शमसद् द्विपदे चतुष्पदे
विश्वं पुष्टं ग्रामे अस्मिन्ननातुरम् ॥ ४८ ॥

imā rudrāya tavase kapardine kṣayadvīrāya pra bharāmahe
matī:| yathā śamasad dvipade catuṣpade
viśvaṃ puṣṭaṃ grāme asminnanāturam || 48 ||

O Lord Rudra, having great prowess with matted locks and the abode of super braves, we submit our intellect to Thee for the well-being of our progeny and cattle and for all the beings in this village to be stout, and to remain free from calamity. (48)

❍ ❍ ❍

या ते रुद्र शिवा तनूः शिवा विश्वाहा भेषजी ।
शिवा रुतस्य भेषजी तया नो मृड जीवसे ॥ ४९ ॥

yā te rudra śivā tanū: śivā viśvāhā bheṣajī |
śivā rutasya bheṣajī tayā no mṛḍa jīvase || 49 ||

O Lord Rudra! By Thy graciousness, make our life happy; Thou art calm and ever gratifying.

O Lord Rudra! Thou shalt make us lead a full and happy life with Thy calm and ever gracious and auspicious form, as eradicator of the miseries of the world, and as super panacea for physical ailments. (49)

❍ ❍ ❍

परि नो रुद्रस्य हेतिर्वृणक्तु परि त्वेषस्य दुर्मतिरघायोः ।
अव स्थिरा मघवद्भ्यस्तनुष्व
मीढ्वस्तोकाय तनयाय मृड ॥ ५० ॥

pari no rudrasya hetirvṛṇattu pari tveṣasya durmatiraghāyo: |
ava sthirā maghavadbhyastanuṣva
mīḍhvastokāya tanayāya mṛḍa || 50 ||

May the weapons of Lord Rudra leave us, and may our angry adversaries spare us (meaning thereby they do not cause us pain). O Rudra! Who pours like rains the desirables to the people and let Thy patrons go fearless by unstringing Thy bow, and let their progenies be happy and fearless. (50)

❍ ❍ ❍

मीढुष्टम शिवतम शिवो नः सुमना भव ।
परमे वृक्ष आयुधं निधाय कृत्तिं वसान
आ चर पिनाकं बिभ्रदा गहि ॥ ५१ ॥

mīḍhuṣṭama śivatama śivo na: sumanā bhava |
parame vṛkṣa āyudhaṃ nidhāya kṛttiṃ vasāna
ā cara pinākaṃ bibhradā gahi || 51 ||

O Rudra! Who showers in abundance the desirables and auspiciousness, be benevolently happy on us and place Thy trident etc. and weapons on some distant trees, and get engaged in penance, adorning elephant's skin and bear Thy bow just for the sake of show. (51)

❍ ❍ ❍

विकिरिद्र विलोहित नमस्ते अस्तु भगवः ।
यास्ते सहस्त्रꣳ हेतयोऽन्यमस्मन्नि वपन्तु ताः ॥ ५२ ॥

vikiridra vilohita namaste astu bhagava: |
yāste sahasraꣳ hetayo'nyamasmanni vapantu tā: || 52 ||

O Rudra! The destroyer of diverse kinds of possible disturbances, having brilliant form (unmixed, clean), our obeisances to Thee, Bhagavān*, Let Thy numberless weapons spare us and hit our enemies. (52)

* bedecked with opulences.

❍ ❍ ❍

सहस्त्राणि सहस्त्रशो बाह्वोस्तव हेतयः ।
तासामीशानो भगवः पराचीना मुखा कृधि ॥ ५३ ॥

sahasrāṇi sahasraśo bāhvostava hetaya: |
tāsāmīśāno bhagava: parācīnā mukhā kṛdhi || 53 ||

O Lord of the universe Rudra! Adorned with excellences and sovereignty, turn the faces of thousands kinds of numberless weapons in Thy hands to the opposite direction (meaning thereby do not use them on us). (53)

❍ ❍ ❍

असंख्याता सहस्त्राणि ये रुद्रा अधि भूम्याम् ।
तेषाꣳ सहस्त्रयोजनेऽव धन्वानि तन्मसि ॥ ५४ ॥

asaṃkhyātā sahasrāṇi ye rudrā adhi bhūmyām |
teṣāꣳ sahasrayojane'va dhanvāni tanmasi || 54 ||

Thousands of Rudras, who live on the earth, we will loosen the strings of their bows, and shall deposit them thousands of miles far away from us. (54)

❍ ❍ ❍

अस्मिन् महत्यर्णवे ऽन्तरिक्षे भवा अधि ।
तेषाꣳ सहस्त्रयोजनेऽव धन्वानि तन्मसि ॥ ५५ ॥

asmin mahatyarṇave 'ntarikṣe bhavā adhi |
teṣāꣳ sahasrayojane'va dhanvāni tanmasi || 55 ||

The Rudras, who live in the vast space filled with the clusters of clouds, we will loosen the strings of their countless bows and deposit them thousands of miles away on a distant path, beyond reach.

❍ ❍ ❍

नीलग्रीवाः शितिकण्ठा दिवꣳ रुद्रा उपश्रिताः ।
तेषाꣳ सहस्त्रयोजनेऽव धन्वानि तन्मसि ॥ ५६ ॥

nīlagrīvā: śitikaṇṭhā divaꣳ rudrā upaśritā: |
teṣāꣳ sahasrayojane'va dhanvāni tanmasi || 56 ||

The Rudras, whose throats are partly blue and partly white complexioned, living in the heaven, we will loosen the strings on their numberless bows and deposit them thousnds of miles away on a distant path, beyond reach. (56)

❍ ❍ ❍

नीतग्रीवाः शितिकण्ठाः शर्वा अधः क्षमाचराः ।
तेषाꣳ सहस्त्रयोजनेऽव धन्वानि तन्मसि ॥ ५७ ॥

nītagrīvā: śitikaṇṭhā: śarvā adha: kṣamācarā: |
teṣāꣳ sahasrayojane'va dhanvāni tanmasi || 57 ||

The Rudras, whose throats are partly blue and partly white complexioned, living in the nether regions of the land, we will loosen the strings on their countless bows and deposit them thousnds of miles away on a distant path, beyond reach. (57)

❍ ❍ ❍

ये वृक्षेषु शष्पिञ्जरा नीलग्रीवा विलोहिताः ।
तेषाꣳ सहस्रयोजनेऽव धन्वानि तन्मसि ॥ ५८ ॥

ye vṛkṣeṣu śaṣpiñjarā nīlagrīvā vilohitā: |
teṣāꣳ sahasrayojane'va dhanvāni tanmasi || 58 ||

The Rudras, having green complexion, like that of tender sprouting grass, partly green, blue and white, who are devoid of blood (because of their supreme energy, blood and flesh diminish) and live on trees, like peepal (holy fig tree) etc., we will loosen the strings from their countless bows and deposit them thousnds of miles away beyond a distant pathway. (58)

❍ ❍ ❍

ये भूतानामधिपतयो विशिखासः कपर्दिनः ।
तेषाꣳ सहस्रयोजनेऽव धन्वानि तन्मसि ॥ ५९ ॥

ye bhūtānāmadhipatayo viśikhāsa: kapardina: |
teṣāꣳ sahasrayojane'va dhanvāni tanmasi || 59 ||

The Rudras, who have matted locks and no hair on head, and who are chiefs of the goblins (mischievous and ugly creatures), we will take off the strings from their bows and deposit them thousands of miles away, beyond a distant pathway. (59)

❍ ❍ ❍

ये पथां पथिरक्षय ऐलबृदा आयुर्युधः ।
तेषाꣳ सहस्त्रयोजनेऽव धन्वानि तन्मसि ॥ ६० ॥

ye pathāṃ pathirakṣaya ailabṛdā āyuryudha: |
teṣāꣳ sahasrayojane'va dhanvāni tanmasi || 60 ||

The Rudras, who are protectors of mundane and righteous Vedic pathways, and nourishers of beings, giving food to them, we shall deposit their bows making them off-strings, thousands of miles away, beyond a distant pathway. (60)

❍ ❍ ❍

ये तीर्थानि प्रचरन्ति सृकाहस्ता निषङ्गिणः ।
तेषाꣳ सहस्त्रयोजनेऽव धन्वानि तन्मसि ॥ ६१ ॥

ye tīrthāni pracaranti sṛkāhastā niṣaṅigaṇa: |
teṣāꣳ sahasrayojane'va dhanvāni tanmasi || 61 ||

The Rudras, who move around in sacred places, bearing weapons like thunder-bolt and sword in hands, we shall take off the strings from their bows and deposit the bows thousnds of miles away, beyond a distant pathway. (61)

❍ ❍ ❍

येऽन्नेषु विविध्यन्ति पात्रेषु पिबतो जनान् ।
तेषाꣳ सहस्त्रयोजनेऽव धन्वानि तन्मसि ॥ ६२ ॥

ye'nneṣu vividhyanti pātreṣu pibato janān |
teṣāꣳ sahasrayojane'va dhanvāni tanmasi || 62 ||

The Rudra, who exists in the food-grains, who causes sufferings to the beings, who consume grains; and the Rudra, who is there in the pots of milk and other liquids, who causes ailments to those who drink them, we shall deposit their bows, taking off the strings on them, thousands of miles away, beyond a distant pathway. (62)

❍ ❍ ❍

य एतावन्तश्च भूयाꣳसश्च दिशो रुद्रा वितस्थिरे ।
तेषाꣳ सहस्त्रयोजनेऽव धन्वानि तन्मसि ॥ ६३ ॥

ya etāvantaśca bhūyāꣳsaśca diśo rudrā vitasthire |
teṣāꣳ sahasrayojane'va dhanvāni tanmasi || 63 ||

The Rudras spread over, widely, in all the ten directions, we shall take off strings from their bows, in order to deposit them far off, thousands of miles away, on a distant pathway. (63)

❍ ❍ ❍

नमोऽस्तु रुद्रेभ्यो ये दिवि येषां वर्षमिषवः ।
तेभ्यो दश प्राचीर्दश दक्षिणा दश प्रतीचीर्दशोदीचीर्दशोर्ध्वाः ।
तेभ्यो नमो अस्तु ते नोऽवन्तु ते नो मृडयन्तु ते
यं द्विष्मो यश्च नो द्वेष्टि तमेषां जम्भे दध्मः ॥ ६४ ॥

namo'stu rudrebhyo ye divi yeṣāṃ varṣamiṣava: |
tebhyo daśa prācīrdaśa dakṣiṇā daśa
pratīcīrdaśodīcīrdaśordhvā: |
tebhyo namo astu te no'vantu te no mṛḍayantu te
yaṃ dviṣmo yaśca no dveṣṭi tameṣāṃ
jambhe dadhma: || 64 ||

Salutations to Rudras, who dwell in heaven, and who are in the form of rains. Towards those Rudras, present in all the directions (east, west, north, south, and upward), we offer our obeisances with folded hands, having all the ten fingers joined together (we pray) to those Rudras to protect us and make us happy. The man, whom the Rudras hate, whom we hate, and who hates us, we consign that man into the mouth of Rudras, who have terrifying teeth. (meaning thereby, the Rudras devour the man who hates us.) (64)

❍ ❍ ❍

नमोऽस्तु रुद्रेभ्यो येऽन्तरिक्षे येषां वात इषवः ।
तेभ्यो दश प्राचीर्दश दक्षिणा दश प्रतीचीर्दशोदीचीर्दशोर्ध्वाः ।
तेभ्यो नमो अस्तु ते नोऽवन्तु ते नो मृडयन्तु ते
यं द्विष्मो यश्च नो द्वेष्टि तमेषां जम्भे दध्मः ॥ ६५ ॥

namo'stu rudrebhyo ye'ntarikṣe yeṣāṃ vāta iṣava: |
tebhyo daśa prācīrdaśa dakṣiṇā daśa
pratīcīrdaśodīcīrdaśordhvā: |
tebhyo namo astu te no'vantu te no mṛḍayantu te
yaṃ dviṣmo yaśca no dveṣṭi tameṣāṃ
jambhe dadhma: || 65 ||

Salutations to the Rudras who dwell in the space (between the heaven and the earth) and to the Rudras whose arrows are in the form of winds. I bow to them with my ten fingers joined together in the east, the south, the west, the north and upwards (meaning thereby I bow to them in all directions). May those Rudras protect us and make us happy. The man whom the Rudras hate, that whom we hate, and who hates us, we consign that man into the terrifying teethful mouth of those Rudras. (meaning thereby, the Rudras devour the man who hates us.) (65)

❍ ❍ ❍

नमोऽस्तु रुद्रेभ्यो ये पृथिव्यां येषामन्नमिषवः ।
तेभ्यो दश प्राचीर्दश दक्षिणा दश प्रतीचीर्दशोदीचीर्दशोर्ध्वाः ।
तेभ्यो नमो अस्तु ते नोऽवन्तु ते नो मृडयन्तु ते
यं द्विष्मो यश्च नो द्वेष्टि तमेषां जम्भे दध्मः ॥ ६६ ॥

namo'stu rudrebhyo ye pṛthivyāṃ yeṣāmannamiṣava: |
tebhyo daśa prācīrdaśa dakṣiṇā daśa
pratīcīrdaśodīcīrdaśordhvā: |
tebhyo namo astu te no'vantu te no mṛḍayantu te
yaṃ dviṣmo yaśca no dveṣṭi tameṣāṃ
jambhe dadhma: || 66 ||

Salutations to the Rudras who exist on planet earth, and whose arrows are in the form of grains, I bow to them with my ten fingers joined together in the east, the south, the west, the north and upwards (I bow to the Rudras in all directions with folded hands). May those Rudras protect us and make us happy. The man, whom the Rudras hate, and who hates us, we consign that man into the terrifying teethful mouth of these Rudras. (Meaning thereby, the Rudras devour the man who hates us.) (66)

❍ ❍ ❍

Devī Hymns (Vāk Hymns)
देवी सूक्त (वाक्-सूक्त)

'Devī Sūkta' carries very special importance in worshipping the Supreme Goddess 'Parāmbā'. The 125th Sūkta of the 10th part (mandal) of the Rigveda is known as the 'Devī Sūkta'. It is also known as the 'Vāk Sūkta', or 'Ātma Sūkta'. Having realised the Supreme Oversoul (Brahm), the daughter of the sage 'Ambhṛṇa', 'Vāk' reveals herself identified one with the 'Supreme Goddess', through her 'sādhanā' (spiritual practice). In an exalted state of her 'Oneness' with the Supreme, she describes, 'Vāk Devī' is none else other than an emancipated living wisdom in the 'Brahm' form. Her hymns exhibit the unity of the explainer and the explained matter. And here is the text:

ॐ अहं रुद्रेभिर्वसुभिश्चराम्यहमादित्यैरुत विश्वदेवैः ।
अहं मित्रावरुणोभा बिभर्म्यहमिन्द्राग्नी अहमश्विनोभा ॥ १ ॥

oṃ ahaṃ rudrebhirvasubhiścarāmyahamādityairuta viśvadevai: |
ahaṃ mitrāvaruṇobhā bibharmyahamindrāgnī ahamaśvinobhā || 1 ||

Om! I move along in the form of Rudra, Vasus, Ādityās and all other Devās (Gods). As the Supreme (Brahma), I bear Mitra, Varuṇa, Indra and Agni, and as such also the two Ashwini Kumarās (all of these are the Gods.)

❍ ❍ ❍

अहं सोममाहनसं बिभर्म्यहं त्वष्टारमुत पूषणं भगम् ।
अहं दधामि द्रविणं हविष्मते सुप्राव्ये यजमानाय सुन्वते ॥ २ ॥

ahaṃ somamāhanasaṃ bibharmyahaṃ tvaṣṭāramuta pūṣaṇaṃ bhagam |

ahaṃ dadhāmi draviṇaṃ haviṣmate suprāvye yajamānāya sunvate || 2 ||

I am sacrificial Soma, Candramā, Mana (mind) or Śiva, and all are being nourished by me, as they are destroyers of enemies and eradicators of demerits and faults (like endless desires, etc.)* I bear Twashtā**, Pūṣā*** and Bhaga**** also, and I am the bestower of fruits of joys of the two worlds on the performers of sacrifices (yajña), who offer oblations and somarasa (juice of soma plant) etc. which is very pleasing to the Gods. (2)

* providing extreme pleasure.
** Divine builder (Twashtā), Vishwakarmā
*** Sun
**** Divine Luster

❍ ❍ ❍

अहं राष्ट्री संगमनी वसूनां चिकितुषी प्रथमा यज्ञियानाम् ।
तां मा देवा व्यदधुः पुरुत्रा भूरिस्थात्रां भूर्य्यावेशयन्तीम् ॥ ३ ॥

ahaṃ rāṣṭrī saṃgamanī vasūnāṃ cikituṣī prathamā yajñiyānām |
tāṃ mā devā vyadadhu: purutrā bhūristhātrāṃ bhūryyāveśayantīm || 3 ||

I am the Goddess of the Universe (Rashtrī). I make available the desired (vasu) wealth to the worshippers. By experiencing the Supreme, the real object of the seekers, I have realised* in My-self. I am the superb of the deities for whom the sacrifices are performed. I am the one who manifests as many in the entire visible creation. I am entering the bodies of the entire lot of beings as life-soul (Jīvātmā). Whatever is taking place in different places, times, things and beings, or is being done, that all is done in me and for me. Since I pervade the entire universe, whatever activity one does, its all me. (3)

* The Supreme Brahma

❍ ❍ ❍

मया सो अन्नमत्ति यो विपश्यति यः प्राणिति य ईं शृणोत्युक्तम् ।
अमन्तवो मां त उप क्षियन्ति श्रुधि श्रुत श्रद्धिवं ते वदामि ॥ ४ ॥

mayā so annamatti yo vipaśyati ya: prāṇiti ya riṃśṛṇotyuktam |
amantavo māṃ ta upa kṣiyanti śrudhi śruta śraddhivaṃ te vadāmi || 4 ||

I am the real power, and whoever enjoys the wordly fruits, enjoys through my enjoying power alone. Through me, one sees, breathes and hears. Those, who do not understand my existence as that of the Supreme consciousness (inner witness) who resides in every being, are bereft of wisdom, and become poor and lean. O dear friend! (an address to a devotee worshipper) Hear my exhortation for you on the Supreme, which is available only through devotion. (4)

❍ ❍ ❍

अहमेव स्वयमिदं वदामि जुष्टं देवेभिरुत मानुषेभिः ।
यं कामये तं तमुग्रं कृणोमि तं ब्रह्माणं तमृषिं तं सुमेधाम् ॥ ५ ॥

ahameva svayamidaṃ vadāmi juṣṭaṃ devebhiruta mānuṣebhi: |
yaṃ kāmaye taṃ tamugraṃ kṛṇomi taṃ brahmāṇaṃ tamṛṣiṃ taṃ sumedhām || 5 ||

I myself exhort on this Supreme knowledge. The Gods and men have cherished this. I am Brahm myself. I make one, the greatest, whom I like to be secured. I can elevate one to the position of creator – Brahmā, introspecting sage and as enlightened and intelligent as Brihaspati. I am myself singing of my form as inseparable from Brahm. (5)

❍ ❍ ❍

अहं रुद्राय धनुरा तनोमि ब्रह्मद्विषे शरवे हन्तवा उ ।
अहं जनाय समदं कृणोम्यहं द्यावापृथिवी आ विवेश ॥ ६ ॥

ahaṃ rudrāya dhanurā tanomi brahmadviṣe śarave hantavā u |
ahaṃ janāya samadaṃ kṛṇomyahaṃ dyāvāpṛthivī ā viveśa || 6 ||

I put on the string on the bow of Rudra in order to kill the hateful, violent bragger of 'Triguṇās' (The three guṇās as Sat, Raj and Tama), the ego-demon (inhabiting Tripur), the enemy of the enlightened beings (Brahmajnānis). I defeat the enemies of my curious praisers (followers, worshippers). I have entered, pervading the heavens and the earth in the form of the inner consciousness (inner witness). (6)

❍ ❍ ❍

अहं सुवे पितरमस्य मूर्धन् मम योनिरप्स्वन्तः समुद्रे ।
ततो वि तिष्ठे भुवनानु विश्वोतामूं द्यां वर्ष्मणोप स्पृशामि ॥ ७ ॥

ahaṃ suve pitaramasya mūrdhan mama yonirapsvanta: samudre |
tato vi tiṣṭhe bhuvanānu viśvotāmūṃ dyāṃ varṣmaṇopa spṛśāmi || 7 ||

I beget (create) the heavens existing on top of the universe or the fatherly (for all beings) Āditya form. The manifestation of all creation, like the sky as the spread over threads of cloth, is the result of the same cause. The divine water-form ocean, where from all beings and materials come out and merge with, is my Supreme Brahm-conscious habitat. By that I am present in the entire worldly matter, pervading all, and I touch all that is visible with my causal illusionary body. (7)

❍ ❍ ❍

अहमेव वात इव प्रवाम्यारभमाणा भुवनानि विश्वा ।
परो दिवा पर एना पृथिव्यैतावती महिना संबभूव ॥ ८ ॥
[ऋक्० १० । १२५]

ahameva vāta iva pravāmyārabhamāṇā bhuvanāni viśvā |
paro divā para enā pṛthivyaitāvatī mahinā saṃbabhūva || 8 ||
[ṛv. 10 | 125]

I begin creating the worlds as the causal form, not being led or established by any other, as the winds blow on their own, not directed by any other cause. I am beyond the earth and the sky. I am beyond transformations, unconnected and indifferent and the (highest) Supreme Consciousness (Kūtastha Brahmacaitanya). In this Supreme form of mine, I exist and conduct the entire creation. (8)

❍ ❍ ❍

Wakefulness (enlightenment) is divinity. Sleepiness (lethargy) is the root of wretchedness (extreme poverty). **(Yaj. 30|17)**

❍ ❍ ❍

Beget intellect, competent in performing many distinguished feats. **(Sām 861)**

❍ ❍ ❍

Those who expand truth, contact truth, accomplish great tasks by the truth itself. **(Sām 848)**

❍ ❍ ❍

Goddess Saraswatī, Accomplishes Supreme and Real Wisdom

Saraswatī Hymns (Saraswatī Rahasyopaniṣad) (सरस्वती सूक्त)

The practice of the Goddess Saraswatī-worship is the super most means of accomplishing the supreme-wisdom, as per the Vedic tradition of 'The Saraswatī Rahasyopaniṣad'. The sage āshwalāyana accomplished the 'Real-wisdom' through this. With the grace of mother Saraswatī the impediments in our way of attaining enlightenment disappear, especially, with the removal of stupor (inactivity), Her (divine) grace is achieved. The Vedic-hymns of Mother Saraswatī follow:

ॐ वाङ् मे मनसि प्रतिष्ठिता मनो मे वाचि प्रतिष्ठितमाविरावीर्म एधि। वेदस्य म आणीस्थः श्रुतं मे मा प्रहासीः। अनेनाधीतेनाहोरात्रान् संदधाम्यृतं वदिष्यामि। सत्यं वदिष्यामि। तन्मामवतु। तद्वक्तारमवतु। अवतु मामवतु वक्तारमवतु वक्तारम्।। ॐ शान्तिः! शान्तिः!! शान्तिः!!

oṃ vāṅ me manasi pratiṣṭhitā mano me vāci pratiṣṭhitamāvirāvīrma edhi| vedasya ma āṇīstha: śrutaṃ me mā prahāsī:| anenādhītenāhorātrān saṃdadhāmyṛtaṃ vadiṣyāmi| satyaṃ vadiṣyāmi| tanmāmavatu| tadvattāramavatu| avatu māmavatu vattāramavatu vattāram|| oṃ śānti:! śānti:!! śānti:!!

It is a Rigvedic mantra, invoking Paramātmā (the Oversoul) with a prayer for peace against all kinds of impediments which may likely arise during their vedic-studies of scriptures.

O Paramātmā (The Oversoul)! (the unified form of Existence-Consciousness-Bliss-Saccidānand) Let my speech be established in my mind and my mind be established in my speech, in order to have the unison of both of them. Speech is to be similar to the thoughts, and the thoughts, the same as the speech. The speech and the thought should follow each other, mutually. O Self-Radiant Oversoul! Manifest Thyself for me, remove the veil of illusion lying before me. In such a state of things, the speaker asks the speech and the mind in unison to fetch the Vedic-Enlightenment in order to be able to acquire deep Vedic-knowledge. Whatever I have heard from the Guru and what I have experienced personally, let that not forsake me. May I keep remembering that forever, and never forget that. I desire, ardently, to bring day and night together, in this endeavour for studies. This is like, studying and contemplating over Brahm-Enlightenment, day and night; and no time ends up futilely. I shall always give utterance to noble and elevated words, devoid of blemishes (ऋतम्). I shall speak, nothing but truth. Resolving this way, firmly, I pray, O Paramātmā (Oversoul)! Protect me. Protect my Guru. Protect me and my preceptor, enlightening me. O Lord! Protect my preceptor.

This is followed by the prayer for peace in order to prevent the possible onslaught of the three kinds of (tapās) sufferings, if any, arising in future. Om Peace! Peace!! Peace!!!

Harihi Om! The story goes as: Once upon a time, expressing due reverence to holy āshwalāyana, the 'sages' enquired of him: 'Holiness! How is that knowledge gained which discovers the word 'Tat', illumining Paramātmā? Tell us, by meditation on which Divinity did you realise the Truth. The Divine āshwalāyana said, 'Best of sages! I accomplished salvation by exalting Saraswatī, through recitation of ten-stanza with seed-syllables-hymns on Her alongwith the telling of mahāmantrā. The sages enquired of him, O sage, observer of great austerity, how could, with what meditation can the accomplishment of the Saraswatī mantrā be won?

Tell us the way Goddess Saraswatī got pleased. The renowned sage said: I, āshwalāyan, am the seer of this ten-verse great mantrā on Lustrous Saraswatī, the eight-syllable Anuṣtup is the metre, the holy Vāgishwarī the divinity, 'Vadvāg' is the seed, 'Devīm vācam' the power, 'prāṇodevī' is the pivotal pin, and the application (of the mantra) is to please the Deity Vāgeshwarī. The placement of the limbs (Anganyās) is made by invoking the name śraddhā, medhā, prajñā, dhāraṇā, the Deity of speech and Supreme-Saraswatī. The mantrās like, **"Om śraddhāyai namo hridayāy namah, Om Medhāyai namah śirase, swāhā, Om prajñayai namah śikhāyai vaṣat, Om Dhāraṇāyai namah kavachāy hum, Om Vāgdevatāyai namo netratrayāy vauṣat, Om Mahāsaraswattyai namah astrāy phat."**

अस्य श्रीसरस्वतीदशश्लोकीमहामन्त्रस्य अहमाश्वलायन ऋषिः।
अनुष्टुप् छन्दः। श्रीवागीश्वरी देवता। यद्वागिति बीजम्। देवीं
वाचमिति शक्तिः। प्र णो देवीति कीलकम्। विनियोगस्तत्प्रीत्यर्थे।
श्रद्धा मेधा प्रज्ञा धारणा वाग्देवता महासरस्वतीत्येतैरङ्गन्यासः।।

asya śrīsarasvatīdaśaślokīmahāmantrāsya
ahamāśvalāyana ṛṣi:| anuṣṭup chanda:| śrīvāgīśvarī
devatā| yadvāgiti bījam| devīṃ vācamiti śatti:|
pra ṇo devīti kīlakam| viniyogastatprītyarthe|
śraddhā medhā prajñā dhāraṇā vāgdevatā
mahāsarasvatītyetairaṅganyāsa:||

ध्यान

नीहारहारघनसारसुधाकराभां
कल्याणदां कनकचम्पकदामभूषाम् ।
उत्तुङ्गपीनकुचकुम्भमनोहराङ्गी
वाणीं नमामि मनसा वचसा विभत्यै ।।

dhyāna

nīhārahāraghanasārasudhākarābhāṃ
kalyāṇadāṃ kanakacampakadāmabhūṣām |
uttuṅgapīnakucakumbhamanoharāṅgī
vāṇīṃ namāmi manasā vacasā vibhatyai ||

Meditation

I salute Goddess Saraswatī (desiring eight fold opulences and salvation), who shines like snow, wears necklace of pearls, anointed with camphor, and white like the brightness of moon, who confers auspiciousness and is bedecked with the garland of golden champak flowers, having charming figure with tended, rounded bosom.

ॐ प्र णो देवी सरस्वती वाजेभिर्वाजिनीवती ।
धीनामवित्र्यवतु ॥ १ ॥

oṃ pra ṇo devī sarasvatī vājebhirvājinīvatī |
dhīnāmavitryavatu || 1 ||

The sage of this mantra, 'Oṃ Prā ṇo devī...' is Bharadwāj, metre gāyatri and Śrī Saraswatī, the Deity. 'Om Namah' is the seed, the power and the pivot (all the three). Its application brings about accomplishment of the desired object. The limbs-placement (Anganyās) is made through the mantrā.

'Verily, whose inmost-form (swarūp) is the supreme-essence (Brahmatatva) of the Vedantic philosophy, and who is manifested in various forms and names, May that Saraswatī protect me.'

Oṃ! May the Goddess Saraswatī, bedecked with act of dispensing, having treasure of nourishment (food-grains etc.), guarding devotees, secure us with provisions (of plentiful grains). (1)

❍ ❍ ❍

'ह्रीं' आ नो दिवो बृहतः पर्वतादा
सरस्वती यजता गन्तु यज्ञम् ।
हवं देवी जुजुषाणा घृताची
शग्मां नो वाचमुशती शृणोतु ॥ २ ॥

'hrīṃ' ā no divo bṛhata: parvatādā
sarasvatī yajatā gantu yajñam |
havaṃ devī jujuṣāṇā ghṛtācī
śagmāṃ no vācamuśatīśṛṇotu || 2 ||

'Aā no divah' – The seer of this mantra is Atri, the metre triṣtup, the Deity Saraswatī, – 'Hrīṃ' – is the seed, the power and the pivot, all the three. Its application is made to realise the desired object. This mantrā is also applied for placement of limbs (Anganyās).

'May the only one extolled in the four Vedās and their āgam*, the non-dual potency of Brahm, (That) Goddess Saraswatī protect us.'

'HRĪṂ' – May Goddess Saraswatī come in our yajña ceremony from the brilliant heavens through the mountaneous cluster of clouds. Jubilant with our prayers, May She, willfully, listen to our pleasant hymns.

* six other related subjects

❍ ❍ ❍

'श्रीं' पावका नः सरस्वती वाजेभिर्वाजिनीवती ।
यज्ञं वष्टु धिया वसुः ॥ ३ ॥

'śrīṃ' pāvakā na: sarasvatī vājebhirvājinīvatī |
yajñaṃ vaṣṭu dhiyā vasu: || 3 ||

'Pāvakā nah' – The seer of this mantra is Madhucchandā, Gāyatrī, the metre, Saraswatī is the Deity; SHRĪṂ is the seed, the power and the pivot, all the three. The application of this mantra is made to achieve the desired accomplishments. The mantra is (also) applied for placement of limbs (Anganyās).

'Goddess Saraswatī, Who is, verily, all pervading, without beginning and end, in the form of letter, word and sentence and their meaning, and Who is having the form of infinite Self, May She protect me.'

‘SHRĪṂ’ – Goddess Saraswatī, the purger of all, the cause of bestowing plentiful grains and wealth, available through Karma, may She be willing to kindly grace our sacrifice (yajña) by Her presence (meaning thereby, to support in completing sacrifice by Her compassion). (3)

❍ ❍ ❍

‘ब्लूं’ चोदयित्री सूनृतानां चेतन्ती
सुमतीनाम् यज्ञं दधे सरस्वती ॥ ४ ॥

‘blūṃ’ codayitrī sūnṛtānāṃ cetantī
sumatīnām yajñaṃ dadhe sarasvatī || 4 ||

‘codayitrī’ – the sage of this mantra is Madhucchandā, the metre Gāyatrī, Saraswatī, the Deity. ‘BLŪṂ’ is the seed of the mantra, and its power and the pivot, all the three. In order to gain the aspired-accomplishment (सिद्धि Siddhi), it is applied. The placement of limbs (Anganyās) is also made by the mantra.

‘May the Goddess Sarawatī, as the Self and the presiding deity, who is the sovereign Goddess in the midst of gods, meaning thereby the inspiring source of gods, dwelling in us as the speech, protect me.’

‘Blūṃ’ – (the seed) Inspirer of truthful speech, and the guide, and awakening the duty-bound good and wise men, May (that) Goddess Saraswatī take up command of this yajña. (4)

❍ ❍ ❍

‘सौः’ महो अर्णः सरस्वती प्र चेतयति केतुना ।
धियो विश्वा वि राजति ॥ ५ ॥

‘sau:’ maho arṇa: sarasvatī pra cetayati ketunā |
dhiyo viśvā vi rājati || 5 ||

‘maho arṇah’ the sage of this mantra is (also) Madhucchandā, the metre, Gāyatrī, the Deity Saraswatī. ‘SAUH’, The seed, the power and the pivot, all the three. The placement (nyās) is with the mantrā (itself). She is the inner consciousness, controller in command of the three worlds, who dwells as Rudra, the Sun and other deities, May that Goddess Saraswati protect us.'

'SAUH' – (The river form of Saraswatī is being prayed in this mantra). Appearing as the river, Goddess Saraswatī displays Her karma by flowing in the immeasurable waters (in it), who in Divinity-form enlivens wisdom, inculcating sense of duty (in mankind).

❍ ❍ ❍

'ऐं' चत्वारि वाक् परिमिता पदानि
तानि विदुर्ब्राह्मणा ये मनीषिणः ।
गुहा त्रीणि निहिता नेङ्गयन्ति
तुरीयं वाचो मनुष्या वदन्ति ॥ ६ ॥

'aiṃ' catvāri vāv parimitā padāni
tāni vidurbrāhmaṇā ye manīṣiṇa: |
guhā trīṇi nihitā neṅgayanti
turīyaṃ vāco manuṣyā vadanti || 6 ||

'catvārivāk' – The sage of this mantra is Ucathya's son Dīrghatamā, the metre 'Triṣtup', Saraswatī, the Divinity. 'aiṃ' – is the seed, the power and the pivot, all the three. The application of the mantra is made to realise aspired accomplishment. The placement (nyās) is performed with the mantra (itself).

'The One, Who is being experienced by the introspecting beings in a number of forms, Who is the only one known, pervading everywhere in the wisdom-form, May That Goddess Saraswatī protect me.'

'aiṃ' – (seed) Speech has four parts, meaning thereby the speech has four divisions – parā (परा), paśyantī (पश्यंती), maddhyamā (मध्यमा) and Vaikharī (वैखरी). All this is known to the learned brāhmins. The first three, parā, paśyantī and maddhyamā exist in the inner region of heart, hence not apparent, outwardly. But the fourth speech Vaikharī is spoken by man. (This is, in a way, adoration of Goddess Saraswatī in the speech-form) (6)

❍ ❍ ❍

'क्लीं' यद् वाग्वदन्त्यविचेतनानि
राष्ट्री देवानां निषसाद मन्द्रा ।
चतस्त्र ऊर्जं दुदुहे पयांसि
क्व स्विदस्याः परमं जगाम ॥ ७ ॥

'klīṃ' yad vāgvadantyavicetanāni
rāṣṭrī devānāṃ niṣasāda mandrā |
catasra ūrjaṃ duduhe payāṃsi
kva svidasyā: paramaṃ jagāma || 7 ||

'Yadvāgavadanti' – The sage, seer of this mantrā is Bhārgava, the metre Triṣtup, (and) the Divinity is Saraswatī. 'Klīṃ' is the seed, the power and the pivot, all the three. The placement (nyāsa) is performed by the mantrā (itself).

'Who is being conceived eight-fold as in name, kind etc., and at the same time, is being exhibited as changeless, May That Goddess Saraswatī protect us.'

'Klīṃ' – 'Rāṣtrī' meaning the speech of divinity, which unfolds the divine intent and pleases most, the Gods. That Goddess Saraswatī gets seated in sacrifice (yajña), imparting knowledge to the ignorants; at that time, She fetches food-grains and water for the four directions, and what is superb in the 'madhyamā-vāk' (the speech in the heart-region), where does it go? (7)

❍ ❍ ❍

'सौः' देवीं वाचमजनयन्त देवास्तां
विश्वरूपाः पशवो वदन्ति ।
सा नो मन्द्रेषमूर्जं दुहाना
धेनुर्वागस्मानुप सुष्टुतैतु ॥ ८ ॥

**'sau:' devīṃ vācamajanayanta devāstāṃ viśvarūpā: paśavo vadanti |
sā no mandreṣamūrjaṃ duhānā
dhenurvāgasmānupa suṣṭutaitu || 8 ||**

'Devīṃ vācam' – This mantra's sage is Bhārgava, the metre 'Triṣtup', and the Deity is Saraswatī. 'SAUH' is the seed, the power and the pivot. The placement (nyās) is also performed with this mantra (itself).

'That Goddess Saraswati, who lends power of speech to the Gods and all other beings with manifested and unmanifested speech, who grants all desired objects as 'Kāmadhenu'* provides milk (in plenty), May She protect me.

'SAUH' - 'Vaikharī', spoken by various beings, was manifested by the grace of the life-giving Gods. May that beautiful voiced Goddess Saraswatī, who has bestowed upon us happiness, nourishments (grains, etc.) and strength and is like 'kāmadhenu'*, be pleased with our (hymns) (prayers), and come to us.

* a scripture cow, yielding desires.

❍ ❍ ❍

**'सं' उत त्वः पश्यन्न ददर्श वाच-
मुत त्वः शृण्वन् न शृणोत्येनाम् ।
उतो त्वस्मै तन्वं विसस्रे
जायेव पत्य उशती सुवासाः ॥ ९ ॥**

**'saṃ' uta tva: paśyanna dadarśa vāca-
muta tva:śṛṇvan naśṛṇotyenām |
uto tvasmai tanvaṃ visasre
jāyeva patya uśatī suvāsā: || 9 ||**

'saṃ' some (people) do not see the speech, (even after seeing it) (meaning thereby, they do not understand, even after understanding), some do not hear, even after hearing it, but to some the Goddess of speech manifests Herself in fullness, just as a beautifully dressed, ardently loving wife disrobes herself before her husband. (9)

❍ ❍ ❍

'ऐं' अम्बितमे नदीतमे देवितमे सरस्वति ।
अप्रशस्ता इव स्मसि प्रशस्तिमम्ब नस्कृधि ॥ १० ॥

'aiṃ' ambitame nadītame devitame sarasvati |
apraśastā iva smasi praśastimamba naskṛdhi || 10 ||

The sage of this mantrā is Gritsmad (गृत्समद), the metre is 'anuṣtup', and the deity is Saraswatī. (ऐं) aiṃ is the seed, power and the pivot, all the three. The placement (nyāsa) is done by the mantrā itself. In whom, the Brahm-realised persons, having invoked this entire creation of name and form, further contemplate upon, That only Supreme Form Saraswatī Devī protect me.

(ऐं) aiṃ: O Saraswatī Devī! Best among mothers, best among rivers, and best among Goddesses, we are getting censored or unpopular for paucity of wealth. Mother! (most benevolent) Bless us with wealth and prosperity in order to be praiseworthy. (10)

❍ ❍ ❍

चतुर्मुखमुखाम्भोजवनहंसवधूर्मम
मानसे रमतां नित्यं सर्वशुक्ला सरस्वती ॥ १ ॥

caturmukhamukhāmbhojavanahaṃsavūdhūrmama
mānase ramatāṃ nityaṃ sarvaśuklā sarasvatī || 1 ||

May the glowing-white complexioned from all around, Saraswatī Devī, roaming as a Royal swan in the forest of lotuses, like Brahmā's face, engross my mind forever. (1)

❍ ❍ ❍

नमस्ते शारदे देवि काश्मीरपुरवासिनि ।
त्वामहं प्रार्थये नित्यं विद्यादानं च देहि मे ॥ २ ॥

namaste śārade devi kāśmīrapuravāsini |
tvāmahaṃ prārthaye nityaṃ vidyādānaṃ ca dehi me || 2 ||

O Śāradā Devī! Salutatios to Thee, living in Thy abode in Kaśmīrpur. I pray Thee always. Bless me with enlightenment. (2)

❍ ❍ ❍

अक्षसूत्राङ्कुशधरा पाशपुस्तकधारिणी ।
मुक्ताहारसमायुक्ता वाचि तिष्ठतु मे सदा ॥ ३ ॥

akṣasūtrāṅkuśadharā pāśapustakadhāāriṇī |
muktāhārasamāyuktā vāci tiṣṭhatu me sadā || 3 ||

May Saraswatī Devī, bearing rosary, pointed piercing rod, a trap and a book in Her four hands, and bedecked with garland of pearls, grace my speech with Her presence always. (3)

❍ ❍ ❍

कम्बुकण्ठी सुताम्रोष्ठी सर्वाभरणभूषिता ।
महासरस्वतीदेवी जिह्वाग्रे सन्निविश्यताम् ॥ ४ ॥

kambukaṇṭhī sutāmroṣṭhī sarvābharaṇabhūṣitā |
mahāsarasvatīdevī jihvāgre sanniviśyatām || 4 ||

Bedecked with all kinds of decoration, having conch like beautiful neck and reddish lips, May Supreme Saraswatī Devī, superbly decorated, be joyously seated on the front part of my tongue. (4)

❍ ❍ ❍

या श्रद्धा धारणा मेधा वाग्देवी विधिवल्लभा ।
भक्तजिह्वाग्रसदना शमादिगुणदायिनी ॥ ५ ॥

yā śraddhā dhāraṇā medhā vāgdevī vidhivallabhā |
bhaktajihvāgrasadanā śamādiguṇadāyinī || 5 ||

The beloved of Brahmā, Saraswatī Devī is personified faith, understanding and intellect, and residing in the front part of Her devotees' tongue, She grants attributes of peace and self-restraint. (5)

❍ ❍ ❍

नमामि यामिनीनाथलेखालंकृतकुन्तलाम् ।
भवानीं भवसंतापनिर्वापणसुधानदीम् ॥ ६ ॥

namāmi yāminīnāthalekhālaṃkṛtakuntalām |
bhavānīṃ bhavasaṃtāpanirvāpaṇasudhānadīm || 6 ||

I offer my obeisances to Goddess Bhavānī, who is in the form of Saraswatī, and is bedecked with locks (ringlets) of beautiful hair and attributes of moon; and is also river of nectar, pacifying worldly afflictions. (6)

❍ ❍ ❍

यः कवित्वं निरातङ्कं भुक्तिमुक्ती च वाञ्छति ।
सोऽभ्यर्च्यैनां दशश्लोक्या भक्त्या स्तौति सरस्वतीम् ॥ ७ ॥

ya: kavitvaṃ nirātaṅkaṃ bhuktimuktī ca vāñchati |
sau'bhyaccainām daśaślaukyā bhaktyā satauti sarasvatīma || 7 ||

He, who aspires to be intelligent and composer of songs, hymns etc., and to be fearless, indulging in pleasures and desiring emancipation, he must worship Saraswatī Devī with deep devotion with these ten mantrās. (7)

❍ ❍ ❍

तस्यैवं स्तुवतो नित्यं समभ्यर्च्य सरस्वतीम् ।
भक्तिश्रद्धाभियुक्तस्य षण्मासात् प्रत्ययो भवेत् ॥ ८ ॥

**tasyaivaṃ stuvato nityaṃ samabhyarcya sarasvatīm |
bhaktiśraddhābhiyuktasya ṣaṇmāsāt
pratyayo bhavet || 8 ||**

A devotee, worshipping Saraswatī Devī, daily with faith as per given practice, shall realise (feel) Her grace within six months. (8)

❍ ❍ ❍

ततः प्रवर्तते वाणी स्वेच्छया ललिताक्षरा ।
गद्यपद्यात्मकैः शब्दैरप्रमेयैर्विवक्षितैः ॥ ९ ॥

**tata: pravartate vāṇī svecchayā lalitākṣarā |
gadyapadyātmakai: śabdairaprameyairvivakṣitai: || 9 ||**

Later, his speech (the devotee of Goddess Sarawati), automatically, acquires unparalleled, elegantly composed prosaic-poetic words. (9)

❍ ❍ ❍

अश्रुतो बुध्यते ग्रन्थः प्रायः सारस्वतः कविः ।
इत्येवं निश्चयं विप्राः सा होवाच सरस्वती ॥ १० ॥

**aśruto budhyate grantha: prāya: sārasvata: kavi: |
ityevaṃ niścayaṃ viprā: sā hovāca sarasvatī || 10 ||**

A devotee-poet of Goddess Saraswatī, generally, understands the purport of literary-works without hearing them from others. O Brahmins! (The Learned Ones) The Goddess Saraswatī Herself manifested this resoluteness. (10)

❍ ❍ ❍

आत्मविद्या मया लब्धा ब्रह्मणैव सनातनी ।
ब्रह्मत्वं मे सदा नित्यं सच्चिदानन्दरूपतः ॥ ११ ॥

**ātmavidyā mayā labdhā brahmaṇaiva sanātanī |
brahmatvaṃ me sadā nityaṃ saccidānandarūpata: || 11 ||**

I received initiation in eternal self-realisation from Lord Brahmā, the creator Himself, and I exist ever in Truth-Consciousness-Bliss (sat-cit-ānand), lending me 'Brahmatva' (His lasting lustre). (11)

❍ ❍ ❍

प्रकृतित्वं ततः सृष्टिं सत्त्वादिगुणसाम्यतः
सत्यमाभाति चिच्छाया दर्पणे प्रतिबिम्बवत् ॥ १२ ॥

prakṛtitvaṃ tata: sṛṣṭiṃ sattvādiguṇasāmyata:
satyamābhāti cicchāyā darpaṇe pratibimbavat || 12 ||

Later on, the equalibrium of three, Sat, Raj, Tam (goodness, passion and ignorance) caused the creation to come into existence. As a mirror reflects an object outside, so does creation, the reflection of consciousness, appears to be true. (12)

❍ ❍ ❍

तेन चित्प्रतिबिम्बेन त्रिविधा भाति सा पुनः ।
प्रकृत्यवच्छिन्नतया पुरुषत्वं पुनश्च ते ॥ १३ ॥

tena citpratibimbena trividhā bhāti sā puna: |
prakṛtyavacchinnatayā puruṣatvaṃ punaśca te || 13 ||

The reflection of that consciousness appears manifested in the nature in three ways; the inseparability from nature is the cause of your individual soul (जीव) coming into existence. (13)

❍ ❍ ❍

शुद्धसत्त्वप्रधानायां मायायां बिम्बितो ह्यजः ।
सत्त्वप्रधाना प्रकृतिर्मायेति प्रतिपाद्यते ॥ १४ ॥

śuddhasattvapradhānāyāṃ māyāyāṃ bimbito hyaja: |
sattvapradhānā prakṛtirmāyeti pratipādyate || 14 ||

Nature, pure and full of goodness is called illusion (māyā). Reflection of the consciousness in that purely, goodness infused māyā (illusion) is called Brahmā (the unborn Eternal One). (14)

❍ ❍ ❍

सा माया स्ववशोपाधिः सर्वज्ञस्येश्वरस्य हि ।
वश्यमायत्वमेकत्वं सर्वज्ञत्वं च तस्य तु ॥ १५ ॥

sā māyā svavaśopādhi: sarvajñasyeśvarasya hi |
vaśyamāyatvamekatvaṃ sarvajñatvaṃ ca tasya tu || 15 ||

Under the command of the Omniscient Lord that māyā (illusion) is a substitute (upādhi). These are the attribues of the Lord to keep that illusion under control, to be one (with it) and be Omniscient. (15)

❍ ❍ ❍

सात्त्विकत्वात् समष्टित्वात् साक्षित्वाज्जगतामपि ।
जगत्कर्तुमकर्तुं वा चान्यथा कर्तुमीशते ॥ १६ ॥

sāttvikatvāt samaṣṭitvāt sākṣitvājjagatāmapi |
jagatkartumakartuṃ vā cānyathā kartumīśate || 16 ||

That Supreme Being has (all) competence to create or not to create the universe, and to do otherwise, because of predominance of His sattvaguṇa (the Reality), His 'wholeness Form' (The Universe), His being 'Self-spectator' of the worlds. (16)

❍ ❍ ❍

यः स ईश्वर इत्युक्तः सर्वज्ञत्वादिभिर्गुणैः ।
शक्तिद्वयं हि मायाया विक्षेपावृतिरूपकम् ॥ १७ ॥

ya: sa īśvara ityutta: sarvajñatvādibhirguṇai: |
śattidvayaṃ hi māyāyā vikṣepāvṛtirūpakam || 17 ||

Thus, having attributes of Omniscience etc. That Consciousness is known as the Supreme. There are two powers of illusion (māyā) – distraction (confusion) and concealment (आवरण) (विक्षेप). (17)

❍ ❍ ❍

विक्षेपशक्तिर्लिङ्गादि ब्रह्माण्डान्तं जगत् सृजेत् ।
अन्तर्दृग्दृश्ययोर्भेदं बहिश्च ब्रह्मसर्गयोः ॥ १८ ॥

vikṣepaśattirliṅdi brahmāṇḍāntaṃ jagat sṛjet |
antardṛgdṛśyayorbhedaṃ bahiśca
brahmasargayo: || 18 ||

The distraction-power (vikśep-śakti) creates from the symbolic body (Linga-śarīra) upto the worlds of the universe. The other, the power of concealment, (covering āvaraṇ-śakti) covers the difference between the inner seer and the scene, and the external powers of concealment covers, the difference between Brahmā and the creation (śriṣti). (18)

❍ ❍ ❍

आवृणोत्यपरा शक्तिः सा संसारस्य कारणम् ।
साक्षिणः पुरतो भातं लिङ्गदेहेन संयुतम् ॥ १९ ॥

āvṛṇotyaparā śakti: sā saṃsārasya kāraṇam |
sākṣiṇa: purato bhātaṃ liṅgadehena saṃyutam || 19 ||

The concealing power (āvaraṇ śakti) is the cause of worldly bondage, which makes the Brahm appear like a symbolic-body (linga deha) to the living-being (jīvātmā). (19)

❍ ❍ ❍

चितिच्छायासमावेशाज्जीवः स्याद्व्यावहारिकः ।
अस्य जीवत्वमारोपात् साक्षिण्यप्यवभासते ॥ २० ॥

citicchāyāsamāveśājjīva: syādvyāvahārika: |
asya jīvatvamāropāt sākṣiṇyapyavabhāsate || 20 ||

The inclusion of reflection of consciousness in the causal creation results in the appearance of living beings in this practical world, and by imposition this sentient jīva gets reflected in the Brahm also. (20)

❍ ❍ ❍

आवृतौ तु विनष्टाया भेदे भाते प्रयाति तत् ।
तथा सर्गब्रह्मणोश्च भेदमावृत्य तिष्ठति ॥ २१ ॥

āvṛtau tu vinaṣṭāyā bhede bhāte prayāti tat |
tathā sargabrahmaṇośca bhedamāvṛtya tiṣṭhati || 21 ||

या शक्तिस्तद्वशाद्ब्रह्म विकृतत्वेन भासते ।
अत्राप्यावृतिनाशेन विभाति ब्रह्मसर्गयोः ॥ २२ ॥

yā śaktistadvaśādbrahma vikṛtatvena bhāsate |
atrāpyāvṛtināśena vibhāti brahmasargayo: || 22 ||

When obscurity vanishes, the difference becomes evident (the animate and the inanimate do not have oneness any longer), so the state of being a jīva (living being) disappears, and the power that obscures the difference between the creation and the Brahm, under whose sway, Brahm appears to be transforming (विकार युक्त), there also, when obscurity vanishes, the difference between the creation and the Brahm, becomes clearly evident. (21-22)

❍ ❍ ❍

भेदस्तयोर्विकारः स्यात् सर्गे न ब्रह्मणि क्वचित् ।
अस्ति भाति प्रियं रूपं नाम चेत्यंशपञ्चकम् ॥ २३ ॥

bhedastayorvikāra: syāt sarge na brahmaṇi kvacit |
asti bhāti priyaṃ rūpaṃ nāma cetyaṃśapañcakam || 23 ||

Between the two, the transformation (vikār) is caused in the creation (सृष्टि), not in Brahm. 'Asti' means, 'is', 'bhāti' means, 'appears or seems', 'priya' means, 'blissful', 'form' and 'name' – these are five part and parcel. (23)

❍ ❍ ❍

आद्यत्रयं ब्रह्मरूपं जगद्रूपं ततो द्वयम् ।
अपेक्ष्य नामरूपे द्वे सच्चिदानन्दतत्परः॥ २४ ॥

ādyatrayaṃ brahmarūpaṃ jagadrūpaṃ tato dvayam |
apekṣya nāmarūpe dve saccidānandatatpara:|| 24 ||

Of the five, 'is' (asti), 'seems or appears' (bhāti) and 'blissful' (Priya-Anand māyā) are the self-form of Brahm, and 'Name' and 'Form' (physical) are those of the world (Jagat). The Oversoul, Para Brahm transforms into the world (Jagat) with togetherness of 'Name' and 'Form'. (24)

❍ ❍ ❍

समाधिं सर्वदा कुर्याद्धृदये वाथ वा बहिः ।
सविकल्पो निर्विकल्पः समाधिर्द्विविधो हृदि ॥ २५ ॥

samādhiṃ sarvadā kuryāddhṛdaye vātha vā bahi: |
savikalpo nirvikalpa: samādhirdvividho hṛdi || 25 ||

In his inner-heart or externally, the researcher (sādhak) should always be engaged in meditation (concentration – samādhi). Internally, (in the heart) there are two kinds of samādhis (concentration). Wavering concentration (savikalpa, with alternative) and unwavering concentration (Nirvikalpa – samādhi), without any alternative. (25)

❍ ❍ ❍

दृश्यशब्दानुभेदेन सविकल्पः पुनर्द्विधा ।
कामाद्याश्चित्तगा दृश्यास्तत्साक्षित्वेन चेतनम् ॥ २६ ॥

dṛśyaśabdānubhedena savikalpa: punardvidhā |
kāmādyāścittagā dṛśyāstatsākṣitvena cetanam || 26 ||

The wavering-concentration (savikalpa – with alternative) is also of two kinds – one, concentration, pierced by vision, two, concentration pierced by sound (words). The aspirations, created inside the conciousness are scenes, and the conscious-self (चेतन आत्मा) is the witness. This is how one should concentrate. This is savikalpa-samadhi (wavering-concentration) pierced by visions. (26)

❍ ❍ ❍

ध्यायेद् दृश्यानुविद्धोऽयं समाधिः सविकल्पकः ।
असङ्गः सच्चिदानन्दः स्वप्रभो द्वैतवर्जितः ॥ २७ ॥

dhyāyed dṛśyānuviddho'yaṃ samādhi: savikalpaka: |
asaṅga: saccidānanda: svaprabho dvaitavarjita: || 27 ||

This be viewed thus, this is wavering-concentration (savikalpa-samadhi) pierced by visions. I am unattached, Self form of Reality (Truth), Consciousness-Bliss (saccidānand), Self-illumined and indivisible-self. (27)

❍ ❍ ❍

अस्मीतिशब्दविद्धोऽयं समाधिः सविकल्पकः ।
स्वानुभूतिरसावेशाद् दृश्यशब्दाद्यपेक्षितुः ॥ २८ ॥

asmītiśabdaviddho'yaṃ samādhi: savikalpaka: |
svānubhūtirasāveśād dṛśyaśabdādyapekṣitu: || 28 ||

This kind of wavering-concentration (savikalpa-samādhi) is known as concentration pierced by words (sound). The researcher (sādhak), who avoids vision and words, swayed by the bliss of self-experience, exists in unwavering-concentration (nirvikalpa-samādhi). (28)

❍ ❍ ❍

निर्विकल्पः समाधिः स्यान्निवातस्थितदीपवत् ।
हृदीयं बाह्यदेशेऽपि यस्मिन् कस्मिंश्च वस्तुनि ॥ २९ ॥

nirvikalpa: samādhi: syānnivātasthitadīpavat |
hṛdīyaṃ bāhyadeśe'pi yasmin kasiṃmaśca vastuni || 29 ||

During unwavering-concentration (nirvikalpa-samādhi), the position of the yogī (meditator) is like that of unwavering flame of a lamp in a zero-wind zone. So, in the external world also, whichever object the mind becomes focused on, one attains the stage of concentration (samādhi). (29)

❍ ❍ ❍

समाधिराद्यदृङ्मात्रा नामरूपपृथक् कृतिः ।
स्तब्धीभावो रसास्वादात् तृतीयः पूर्ववन्मतः ॥ ३० ॥

samādhirādyadṛṅamātrā nāmarūpapṛthav kṛti: |
stabdhībhāvo rasāsvādāt tṛtīya: pūrvavanmata: || 30 ||

The first stage of concentration (samādhi) is caused with the wisdom of the seer and the scene; to oversee the underneath basis of consciousness in an object separating it from its name and form, is the second kind of concentration, samādhi; and the third is as earlier one, wherein swayed by experiencing an all pervading blissfulness, stillness (of mind) prevails. (30)

❍ ❍ ❍

एतैः समाधिभिः षड्भिर्नयेत् कालं निरन्तरम् ।
देहाभिमाने गलिते विज्ञाते परमात्मनि ।
यत्र यत्र मनो याति तत्र तत्र परामृतम् ॥ ३१ ॥

etai: samādhibhi: ṣaḍbhirnayet kālaṃ nirantaram |
dehābhimāne galite vijñāte paramātmani |
yatra yatra mano yāti tatra tatra parāmṛtam || 31 ||

When body-consciousness vanishes, and self-realisation is attained, wherever mind goes, the supreme-nectar is realised. One has to spend one's time, regularly, in venturing on these six kinds of concentrations (samādhis). (31)

❍ ❍ ❍

भिद्यते हृदयग्रन्थिश्छिद्यन्ते सर्वसंशयाः ।
क्षीयन्ते चास्य कर्माणि तस्मिन् दृष्टे परावरे ॥ ३२ ॥

bhidyate hṛdayagranthiśchidyante sarvasaṃśayā: |
kṣīyante cāsya karmāṇi tasmin dṛṣṭe parāvare || 32 ||

The knots (inside) of the heart get loosened, all doubts vanish, and on realisation of Brahm (the Supreme), indivisble and divisible (निष्कल एवं सकल), the actions (karmas) of the wise diminish. (32)

❍ ❍ ❍

मयि जीवत्वमीशत्वं कल्पितं वस्तुतो नहि ।
इति यस्तु विजानाति स मुक्तो नात्र संशयः ॥ ३३ ॥
mayi jīvatvamīśatvaṃ kalpitaṃ vastuto nahi |
iti yastu vijānāti sa mutto nātra saṃśaya: || 33 ||

'Existentialism* and Divinity** in me is notional (not real)'. Those who are aware of this, are liberated. There is not a slightest doubt in this. (33)

* individual existence (Jīvatva)
** Divinity (Īshwaratva – as God)

❍ ❍ ❍

॥ ॐ वाङ् मे मनसीति शान्तिः ॥
[ऋग्वेदीय सरस्वतीरहस्योपनिषद्]
|| oṃ vāṅ me manasīti śānti: ||
[ṛgvedīya sarasvatīrahasyopaniṣad]

Om! May my speech and mind* be in unison, śantih.

* मनसा वाचा एकत्व

❍ ❍ ❍

Medhā (Intellect) Hymns (A)

मेधा सूक्त (क)

Some mantrās, on the faculty of retentive power of mind, are available in the 32nd Chapter of the Yajurvedra. These are known as 'The Intellect-Hymns' (Medhā-Sūkta). The term 'Medhā' simply means faculty of retaining in mind. Retentiveness (Medhā) is a special power of mind. This retains the acquired knowledge, and has ability to express it when needed. In order to acquire this power, these mantrās are practised. The Gods such as Agni, Varuṇa, Prajāpati, Indira, Vāyu (wind), Dhātā etc. are worshipped in these mantrās. The recitation of the mantrās help in widening intelligence and bring in purity. Of these, there is a very popular mantrā, as follows here:

'मेधां मे वरुणो ददातु मेधामग्निः प्रजापतिः ।
मेधामिन्द्रश्च वायुश्च मेधां धाता ददातु मे स्वाहा ॥'

**'medhāṃ me varuṇo dadātu medhāmagni: prajāpati: |
medhāmindraśca vāyuśca medhāṃ dhātā
dadātu me svāhā ||'**

In the Vedic culture, of the sixteen known rites, 'Jāt Karma' rite is performed on the birth-time of a child before umbilical cord is separated. The two special rites, at this juncture, concern rejuvenating intellect and attaining longivity of life for the child. In order to attain intelligence and wisdom of discrimination, for the child, clarified butter (Ghrit) and honey are put in the mouth with ring finger to lick by the child, chanting mantra 'ॐ भूतस्त्वयि दधामि' etc. and for his longivity of life, another mantra 'ॐ अग्निरायुष्मान' etc. are recited in the right ear of the child or near his navel-cord.

Thus, the mantrās of 'the Medhā Sūkta' carry paramount importance for the benefit of widening intelligence. The text follows:

सदसस्पतिमद्भुतं प्रियमिन्द्रस्य काम्यम् ।
सनिं मेधामयासिषꣳ स्वाहा ॥ १ ॥

sadasaspatimadbhutaṃ priyamindrasya kāmyam |
saniṃ medhāmayāsiṣaꣳ svāhā || 1 ||

I pray to the cherished and loving power of the Supreme Lord, God of fire (Agni), the protector of the house-hold performing sacrifice (yajña), endowed with inconceivable power to fetch (for me) wealth-prosperity and intellect (Medha-wisdom with retentive power). For which, this best oblation, may kindly be accepted. (1)

❍ ❍ ❍

यां मेधां देवगणाः पितरश्चोपासते ।
तया मामद्य मेधयाऽग्ने मेधाविनं कुरु स्वाहा ॥ २ ॥

yāṃ medhāṃ devagaṇā: pitaraścopāsate |
tayā māmadya medhayā'gne medhāvinaṃ
kuru svāhā || 2 ||

O God of Fire! Bless me with that intellect (retentive power of mind) in order to have the wisdom, which the group of devatās and the ancestors utilise. For Thee, this best oblation is offered. (2)

❍ ❍ ❍

मेधां मे वरुणो ददातु मेधामग्निः प्रजापतिः ।
मेधामिन्द्रश्च वायुश्च मेधां धाता ददातु मे स्वाहा ॥ ३ ॥

medhāṃ me varuṇo dadātu medhāmagni: prajāpati: |
medhāmindraśca vāyuśca medhāṃ dhātā dadātu
me svāhā || 3 ||

O Varuṇa! (God of water and that of the West direction) Bless me with the wisdom capable of comprehending the quintessence (the highest element of knowledge), Agni and Prajāpati! Bless me with wisdom, Indra and Vāyu! Bless me with intellect. O Dhātā! Bless me with wisdom. For all of Thee, hereby, I offer my excellent oblation. (3)

❍ ❍ ❍

इदं मे ब्रह्म च क्षत्रं चोभे श्रियमश्नुताम् ।
मयि देवा दधतु श्रियमुत्तमां तस्यै ते स्वाहा ॥ ४ ॥
[शु॰ यजु॰ ३२ । १३-१६]

idaṃ me brahma ca kṣatraṃ cobhe śriyamaśnutām |
mayi devā dadhatu śriyamuttamāṃ tasyai te svāhā || 4 ||
[śu. yaju. 32 | 13-16]

This clan of the brāhmins and that of the kśatriyās – both of them, together, enjoy my prosperity (wealth). O Devagaṇa! (group of Gods) Bless me with excellent wealth. This excellent oblation is offered by me to Goddess Lakśami in order to have wealth. (4)

❍ ❍ ❍

Medhā (Intellect) Hymns (B)
मेधा सूक्त (ख)

There is another 'MedhāSūkta' available in the 'Mahānarayaṇopaniṣad' in the Kṛṣṇa Yajurveda. These four mantrās are being given hereunder:

मेधादेवी जुषमाणा न आगाद्विश्वाची भद्रा सुमनस्य माना ।
त्वया जुष्टा नुदमाना दुरुक्तान् बृहद्वदेम विदथे सुवीराः ।
त्वया जुष्ट ऋषिर्भवति देवि त्वया ब्रह्माऽऽगतश्रीरुत त्वया ।
त्वया जुष्टश्चित्रं विन्दते वसु सा नो जुषस्व द्रविणो न मेधे ॥ १ ॥

medhādevī juṣamāṇā na āgādviśvācī bhadrā sumanasya mānā |
tvayā juṣṭā nudamānā duruttān bṛhadvadema vidathe suvīrā: |
tvayā juṣṭa ṛṣirbhavati devi tvayā brahmā" gataśrīruta tvayā |
tvayā juṣṭaścitraṃ vindate vasu sā no juṣasva draviṇo na medhe || 1 ||

May the rejoicing Goddess Medhā (intellect) and benevolent Goddess Viśvācī, having, beautiful mindset, grace us by their presence, near us. Being gratified and motivated by Thee, let us speak in excellent words with untruth-speaking men, and let us be highly valorous. O Goddess! With Thy grace, a man becomes a sage (seer of mantrās); he becomes enlightened, blessed with Supreme wisdom and becomes prosperous. Thy grace provides unique wealth (to Thy devotee). O such a Goddess Medhā! Be happy (graceful) on us and bless us with wealth. (1)

❍ ❍ ❍

मेधां म इन्द्रो दधातु मेधां देवी सरस्वती ।
मेधां मे अश्विनावुभावाधत्तां पुष्करस्त्रजा ।
अप्सरासु च या मेधा गन्धर्वेषु च यन्मनः ।
दैवीं मेधा सरस्वती सा मां मेधा सुरभिर्जुषतां स्वाहा ॥ २ ॥

medhāṃ ma indro dadhātu medhāṃ devī sarasvatī |
medhāṃ me aśvināvubhāvādhattāṃ puṣkarasrajā |
apsarāsu ca yā medhā gandharveṣu ca yanmana: |
daivīṃ medhā sarasvatī sā māṃ medhā
surabhirjuṣatāṃ svāhā || 2 ||

May Indra bless us with intellect, May Goddess Sarawatī bless us with intellect, May the two Aświnī Kumars, adorned with lotus garlands, provide us with intellect. The intellect, available in fairies (अप्सराएं), (intellect) which glows in the heart of heavenly choristers (Gandharvās), May (all this) the power of intellect of Goddess Saraswatī, spread over like fragrance on me, and be favourable to me. (2)

❍ ❍ ❍

आ मां मेधा सुरभिर्विश्वरूपा हिरण्यवर्णा जगती जगम्या ।
ऊर्जस्वती पयसा पिन्वमाना सा मां मेधा सुप्रतीका जुषन्ताम् ॥ ३ ॥
[कृष्णयजुर्वेदीय महानारायणोपनिषद्]

ā māṃ medhā surabhirviśvarūpā hiraṇyavarṇā
jagatī jagamyā |
ūrjasvatī payasā pinvamānā sā māṃ medhā
supratīkā juṣantām || 3 ||
[kṛṣṇayajurvedīya mahānārāyaṇopaniṣad]

Manifested in many forms like fragrance, brilliantly shining (Tejaswin – तेजोमयी) like gold, all pervading in the universe, vibrant Goddess Medha (of intellect), adorned with symbols of beauty, feeding the milk of wisdom; may She be happy with me. (3)

❍ ❍ ❍

The Sun Hymns (A)
सूर्य सूक्त (क)

This is Rigveda Sūkta (1/115). The sage of the Sūkta is 'Kutsa Angiras', the Divinity, Sun and the metre 'Triṣtup'. The Sun is the light of the eyes, of all life-energy in the entire planets of this solar-world. Sun is the soul of the world and the God, inspiring the entire beings to get engaged in virtuous deeds. The sun enjoys the highest and most important place in the congregation of gods; the reason being, for all living beings, He is the only visible God. He lends wellness to all and is the chief-source of welfare in every manner. Thus, the sun is venerable and adorable for all living beings. The text follows:

चित्रं देवानामुदगादनीकं चक्षुर्मित्रस्य वरुणस्याग्नेः ।
आप्रा द्यावापृथिवी अन्तरिक्षꣳ सूर्य आत्मा जगतस्तस्थुषश्च ॥ १ ॥

citraṃ devānāmudagādanīkaṃ cakṣurmitrasya varuṇasyāgne: |
āprā dyāvāpṛthivī antarikṣaꣳ sūrya ātmā jagatastasthuṣaśca || 1 ||

A cluster of brilliant rays or a heap-on aggregation of Gods are rising in the form of the solar-circle. These, Mitra, Varuṇa, Agni are the brilliant eyes of the entire world. These (bodies) have filled the heaven, the earth and the space with their radiant (dedīpyamān) brilliance (tejas) by their ascent. The Sun in this circle, being the inmost-soul (antaryāmī), is the inspirational Oversoul, and is the soul of the animate and inanimate creation (of the world). (1)

❍ ❍ ❍

सूर्यो देवीमुषसं रोचमानां मर्त्यो न योषामभ्येति पश्चात् ।
यत्रा नरो देवयन्तो युगानि वितन्वते प्रति भद्राय भद्रम् ॥ २ ॥

sūryo devīmuṣasaṃ rocamānāṃ martyo na yoṣāmabhyeti paścāt |
yatrā naro devayanto yugāni vitanvate prati bhadrāya bhadram || 2 ||

The sun follows behind the virtuous and brilliant Aurora (goddess of dawn), as if a man were pursuing an all charming woman. When the beautiful Aurora incarnates, men dedicate themselves to their duties in order to worship the God of Light, the Sun. The Sun is an embodiment of generosity and His worshipping inspires dutifulness, which provides wellness (in all fields). (2)

○ ○ ○

भद्रा अश्वा हरितः सूर्यस्य चित्रा एतग्वा अनुमाद्यासः ।
नमस्यन्तो दिव आ पृष्ठमस्थुः परि द्यावापृथिवी यन्ति सद्यः ॥ ३ ॥

bhadrā aśvā harita: sūryasya citrā etagvā anumādyāsa: |
namasyanto diva ā pṛṣṭhamasthu: pari dyāvāpṛthivī yanti sadya: || 3 ||

Like a horse, this circle of rays of the Sun reaches out everywhere in the form of wellness in a wonderful manner. The Sun moves on His own track everyday (uninterrupted) and is worthy of being worshipped and is venerable. This inspires us to respect Him by doing praṇām. His abode is above heaven. He, instantly, illuminates the heaven and the earth with brilliant rays. (3)

○ ○ ○

तत् सूर्यस्य देवत्वं तन्महित्वं मध्या कर्तोर्विततं सं जभार ।
यदेदयुक्त हरितः सधस्थादाद्रात्री वासस्तनुते सिमस्मै ॥ ४ ॥

tat sūryasya devatvaṃ tanmahitvaṃ madhyā kartorvitataṃ saṃ jabhāra |
yadedayutta harita: sadhasthādādrātrī vāsastanute simasmai || 4 ||

It is godlike and important of the inspiring Universal-soul, the Sun to assimilate all His rays, when setting, leaving behind all the deeds, which were started and those which were unfinished, and remained unfinished. He engages His juice-extracting rays and horses elsewhere, withdrawing them from one place. At that time, night enwraps all with the cover of darkness. (4)

❍ ❍ ❍

तन्मित्रस्य वरुणस्याभिचक्षे सूर्यो रूपं कृणुते द्योरुपस्थे ।
अनन्तमन्यद् रुशदस्य पाजः कृष्णमन्यद्धरितः सं भरन्ति ॥ ५ ॥

tanmitrasya varuṇasyābhicakṣe sūryo rūpaṃ kṛṇute dyorupasthe |
anantamanyad ruśadasya pāja: kṛṣṇamanyaddharita: saṃ bharanti || 5 ||

The stimulating Sun incarnates His brilliant form in the eastern horizon of the sky in order to illuminate Mitra, Varuṇa and the entire creation from the front. His juice-extracting rays (power to dry) and green-horses bear unique glow, capable in dispelling the darkness of night. (5)

❍ ❍ ❍

अद्या देवा उदिता सूर्यस्य निरंहसः पिपृता निरवद्यात् ।
तन्नो मित्रो वरुणो मामहन्तामदितिः सिन्धुः पृथिवी उत द्यौः ॥ ६ ॥
[ऋक्० १ । ११५]

adyā devā uditā sūryasya niraṃhasa: pipṛtā niravadyāt |
tanno mitro varuṇo māmahantāmaditi: sindhu: pṛthivī uta dyau: || 6 ||
[ṛv. 1 | 115]

O luminous Sun-rays! Save us from sins by scattering hither and thither at sunrise, today. Save us, not only from sins, but also from all that is despicable, reproachable, sad and wretched. Whatever we speak, May Mitra, Varuṇa, Aditi, Sindhu, Prithvī (Earth) and the presiding deity of heaven give it honour and endorse it, May they also protect us.

The Sun Hymns (B)

सूर्य सूक्त (ख)

This is Śukla Yajurveda sūkta. The sage of this sūkta is 'vibhrāḍ', the deity is Sun and the metre 'Jagatī'. This is the visible God of the solar-circle, everyone has daily view of Him, regularly. There is a tradition of recitation of 'Sūrya Sūkta' in the 'abode' (upasthān उपस्थान) and 'worship' of the God, 'Sūrya Nārāyaṇ'. This Sūkta has an unprecedented power in providing relief from physical ailments.

The Text follows as under:

विभ्राड् बृहत्पिबतु सोम्यं मध्वायुर्दधद्यज्ञपताववि‍ह्रुतम् ।
वातजूतो यो अभिरक्षति त्मना प्रजाः पुपोष पुरुधा वि राजति ॥ १ ॥

vibhrāḍ bṛhatpibatu somyaṃ
madhvāyurdadhadyajñapatāvavihradbhatam |
vātajūto yo abhirakṣati tmanā prajā: pupoṣa purudhā
vi rājati || 1 ||

Stimulated by the wind, the soul, with which the great Sun radiates, who protects and nourishes subjects (Prajā), and acquires brilliance, May that (Sun) taste sweet 'somarasa' (juice of a plant, which makes one immortal), providing unbroken life. (1)

❍ ❍ ❍

उदु त्यं जातवेदसं देवं वहन्ति केतवः ।
दृशे विश्वाय सूर्यम् ॥ २ ॥

udu tyaṃ jātavedasaṃ devaṃ vahanti ketava: |
dṛśe viśvāya sūryam || 2 ||

Like the flame of fire, the Sun is being kept lifted upward by

'Brahm jyoties' (lustre of Brahm) in order to perform viewing-process (darshan-kriyā) of the world. (2)

❍ ❍ ❍

येना पावक चक्षसा भुरण्यन्तं जनाँ२ अनु ।
त्वं वरुण पश्यसि ॥ ३ ॥

**yenā pāvaka cakṣasā bhuraṇyantaṃ janāṁ2 anu |
tvaṃ varuṇa paśyasi || 3 ||**

O Sun God! In the form of Pāvak (Fire) and Varuṇa (water), as Thou looketh upon those who go to the elevated spheres, do look upon all the beings with the same merciful glance. (3)

❍ ❍ ❍

दैव्यावध्वर्यू आ गतꣳ रथेन सूर्यत्वचा ।
मध्वा यज्ञꣳ समञ्जाथे। तं प्रत्नथा ऽयं वेनश्चित्रं देवानाम् ॥ ४ ॥

**daivyāvadhvaryū ā gataꣳ rathena sūryatvacā |
madhvā yajñaꣳ samañjāthe| taṃ pratnathā 'yaṃ
venaścitraṃ devānām || 4 ||**

O Divine Aśvinikumārās! May Thou also come in a chariot, splendrous as that of the Sun, and complete the sacrfice (yajña) with oblations, that which has been made unique with ancient ways by the moon, of the celestial spectacles (jyotishman). (4)

❍ ❍ ❍

तं प्रत्नथा पूर्वथा विश्वथेमथा ज्येष्ठतातिं बर्हिषदꣳस्वर्विदम् ।
प्रतीचीनं वृजनं दोहसे धुनिमाशुं जयन्तमनु यासु वर्धसे ॥ ५ ॥

**taṃ pratnathā pūrvathā viśvathemathā jyeṣṭhatātiṃ
barhiṣadaꣳsvarvidam |
pratīcīnaṃ vṛjanaṃ dohase dhunimāśuṃ jayantamanu
yāsu vardhase || 5 ||**

First in order in the noble sacrificial ceremonies, (one) dispelling opposite sins, excellent expander, seated on excellent seat, knower of heaven, we worship Thee with ancient, complete and common available ways. (5)

❍ ❍ ❍

अयं वेनश्चोदयत् पृश्निगर्भा ज्योतिर्जरायू रजसो विमाने ।
इममपाᳫंसङ्गमे सूर्यस्य शिशुं न विप्रा मतिभी रिहन्ति ॥ ६ ॥

ayaṃ venaścodayat pṛśnigarbhā jyotirjarāyū rajaso vimāne |
imamapāᳫsaṅgame sūryasya śiśuṃ na viprā matibhī rihanti || 6 ||

In the creation of water, the moon, which is overcast by the brilliant sphere, stimulates water in the space. The brahmins glorify the moon (vena) in common simple words (speech), during the advent of water. (6)

❍ ❍ ❍

चित्रं देवानामुदगादनीकं चक्षुर्मित्रस्य वरुणस्याग्नेः ।
आप्रा द्यावापृथिवी अन्तरिक्षᳫ सूर्य आत्मा जगतस्तस्थुषश्च ॥ ७ ॥

citraṃ devānāmudagādanīkaṃ cakṣurmitrasya varuṇasyāgne: |
āprā dyāvāpṛthivī antarikṣaᳫ sūrya ātmā jagatastasthuṣaśca || 7 ||

What a wonder! This Sun, that is the soul of the animate and inanimate world, and is a cluster of brilliant rays, and the eyes of Gods, Agni, Mitra and Varuṇa, rises pervading the earth, the heaven. (7)

❍ ❍ ❍

आ न इडाभिर्विदथे सुशस्ति विश्वानरः सविता देव एतु ।
अपि यथा युवानो मत्सथा नो विश्वं जगदभिपित्वे मनीषा ॥ ८ ॥

ā na iḍābhirvidathe suśasti viśvānara: savitā deva etu |
api yathā yuvāno matsathā no viśvaṃ jagadabhipitve manīṣā || 8 ||

May the auspicious Sun God come in our laudable sacrifice (yajña) comprising rich food (cooked rise, used in sacrifices). O Ageless Gods! Be thou satiated (appeared by indulging to the full) and satiate our entire cows, intelligently, at (Thy) arrival. (8)

❍ ❍ ❍

यदद्य कच्च वृत्रहन्नुदगा अभि सूर्य ।
सर्वं तदिन्द्र ते वशे ॥ ९ ॥

yadadya kacca vṛtrahannudagā abhi sūrya |
sarvaṃ tadindra te vaśe || 9 ||

O Indra! O Sūrya (Sun)! wherever Thou art risen, all those regions are under Thy command. (9)

❍ ❍ ❍

तरणिर्विश्वदर्शतो ज्योतिष्कृदसि सूर्य ।
विश्वमा भासि रोचनम् ॥ १० ॥

taraṇirviśvadarśto jyotiṣkṛdasi sūrya |
viśvamā bhāsi rocanam || 10 ||

O Sun! The luminaire of the world, in moments, Thou doth invade the world. This brightened world is illumed by Thee. (10)

❍ ❍ ❍

तत् सूर्यस्य देवत्वं तन्महित्वं मध्या कर्तोर्विततꣳ सं जभार ।
यदेदयुक्त हरितः सधस्थादाद्रात्री वासस्तनुते सिमस्मै ॥ ११ ॥

tat sūryasya devatvaṃ tanmahitvaṃ madhyā kartorvitataꣳ saṃ jabhāra |
yadedayutta harita: sadhasthādādrātrī vāsastanute simasmai || 11 ||

This is the Divinity of the Sun that He bears all the planets, existing in the midst of the Supreme's – creation world; and when (He) gets mixed-up with the greenish rays from the sky, night spreads the cover of darkness for all. (11)

❍ ❍ ❍

तन्मित्रस्य वरुणस्याभिचक्षे सूर्यो रूपं कृणुते द्योरुपस्थे ।
अनन्तमन्यद् रुशदस्य पाजः कृष्णमन्यद्धरितः सं भरन्ति ॥ १२ ॥

tanmitrasya varuṇasyābhicakṣe sūryo rūpaṃ kṛṇute dyorupasthe |
anantamanyad ruśadasya pāja: kṛṣṇamanyaddharita: saṃ bharanti || 12 ||

In the lap of heaven, this Sun, in the form of Mitra and Varuṇa, oversees all. He has a different non-dual, infinitely, bright and brilliant form. There is another dual and dark form, which the senses adopt.

❍ ❍ ❍

बण्महाँ२ असि सूर्य बडादित्य महाँ२ असि ।
महस्ते सतो महिमा पनस्यतेऽद्धा देव महाँ२ असि ॥ १३ ॥

baṇmahāṁ2 asi sūrya baḍāditya mahāṁ2 asi |
mahaste sato mahimā panasyate'ddhā deva mahāṁ2 asi || 13 ||

O Paramātmā, in the form of Sun! Thou art, verily, great. O Aditya! Thou art, verily, great. Thy greatness is being sung, because Thou art great in reality (sadrūpa). Thou art, verily, great. (13)

❍ ❍ ❍

बट् सूर्य श्रवसा महाँ२ असि सत्रा देव महाँ२ असि ।
मह्ना देवानामसुर्यः पुरोहितो विभु ज्योतिरदाभ्यम् ॥ १४ ॥

baṭ sūrya śravasā mahāṁ2 asi satrā deva mahāṁ2 asi |
mahnā devānāmaSūrya: purohito vibhu jyotiradābhyam || 14 ||

O Sun! Thou art, verily, great by Thy glory. Great art Thou by sacrifice (yajña) and great by Thy majesty. Thou art propitious and foremost for the Gods, and art untamable, pervading brightness. (14)

❍ ❍ ❍

श्रायन्त इव सूर्यं विश्वेदिन्द्रस्य भक्षत ।
वसूनि जाते जनमान ओजसा प्रति भागं न दीधिम ॥ १५ ॥

śrāyanta iva sūryaṃ viśvedindrasya bhakṣata |
vasūni jāte janamāna ojasā prati bhāgaṃ
na dīdhima || 15 ||

That Sun, we bear in heart, with whose support, the rays devour the entire wealth of rains of Indra, then (re)produce them, in the due form of rains. (15)

❍ ❍ ❍

अद्या देवा उदिता सूर्यस्य निरꣳहसः पिपृता निरवद्यात् ।
तन्नो मित्रो वरुणो मामहन्तामदितिः सिन्धुः पृथिवी उत द्यौः ॥ १६ ॥

adyā devā uditā sūryasya niraꣳ hasa: piprtā niravadyāt |
tanno mitro varuṇo māmahantāmaditi: sindhu: pṛthivī
uta dyau: || 16 ||

O Gods! May the Sun-rise today dispel all our sins and imperfections (inadequacies), and May Mitra, Varuṇa, Aditi, Sindhu, Prithivī and heaven, all of them endorse my eloquence. (16)

❍ ❍ ❍

आ कृष्णेन रजसा वर्तमानो निवेशयन्नमृतं मर्त्यं च ।
हिरण्ययेन सविता रथेना देवो याति भुवनानि पश्यन् ॥ १७ ॥
[शुक्ल यजुर्वेद]

ā kṛṣṇena rajasā vartamāno niveśayannamṛtaṃ martyaṃ ca |
hiraṇyayena savitā rathenā devo yāti bhuvanāni paśyan || 17 ||
[śukla yajurveda]

Inspirator of all, the Sun God, seated in the golden chariot, moving on the path of dark-space, engaging Gods and mankind in their (respective) deeds, is approaching while watching the world. (17)

❍ ❍ ❍

The Supreme is one, and, verily, one. **(Ath. 13|5|20)**

❍ ❍ ❍

Speak sweetly spoken words alone. **(Ath. 1|34|3)**

❍ ❍ ❍

Accumulate with hundreds of hands, and spend with thousands of hands. **(Ath. 3|24|5)**

❍ ❍ ❍

May our powerful sweet speech, never be of wicked nature. **(Ath. 16|2|1)**

❍ ❍ ❍

The Fire Hymns (A)

अग्निसूक्त (क)

The sage of this Sūkta is Vaiśwamitra Madhucchandā, the Deity, Agni (Fire) and the metre, Gāyatrī. The Rig-Veda Sanhitā comprises two hundred Sūktās in adoration of fire. In the beginning of all the sections (mandal) of the Rig-Veda, the presence of 'Agni Sūkta' establishes the importance of this God Agni (Fire). The Fire God is first and foremost, apart from being the chief, and all pervading. The name, 'Jātveda' signifies His speciality. It is said that the chief elements of the region of earth have their relation with fire. The text follows as under:

अग्निमीळे पुरोहितं यज्ञस्य देवमृत्विजम् ।
होतारं रत्नधातमम् ॥ १ ॥

**agnimīḻe purohitaṃ yajñasya devamṛtvijam |
hotāraṃ ratnadhātamam || 1 ||**

Om! I admire Agni, who is well-wisher of all, who is purohit (priest) of Yajña (sacrifice), illuminator of sacrifice, always performing favourale yajña, helper of scholars, i admire Thee Agni.

❍ ❍ ❍

अग्निः पूर्वेभिर्ऋषिभिरीड्यो नूतनैरुत ।
स देवाँ एह वक्षति ॥ २ ॥

**agni: pūrvebhirṛṣibhirīḍyo nūtanairuta |
sa devāṁ eha vakŚati || 2 ||**

Ever being adored, O Agni Dev! (I) invoke Thee. The Gods exist in the body, because of Agni. All the Gods forsake the body, when Agni leaves the body. (2)

❍ ❍ ❍

अग्निना रयिमश्नवत् पोषमेव दिवेदिवे ।
यशसं वीरवत्तमम् ॥ ३ ॥

agninā rayimaśnvaat poṣameva divedive |
yaśasaṃ vīravattamam || 3 ||

It is from Agni, nourishing, healthy and distinctive quality grain is obtained. Agni nourishes, increases glory and valour, and provides wealth.

❍ ❍ ❍

अग्ने यं यज्ञमध्वरं विश्वतः परिभूरसि ।
स इद् देवेषु गच्छति ॥ ४ ॥

agne yaṃ yajñamadhvaraṃ viśvata: paribhūrasi |
sa id deveṣu gacchati || 4 ||

O Agni! The sacrifice, without violence, which Thou maketh successful, that alone goes towards the Devās. (4)

❍ ❍ ❍

अग्निर्होता कविक्रतुः सत्यश्चित्रश्रवस्तमः ।
देवो देवे-भिरा गमत् ॥ ५ ॥

agnirhotā kavikratu: satyaścitraśravastama: |
devo deve-bhirā gamat || 5 ||

Agni, the invoker of Gods, cause of sacrifice (yajña), stimulator of energy in work force in the wise, sticking to the truth, having varied forms and unique eminence, the vibrant God of Fire, alongwith other Gods, has come in the sacrifice (yajña).

❍ ❍ ❍

यदङ्ग दाशुषे त्वमग्ने भद्रं करिष्यसि ।
तवेत् तत् सत्य-मङ्गिरः ॥ ६ ॥

yadaṅga dāśuṣe tvamagne bhadraṃ kariṣyasi |
tavet tat satya-maṅigara: || 6 ||

O Agni (God of Fire)! Thou art propitious to a generous

person. O Agni, infused (well) in body! This, indeed, is Thy truthful deed. (6)

❍ ❍ ❍

उप त्वाग्ने दिवेदिवे दोषावस्तर्धिया वयम् ।
नमो भरन्त एमसि ॥ ७ ॥

upa tvāgne divedive doṣāvastardhiyā vayam |
namo bharanta emasi || 7 ||

O Agni! We come near Thee, with our intelligence, day after day, meaning thereby, we need to glroify* Agni by our hymns, and bow in salutation day and night. (7)

* illuminating and vibrant

❍ ❍ ❍

राजन्तमध्वराणां गोपामृतस्य दीदिविम् ।
वर्धमानं स्वे दमे ॥ ८ ॥

rājantamadhvarāṇāṃ gopāmṛtasya dīdivim |
vardhamānaṃ sve dame || 8 ||

(O Agni!) The protector of bright, violence-free sacrifices, illuminator of Divine Truth (Ṛta), we reach, with salutations, near Thee, who is increasing illumination (of truth) in our houses (within our own hearts). (8)

❍ ❍ ❍

स नः पितेव सूनवे ऽग्ने सूपायनो भव ।
सचस्वा नः स्वस्तये ॥ ९ ॥
[ऋग्वेद]

sa na: piteva sūnave 'gne sūpāyano bhava |
sacasvā na: svastaye || 9 ||
[ṛgveda]

O Agni!, like a father to a son, be Thou supporting in our well-being and in deeds of welfare. (9)

❍ ❍ ❍

The Fire Hymns (B)

अग्नि सूक्त (ख)

This sūkta is part of a chapter in the Sāmveda, known as 'Pūrvācik'. It is Āgneya Parva, exhibiting grandeur of Agni and hymns on the Fire-God. Agni is Reality-incarnate, protector of sacrifice (yajña), highly vibrant and nourisher.

Agni is the backbone of the Vedic-rituals, and Earth is the local God. Agni is depicted as the first among the Gods, as described by the Aitareya-brāhmaṇās:

'अग्निर्वै देवानां प्रथमः'

Agni causes life to exist, infuses movement and energy in the universe. Agni is described as the mouth of Gods, and oblations made to the fire as sacrificial-material reach (directly) the Gods. He, therefore, is known as the benefactor to Gods. The last twelve mantrās in the 'Āgneyaparva' are known as Agnisūkta (The Fire-Hymns). The text follows:

प्र मंहिष्ठाय गायत ऋताव्ने बृहते शुक्रशोचिषे ।
उपस्तुतासो अग्नये ॥ १ ॥

pra maṃhiṣṭhāya gāyata ṛtāvne bṛhate śukraśociṣe |
upastutāso agnaye || 1 ||

O Praisers! By your excellent odes, eulogise the Fire-God. He is the protector of great truth and sacrifice (yajña) and He is highly vibrant, and is the protector. (1)

❍ ❍ ❍

प्र सो अग्ने तवोतिभिः सुवीराभिस्तरति वाजकर्मभिः ।
यस्य त्वं सख्यमाविथ ॥ २ ॥

pra so agne tavotibhi: suvīrābhistarati vājakarmabhi: |
yasya tvaṃ sakhyamāvitha || 2 ||

O Fire God! To whom Thine help is available, those group of praisers receive (by Thy grace) superior progeny, grains, power and prosperity. (2)

❍ ❍ ❍

तं गूर्धया स्वर्णरं देवासो देवमरतिं दधन्विरे ।
देवत्रा हव्यमूहिषे ॥ ३ ॥

taṃ gūrdhayā svarṇaraṃ devāso devamaratiṃ dadhanvire |
devatrā havyamūhiṣe || 3 ||

O Praisers! Eulogise the Fire God, who carries oblations to heaven. The oblation-makers eulogise and make offering materials available to the Gods. (3)

❍ ❍ ❍

मा नो हृणीथा अतिथिं वसुरग्निः पुरुप्रशस्त एषः ।
यः सुहोता स्वध्वरः ॥ ४ ॥

mā no hṛṇīthā atithiṃ vasuragni: purupraśasta eṣa: |
ya: suhotā svadhvara: || 4 ||

Do not take our loving guest-like Fire God far away from the sacrificial-place. He fetches Gods (to the yajña); and is munificient*; and is adorable. (4)

* very liberal अति उदार

❍ ❍ ❍

भद्रो नो अग्निराहुतो भद्रा रातिः सुभग भद्रो अध्वरः ।
भद्रा उत प्रशस्तयः ॥ ५ ॥

bhadro no agnirāhuto bhadrā rāti: subhaga bhadro adhvara: |
bhadrā uta praśastaya: || 5 ||

Pleased with the oblations, O Fire God! May Thou be propitious for us. O Opulent One! (with Thy grace) May we have pure wealth, and may our hynms be auspicious for us. (5)

❍ ❍ ❍

यजिष्ठं त्वा ववृमहे देवं देवत्रा होतारममर्त्यम् ।
अस्य यज्ञस्य सुक्रतुम् ॥ ६ ॥

**yajiṣṭhaṃ tvā vavṛmahe devaṃ devatrā hotāramamartyam |
asya yajñasya sukratum || 6 ||**

O God of Gods, Fire! Thou art highly well-versed in sacrificial rituals. Thou shalt accomplish this sacrifice (yajña) well. We pray to Thee. (6)

❍ ❍ ❍

तदग्ने द्युम्नमा भर यत्सासाहा सदने कं चिदत्रिणम् ।
मन्युं जनस्य दूढ्यम् ॥ ७ ॥

**tadagne dyumnamā bhara yatsāsāhā sadane kaṃ cidatriṇam |
manyuṃ janasya dūḍhyam || 7 ||**

O Fire God! Kindly Grant us sharp energy to enable us to control deeply indulgent wicked people. Thou shalt also prevent the anger of the foolish men, alongwith. (7)

❍ ❍ ❍

यद्वा उ विश्पतिः शितः सुप्रीतो मनुषो विशे ।
विश्वेदग्निः प्रति रक्षांसि सेधति ॥ ८ ॥
[सामवेद, पूर्वार्चिक आग्नेयपर्व १२ । १-८]

**yadvā u viśpati: śita: suprīto manuṣo viśe |
viśvedagni: prati rakṣāṃsi sedhati || 8 ||
[sāmaveda, pūrvārcika āgneyaparva 12 | 1-8]**

The Fire God! The protector of patrons, kindled by the oblations and pleased (well) by it, consecrates in the houldholds of oblation-makers and eliminates all the wicked and immoral people (by His intense lustrous influence).

❍ ❍ ❍

The Golden-Womb Hymns
हिरण्यगर्भ सूक्त (Paramātmā)

'The Golden-Womb Hymns', i.e., 'Hiraṇyagarbha Sūkta' is the 121st sūkta in the 10th section (mandal) of the Rigveda. This Sūkta enunciates the source of the creation of the universe, as per the vedic philosophy, how does the cosmos get manifested.

'Hiraṇyagarbha' is known as the soul of the universe or 'Brahm'. In the vedantic terminology, this is used for the 'Creator', the cause of all causes. In the beginning of the creation, 'Hiraṇyagarbha' is the self-manifested enormous egg-shaped element. This is known as the initial fire-element of creation. 'Hiraṇyagarbha', manifested in the great waters, has three dynamics—1. Waves arising in the waters caused admixture (sameṣaṇ — समेषण). 2. It caused 'onward-movement', action (प्रसर्पण Prasarpaṇ). 3. Floating around, it caused inundation (परिप्लवन Pariplavan). This later broke into two halves, which caused formation of 'Earth' and 'Heaven'. This 'Hiraṇyagarbha' is the root of all creation. In the beginning of the creation, the seer of the mantra expressed his curiousness, 'That which existed before the creation'. The text follows:

हिरण्यगर्भः समवर्तताग्रे भूतस्य जातः पतिरेक आसीत् ।
स दाधार पृथिवीं द्यामुतेमां कस्मै देवाय हविषा विधेम ॥ १ ॥

hiraṇyagarbha: samavartatāgre bhūtasya jāta: patireka āsīt |
sa dādhāra pṛthivīṃ dyāmutemāṃ kasmai devāya haviṣā vidhema || 1 ||

The Oversoul, in whom inhabits the splendour as that of the Sun, was present before the creation and came into being.

That Oversoul (Himself) bears the Earth and the Heaven, and for that God, we offer oblations. (1)

❍ ❍ ❍

य आत्मदा बलदा यस्य विश्व उपासते प्रशिषं यस्य देवाः ।
यस्य छायामृतं यस्य मृत्युः कस्मै देवाय हविषा विधेम ॥ २ ॥

ya ātmadā baladā yasya viśva upāsate praśiṣaṃ yasya devā: |
yasya chāyāmṛtaṃ yasya mṛtyu: kasmai devāya haviṣā vidhema || 2 ||

The Oversoul, who bestows will-power and physical vigour, whose excellent guidance is observed by the Gods, whose shelter blesses with the bliss of liberation, avoidance of whose devotion and dependence causes death, to That God, we offer oblations. (2)

❍ ❍ ❍

यः प्राणतो निमिषतो महित्वैक इद्राजा जगतो बभूव ।
य ईशे अस्य द्विपदश्चतुष्पदः कस्मै देवाय हविषा विधेम ॥ ३ ॥

ya: prāṇato nimiṣato mahitvaika idrājā jagato babhūva |
ya īśe asya dvipadaścatuṣpada: kasmai devāya haviṣā vidhema || 3 ||

The Oversoul, who by His capacity became Himself the Lord of all the beings, animate and inanimate in the world, and who is the Lord of two-footed man, birds, and four-footed animals; we offer, oblations with devotion to that blissful Lord. (3)

❍ ❍ ❍

यस्येमे हिमवन्तो महित्वा यस्य समुद्रं रसया सहाहुः ।
यस्येमाः प्रदिशो यस्य बाहू कस्मै देवाय हविषा विधेम ॥ ४ ॥

yasyeme himavanto mahitvā yasya samudraṃ rasayā sahāhu: |
yasyemā: pradiśo yasya bāhū kasmai devāya haviṣā vidhema || 4 ||

The Oversoul, whose great glory created these snow-clad mountains, whose strength created these enormous oceans; and by whose capacity, the directions and sub-directions which are like arms spread over and around, to That Happy-form*, who nourishes subjects by His divine qualities, we offer oblations. (4)

* Omnipotent-Oversoul

❍ ❍ ❍

येन द्यौरुग्रा पृथिवी च दृळ्हा येन स्वः स्तभितं येन नाकः ।
यो अन्तरिक्षे रजसो विमानः कस्मै देवाय हविषा विधेम ॥ ५ ॥

yena dyaurugrā pṛthivī ca dṛḻhā yena sva: stabhitaṃ yena nāka: |
yo antarikṣe rajaso vimāna: kasmai devāya haviṣā vidhema || 5 ||

That Bliss-form Oversoul, who made the heaven brilliant and the earth strong, who stabilised the light, who provided happiness and blissfulness, who creates worlds in the space, to Him, we offer oblations. None else other than Him is to be worshipped. (5)

❍ ❍ ❍

यं क्रन्दसी अवसा तस्तभाने अभ्यैक्षेतां मनसा रेजमाने ।
यत्राधि सूर उदितो विभाति कस्मै देवाय हविषा विधेम ॥ ६ ॥

yaṃ krandasī avasā tastabhāne abhyaikṣetāṃ manasā rejamāne |
yatrādhi sūra udito vibhāti kasmai devāya haviṣā vidhema || 6 ||

Verily, being stable but in reality dynamic, speedy, vibrating or brilliant, the heaven and the earth observe whom by mental-energy and in whom the rising Sun shines brilliantly, to that Bliss-Form Oversoul, we offer oblations. (6)

❍ ❍ ❍

आपो ह यद्बृहतीर्विश्वमायन् गर्भं दधाना जनयन्तीरग्निम् ।
ततो देवानां समवर्ततासुरेकः कस्मै देवाय हविषा विधेम ॥ ७ ॥

āpo ha yadbṛhatīrviśvamāyan garbhaṃ dadhānā janayantīragnim |
tato devānāṃ samavartatāsureka: kasmai devāya haviṣā vidhema || 7 ||

When the enormous water-body appeared in the world, bearing the womb while manifesting fire, it delivered the life-soul of the Gods. To That God, born of waters, we offer oblations. (7)

❍ ❍ ❍

यश्चिदापो महिना पर्यपश्यद् दक्षं दधाना जनयन्तीर्यज्ञम् ।
यो देवेष्वधि देव एक आसीत् कस्मै देवाय हविषा विधेम ॥ ८ ॥

yaśicadāpo mahinā paryapaśyad dakṣaṃ dadhānā janayantīryajñam |
yo deveṣvadhi deva eka āsīt kasmai devāya haviṣā vidhema || 8 ||

The Oversoul, who begot creation-water, and who initiated creativity-power in the waters and the creation in the form of sacrifice (yajña), meaning thereby, sacrificial creation (यज्ञमय सृष्टि), to That Supreme Being alone, we offer our worship in the form of oblations. (8)

❍ ❍ ❍

मा नो हिंसीज्जनिता यः पृथिव्या यो वा दिवं सत्यधर्मा जजान ।
यश्चापश्चन्द्रा बृहतीर्जजान कस्मै देवाय हविषा विधेम ॥ ९ ॥

mā no hiṃsījjanitā ya: pṛthivyā yo vā divaṃ satyadharmā jajāna |
yaścāpaścandrā bṛhatīrjajāna kasmai devāya haviṣā vidhema || 9 ||

The Supreme Being, the creator of this earth and this

sky, may He not give us sufferings. That Supreme who manifested the rejoicing waters, to Him we offer worship in the form of oblations. (9)

❍ ❍ ❍

प्रजापते न त्वदेतान्यन्यो विश्वा जातानि परि ता बभूव ।
यत् कामास्ते जुहुमस्तन्नो अस्तु वयं स्याम पतयो रयीणाम् ॥ १०॥
[ऋग्वेद १० । १२१]

prajāpate na tvadetānyanyo viśvā jātāni pari tā babhūva |
yat kāmāste juhumastanno astu vayaṃ syāma patayo rayīṇām || 10||
[ṛgveda 10 | 121]

O* Protector of Creation (all beings)! No one other than Thee pervades all the beings. It is inappropriate to pray to any one else for our wishes. May that wish be granted for which we offer oblations, and may we be the masters of treasures (to enable us to be charitable). (10)

* प्रजापति – an address — 'O'

❍ ❍ ❍

The Auspicious Resolution Hymns

शिवसंकल्प सूक्त

(कल्याण सूक्त)

The Auspicious Resolution Hymns

Each sense-organ has a special importance in human-body, but the extraordinary mind has its paramount importance. It is the mind which controls all; it has unique power, and is most effective. The mind pervades everywhere, all the senses of action and knowledge, happiness and sorrow are all under its control. It is, therefore, obvious that the auspicious resolve or 'The Conscious Resolve' of the mind is the key to elevation in man's life; and the seer sage of mantra expresses the same prayer in 'the Auspicious-Resolution Hymns' (Śiva-sankalpa Sūkta). This Sūkta is recited in the 34th chapter of the Śukla-Yajurveda (also known as White Yajurveda). There are six mantrās in this chapter. The text follows:

यज्जाग्रतो दूरमुदैति दैवं तदु सुप्तस्य तथैवैति ।
दूरङ्गमं ज्योतिषां ज्योतिरेकं तन्मे मनः शिवसङ्कल्पमस्तु ॥ १ ॥

yajjāgrato dūramudaiti daivaṃ tadu suptasya tathaivaiti |
dūraṅgamaṃ jyotiṣāṃ jyotirekaṃ tanme mana: śvisaṅkalpamastu || 1 ||

The mind (Mana मन) of a man, when in awoken state, roams afar, and that of a deep sleeping one comes back near him. Mind is the chief means of directly witnessing Oversoul (Parmātmā परमात्मा), the one which alone knows the past, the present, the future, what is close or at hand and customary things; and which alone knows the subjects of ears and those of the sense-organs. It alone enlightens and initiates as a source. May that mind have auspicious and solemn resolution. (1)

❍ ❍ ❍

येन कर्माण्यपसो मनीषिणो यज्ञे कृण्वन्ति विदथेषु धीराः ।
यदपूर्वं यक्षमन्तः प्रजानां तन्मे मनः शिवसङ्कल्पमस्तु ॥ २ ॥

yena karmāṇyapaso manīṣiṇo yajñe kṛṇvanti vidatheṣu dhīrā: |
yadapūrvaṃ yakṣamanta: prajānāṃ tanme mana: śivasaṅkalpamastu || 2 ||

The mind by which diligent and stable-minded scholars acquire knowledge of sacrificial matters and expand sacrifical-rituals, that which is ancestral source of senses and is the innate soul and is most revered residing in all beings; may my that mind have auspicious and solemn resolution. (2)

❍ ❍ ❍

यत्प्रज्ञानमुत चेतो धृतिश्च यज्ज्योतिरन्तरमृतं प्रजासु ।
यस्मान्न ऋते किं चन कर्म क्रियते तन्मे मनः शिवसङ्कल्पमस्तु ॥ ३ ॥

yatprajñānamuta ceto dhṛtiśca yajjyotirantaramṛtaṃ prajāsu |
yasmānna ṛte kiṃ cana karma kriyate tanme mana: śivasaṅkalpamastu || 3 ||

That mind, which is cause of specific knowledge, and is that of common knowledge, which is stable, which lives in the heart of man illuminating all his senses, which remains immortal even when the physical body dies, and without which nothing can be done, may that mind of mine have auspicious and solemn resolution. (3)

❍ ❍ ❍

येनेदं भूतं भुवनं भविष्यत् परिगृहीतममृतेन सर्वम् ।
येन यज्ञस्तायते सप्तहोता तन्मे मनः शिवसङ्कल्पमस्तु ॥ ४ ॥

**yenedaṃ bhūtaṃ bhuvanaṃ bhaviṣyat parigṛhītamamṛtena sarvam |
yena yajñastāyate saptahotā tanme mana: śivasaṅkalpamastu || 4 ||**

That immortal-form-like mind, which can obtain the past, present and future of all the things, and through which the yajña (sacrifice) with seven priests is performed, may that mind have auspicious, solemn, and devotional resolution. (4)

❍ ❍ ❍

**यस्मिन्नृचः साम यजूꣳषि यस्मिन् प्रतिष्ठिता रथनाभाविवाराः ।
यस्मिँश्चित्तꣳ सर्वमोतं प्रजानां तन्मे मनः शिवसङ्कल्पमस्तु ॥ ५ ॥**

**yasminnṛca: sāma yajūꣳṣi yasmin pratiṣṭhitā rathanābhāvivārā: |
yasiṁmaścittaꣳ sarvamotaṃ prajānāṃ tanme mana: śivasaṅkalpamastu || 5 ||**

That mind, which is like the hub of the chariot wheel, establishing spokes of Rigveda, Yajurveda and Sāmaveda, soaked in entire knowledge of all matters, may that mind of mine have auspicious, solemn, and devotional resolution. (5)

❍ ❍ ❍

**सुषारथिरश्वानिव यन्मनुष्यान्नेनीयतेऽभीशुभिर्वाजिन इव ।
हृत्प्रतिष्ठं यदजिरं जविष्ठं तन्मे मनः शिवसङ्कल्पमस्तु ॥ ६ ॥
[शुक्लयजुर्वेद अ० ३४]**

**suṣārathiraśvāniva yanmanuṣyānnenīyate'bhīśubhirvājina iva |
hṛtpratiṣṭhaṃ yadajiraṃ javiṣṭhaṃ tanme mana: śivasaṅkalpamastu || 6 ||
[śuklayajurveda a. 34]**

Just as an apt charioteer drives and holds the reins of horses to run as per his command, so too the mind, living in the heart, never getting old, is very swift; may that well controlled mind of mine, have auspicious, devotional, and solemn resolution. (6)

❍ ❍ ❍

The eyes, ears and other sense organs record data as an instrument, but it is the mind that makes it mean something. And it is our thoughts (arising in our mind) which build up the personality of a man. 'मन एव मनुष्याणां...'

Anger takes away the great and immense asceticism and fame acquired with extreme toil of man.

(Viṣṇu Purāṇa)

❍ ❍ ❍

Pride of wealth destroys wealth, pride of strength destroys strength, and the pride of knowledge destroys knowledge. **(Sām Veda)**

❍ ❍ ❍

The Wedding Hymns
विवाह सूक्त (सोमसूर्यासूक्त)

The Sanātan Vedic Dharma enunciates sixteen important rituals in our way of life. The wedding-rituals occupy paramount significance among them. This 'sanskār' is a lifelong commitment between marrying couples to remain together throughout the span of their life. Their coming together as husband and wife is witnessed by the God of Fire. As per the Vedic instructions, the purpose of the wedding-knot is to pursue the four desirables in life, of Dharma, Artha (possessions), Kāma (physical as well as higher divine goals) and Mokśa (liberation) in unison.

This 'Vivāh Sūkta' is there in the 10th section (mandal) of the Rigaveda as the 85th Sūkta. This is also known as the 'SomaSūrya Sūkta'. As it is important, this comprises 47 mantrās in it. The seer riṣikā of this Sūkta is Sāvitrī Sūrya. It has hymns in adoration of Gods, the Sun and the Moon. During the wedding-sanskār (ritual) a number of mantrās are recited from this sūkta. While the ritual of placement of vermilion (sindūrdān) on the forehead of the bride by the birdegroom, there is a mantra recited, blessing the bride to remain wedded throughout her life, and being most auspicious in the family welfare. There is an exhortation in the mantrā for all to bless the bride and have her glimpse (to look at her beautiful face).

'सुमङ्गलीरियं वधूः०'।

In an other mantrā the bride and the groom are exhorted to remain together and never get separated from one another.

'मा वि यौष्टम्'।

Be blessed with full longlife and enjoy themselves with their children and grand children. The wedding 'sanskār' in the vedic culture is not a simple contract, it is an unbreakable solemn and divine commitment between the wedding-couple.

The text follows:

सत्येनोत्तभिता भूमिः सूर्येणोत्तभिता द्यौः ।
ऋतेनादित्यास्तिष्ठन्ति दिवि सोमो अधि श्रितः ॥ १ ॥

satyenottabhitā bhūmi: sūryeṇottabhitā dyau: |
ṛtenādityāstiṣṭhanti divi somo adhi śrita: || 1 ||

Among the Gods, the Truth, personified Brahmā is bearing the earth in the space, and the Sun has held up heaven, and is bearing it. (And) it is the sacrifice (yajña) which enlivens the Gods. Soma exists in the upper heaven. (1)

❍ ❍ ❍

सोमेनादित्या बलिनः सोमेन पृथिवी मही ।
अथो नक्षत्राणामेषामुपस्थे सोम आहितः ॥ २ ॥

somenādityā balina: somena pṛthivī mahī |
atho nakṣatrāṇāmeṣāmupasthe soma āhita: || 2 ||

It is Soma which empowers Indra and other Gods. The cause of the Earth's greatness is also Soma; and Soma has been placed in the midst of constellation (heavenly bodies or planets). (2)

❍ ❍ ❍

सोमं मन्यते पपिवान् यत् संपिंषन्त्योषधिम् ।
सोमं यं ब्रह्माणो विदुर्न तस्याश्नाति कश्चन ॥ ३ ॥

somaṃ manyate papivān yat saṃpiṃṣantyoṣadhim |
somaṃ yaṃ brahmāṇo vidurna tasyāśnāti kaścana || 3 ||

While grinding the medicinal plant Soma, people believe that they have drunk Soma, but the learned scholars know that Soma cannot be eaten by any one who does not perform sacrifice (yajña). (3)

❍ ❍ ❍

आच्छद्विधानैर्गुपितो बार्हतैः सोम रक्षितः ।
ग्राव्णामिच्छृण्वन् तिष्ठसि न ते अश्नाति पार्थिवः ॥ ४ ॥

ācchadvidhānairgupito bārhatai: soma rakṣita: |
grāvṇāmicchṛṇvan tiṣṭhasi na te aśnāti pārthiva: || 4 ||

O Soma! Thou art guarded by the secret laws and means and art, well secured by the outrageous groups (Dogs, radiance*, etc.). Thou doth keep hearing the sound of the grinding stones. No common man on earth can devour thee.

* heap of charcoal

❍ ❍ ❍

यत् त्वा देव प्रपिबन्ति तत आ प्यायसे पुनः ।
वायुः सोमस्य रक्षिता समानां मास आकृतिः ॥ ५ ॥

yat tvā deva prapibanti tata ā pyāyase puna: |
vāyu: somasya rakṣitā samānāṃ māsa ākṛti: || 5 ||

O Somadeva! When people taste Thee as medicine, Thou art consumed again and again. The air guards Thee Soma, as the months guard the year. (5)

❍ ❍ ❍

रैभ्यासीदनुदेयी नाराशंसी न्योचनी ।
सूर्याया भद्रमिद्वासो गाथयैति परिष्कृतम् ॥ ६ ॥

raibhyāsīdanudeyī nārāśaṃsī nyocanī |
sūryāyā bhadramidvāso gāthayaiti pariṣkṛtam || 6 ||

Raibhi (some of the Vedic mantrās) became the companion of the bride after wedding. The mantrās chanted by mankind became her slaves. The covering-cloth of Sūrya was very beautiful and became adorned by a story. (6)

❍ ❍ ❍

चित्तिरा उपबर्हणं चक्षुरा अभ्यञ्जनम् ।
द्यौर्भूमिः कोश आसीद् यदयात् सूर्या पतिम् ॥ ७ ॥

cittirā upabarhaṇaṃ cakṣurā abhyañjanam |
dyaurbhūmi: kośa āsīd yadayāt sūryā patim || 7 ||

When Sūrya reached her husband's abode, the elevated thoughts were the covering-cloth (ćādar). The eyes were blackish lined with Kājal. The space (sky) and the Earth were her treasures. (7)

❍ ❍ ❍

स्तोमा आसन् प्रतिधयः कुरीरं छन्द ओपशः ।
सूर्याया अश्विना वरा ऽग्निरासीत् पुरोगवः ॥ ८ ॥

stomā āsan pratidhaya: kurīraṃ chanda opaśa: |
sūryāyā aśvinā varā 'gnirāsīt purogava: || 8 ||

The hymns were the spokes of the wheel of the chariot of Sūrya, the metre 'Kurīr' was adorning the chariots; Sūrya's groom were Aświnī Kumārs and the fore-going was Agni. (8)

❍ ❍ ❍

सोमो वधूयुरभवदश्विनास्तामुभा वरा ।
सूर्यां यत् पत्ये शंसन्तीं मनसा सवितादददात् ॥ ९ ॥

somo vadhūyurabhavadaśvināstāmubhā varā |
sūryāṃ yat patye śaṃsantīṃ manasā savitādadāt || 9 ||

Soma was desirous to wed, (but) the two Aświnī Kumārs were accepted as her husbands. Savitā, willingly, gave Sūrya, when she so desired for husband. (9)

❍ ❍ ❍

मनो अस्या अन आसीद् द्यौरासीदुत च्छदिः ।
शुक्रावनड्वाहावास्तां यदयात् सूर्या गृहम् ॥ १० ॥

mano asyā ana āsīd dyaurāsīduta cchadi: |
śukrāvanaḍvāhāvāstāṃ yadayāt sūryā gṛham || 10 ||

When Sūrya reached her husband's abode, then her chariot was her mind (मन - Man), and the sky was the roof. The Sun and the Moon became her charioteers. (10)

❍ ❍ ❍

ऋक्सामाभ्यामभिहितौ गावौ ते सामनावितः ।
श्रोत्रं ते चक्रे आस्तां दिवि पन्थाश्चराचरः ॥ ११ ॥

ṛksāmābhyāmabhihitau gāvau te sāmanāvita: |
śrotraṃ te cakera āstāṃ divi panthāścarācara: || 11 ||

O Surye Devi! The Rig and the Sāma Vedās, who are the chariot of Thy mind, enunciate that the Sun and the Moon like bulls, remain quiet and move on helping each other peacefully. Those two ears became the wheels of the chariot of mind. And the upper-space became the pathway of the chariot. (11)

❍ ❍ ❍

शुची ते चक्रे यात्या व्यानो अक्ष आहतः ।
अनो मनस्मयं सूर्या ऽऽरोहत् प्रयती पतिम् ॥ १२ ॥

śucī te cakera yātyā vyāno akṣa āhata: |
ano manasmayaṃ sūryā "rohat prayatī patim || 12 ||

The two wheels of Thy moving chariot became ears. The Air was the hub of the chariot. Moving toward the abode of her husband, Sūrya rode upon the chariot of mind. (12)

❍ ❍ ❍

सूर्याया वहतुः प्रागात् सविता यमवासृजत् ।
अघासु हन्यन्ते गावो ऽर्जुन्योः पर्युह्यते ॥ १३ ॥

sūryāyā vahatu: prāgāt savitā yamavāsṛjat |
aghāsu hanyante gāvo 'rjunyo: paryuhyate || 13 ||

The treasure of cows etc., given by her father, Sun, with love and affection, had already been sent earlier, when she was going toward her husband's abode. The cows, gifted to the daughter at the departure-time, are herded by a wooden rod during 'Maghā' constellation (Nakśatra), and the bride is escorted to her husband's home during 'Phālguni' constellation. (13)

❍ ❍ ❍

यदश्विना पृच्छमानावयातं त्रिचक्रेण वहतुं सूर्यायाः ।
विश्वे देवा अनु तद्वामजानन् पुत्रः पितराववृणीत पूषा ॥ १४ ॥

yadaśvinā pṛcchamānāvayātaṃ tricakeraṇa vahatuṃ sūryāyā: |
viśve devā anu tadvāmajānan putra: pitarāvavṛṇīta pūṣā || 14 ||

O the two Aświns! When Ye had come in a three-wheeler chariot, asking about the marraige of Sūrya, the Gods had given permission to Thy venture and Thy son, 'Pūṣā' had chosen Thee. (14)

❍ ❍ ❍

यदयातं शुभस्पती वरेयं सूर्यामुप ।
क्वैकं चक्रं वामासीत् क्व देष्ट्राय तस्थथुः ॥ १५ ॥

yadayātaṃ śubhaspatī vareyaṃ sūryāmupa |
kvaikaṃ cakaṃra vāmāsīt kva deṣṭrāya tasthathu: || 15 ||

O the two Aświns! When Ye had come to meet Sūrya, near Savitā, where was one wheel of Thy chariot? You were ready to give and accept mutually, where were Thee, then? (15)

❍ ❍ ❍

द्वे ते चक्रे सूर्ये ब्रह्माण ऋतुथा विदुः ।
अथैकं चक्रं यद्गुहा तदद्धातय इद्विदुः ॥ १६ ॥

dve te cakera sūrye brahmāṇa ṛtuthā vidu: |
athaikaṃ cakraṃ yadguhā tadaddhātaya idvidu: || 16 ||

O Surye! The two wheels of Thy chariot, like Sūrya and Ćandra (like the Sun and the Moon), which are famous, are known to the brāhmins, and the third, the yearly wheel (samvatsar) which was a secret, is known only to the learned. (16)

❍ ❍ ❍

सूर्यायै देवेभ्यो मित्राय वरुणाय च ।
ये भूतस्य प्रचेतस इदं तेभ्योऽकरं नमः ॥ १७ ॥

sūryāyai devebhyo mitrāya varuṇāya ca |
ye bhūtasya pracetasa idaṃ tebhyo'karaṃ nama: || 17 ||

I offer my salutations to Sūryā, Deva, Mitra, Varuṇa and all those who are the well wisher and beneficient to all the beings. (17)

❍ ❍ ❍

पूर्वापरं चरतो माययैतौ शिशू क्रीळन्तौ परि यातो अध्वरम् ।
विश्वान्यन्यो भुवनाभिचष्ट ऋतूँरन्यो विदधज्जायते पुनः ॥ १८ ॥

pūrvāparaṃ carato māyayaitau śiśū krīḻantau pari yāto adhvaram |
viśvānyanyo bhuvanābhicaṣṭa ṛtūṁranyo vidadhajjāyate puna: || 18 ||

These two infants — the Sun and the Moon move around east-west by their energy and, sportingly, reach sacrificial (yajña) place. One of them, the Sūrya (Sun) looks up to all worlds, and the other, the Moon rises time and again creating seasons with time-divisions of two months. (18)

❍ ❍ ❍

नवोनवो भवति जायमानो ऽह्नां केतुरुषसामेत्यग्रम् ।
भागं देवेभ्यो वि दधात्यायन् प्र चन्द्रमास्तिरते दीर्घमायुः ॥ १९ ॥

navonavo bhavati jāyamāno ’hnāṃ
keturuṣasāmetyagram |
bhāgaṃ devebhyo vi dadhātyāyan pra candramāstirate
dīrghamāyu:: || 19 ||

This moon rises everyday as a new one. As indicator of days during the nights of the waning fortnight, it rises before the day dawns, or as the indicator of days, the Sun rises every morning as the new. The Sun rises giving sacrificial (yajña) offering to the Gods. The Moon rises providing happiness, and long-life. (19)

❍ ❍ ❍

सुकिंशुकं शल्मलिं विश्वरूपं हिरण्यवर्णं सुवृतं सुचक्रम् ।
आ रोह सूर्ये अमृतस्य लोकं स्योनं पत्ये वहतुं कृणुष्व ॥ २० ॥

sukiṃśukaṃ śalmaliṃ viśvarūpaṃ hiraṇyavarṇaṃ
suvṛtaṃ sucakram |
ā roha sūrye amṛtasya lokaṃ syonaṃ patye vahatuṃ
kṛṇuṣva || 20 ||

O Surye! Aboard this chairot made of Butea (Kinśuk*) and Sālmalikī* wood having different forms, the golden coloured, decorated with excellent sails and superb wheels and make the immortal world propitious for your husband. (20)

* Kinśuk and Sālmalikī are trees. Wood of these trees used in manufacturing this chariot.

Kinshuk – Flowers with no smell. पलाश-ढाक
Sālmaliki – Silk-cotton tree.

❍ ❍ ❍

उदीर्ष्वातः पतिवती ह्ये३षा विश्वावसुं नमसा गीर्भिरीळे ।
अन्यामिच्छ पितृषदं व्यक्तां स ते भागो जनुषा तस्य विद्धि ॥ २१ ॥

udīrṣvāta: pativatī hye3ṣā viśvāvasuṃ namasā
gīrbhirīḻe |
anyāmiccha pitṛṣadaṃ vyattāṃ sa te bhāgo
januṣā tasya viddhi || 21 ||

O Viśwāvaso (Gandharva)! Rise from this place, as this woman has become wedded to her husband. I eulogise Viśwāvasu with salutations and speeches. You desire for another girl, living with her father's family, she is your part, know her from (her) birth. (21)

❍ ❍ ❍

उदीर्ष्वातो विश्वावसो नमसेळामहे त्वा ।
अन्यामिच्छ प्रफर्व्यं१ सं जायां पत्या सृज ॥ २२ ॥

udīrṣvāto viśvāvaso namaseḻāmahe tvā |
anyāmiccha prapharvyaṃ1 saṃ jāyāṃ patyā sṛja || 22 ||

O Viśwāvaso! Rise from this place; (I) eulogise you with salutation. You desire for another (woman) with wide buttocks, and unite her with her husband. (22)

❍ ❍ ❍

अनृक्षरा ऋजवः सन्तु पन्था येभिः सखायो यन्ति नो वरेयम् ।
समर्यमा सं भगो नो निनीयात् सं जास्पत्यं
सुयममस्तु देवाः ॥ २३ ॥

anṛkṣarā ṛjava: santu panthā yebhi: sakhāyo yanti no vareyam |
samaryamā saṃ bhago no ninīyāt saṃ jāspatyaṃ suyamamastu devā: || 23 ||

All the paths, which lead to the girl's residence, may those be bereft of thorns and be easy for our friends to reach, and may Aryamā and Bhagdeva take us there comfortably. O Gods! May these, wife and husband be good copulating-couple. May the paths of the bride and the groom be bereft of thorns and be easy. May the Gods bless this couple with happiness and prosperity. (23)

❍ ❍ ❍

प्र त्वा मुञ्चामि वरुणस्य पाशाद् येन त्वाबध्नात् सविता सुशेवः ।
ऋतस्य योनौ सुकृतस्य लोके ऽरिष्टां त्वा सह
पत्या दधामि ॥ २४ ॥

pra tvā muñcāmi varuṇasya pāśād yena tvābadhnāt savitā suśeva: |
ṛtasya yonau sukṛtasya loke 'riṣṭāṃ tvā saha patyā dadhāmi || 24 ||

I let thee free from the bonds of Varuṇa which had bound thee by serviceable Savitā (Sun). (I) Let thee be established in the household of truthful and good-conducting man's world, who is not violent by nature. (24)

❍ ❍ ❍

प्रेतो मुञ्चामि नामुतः सुबद्धाममुतस्करम् ।
यथेयमिन्द्र मीढ्वः सुपुत्रा सुभगासति ॥ २५ ॥

preto muñcāmi nāmuta: subaddhāmamutaskaram |
yatheyamindra mīḍhva: suputrā subhagāsati || 25 ||

(I) Let thee be free from father's-clan, not from thy (husband's clan). I bind thee well with them. O benevolent Indira! So that this bride be blessed with superb sons and excellent fortune. (25)

❍ ❍ ❍

पूषा त्वेतो नयतु हस्तगृह्याऽश्विना त्वा प्र वहतां रथेन ।
गृहान् गच्छ गृहपत्नी यथासो वशिनी त्वं विदथमा वदासि ॥ २६ ॥

pūṣā tveto nayatu hastagṛhyā'śvinā tvā pra vahatāṃ rathena |
gṛhān gaccha gṛhapatnī yathāso vaśinī tvaṃ vidathamā vadāsi || 26 ||

May Pūṣā (Sun, the Vedic deity) walk thee holding thy hand, ahead of it, may Aśwideva, help thee sit on the chariot escorting thee (to the destination). Go to thy husband's home. Be thou the mistress of the household, captivating all under hold. Express thyself wisely over there. (26)

❍ ❍ ❍

इह प्रियं प्रजया ते समृध्यतामस्मिन् गृहे गार्हपत्याय जागृहि ।
एना पत्या तन्वं१ सं सृजस्वाऽधा जिव्री विदथमा वदाथः ॥ २७ ॥

iha priyaṃ prajayā te samṛdhyatāmasmin gṛhe gārhapatyāya jāgṛhi |
enā patyā tanvaṃ1 saṃ sṛjasvā'dhā jivrī vidathamā vadātha: || 27 ||

Let fondness increase here with thy progeny, and let thee remain awaken for household duties of this home. Join thy body with husband. On becoming old, both of thee deliver good sermons. (27)

❍ ❍ ❍

नीललोहितं भवति कृत्यासक्तिर्व्यज्यते ।
एधन्ते अस्या ज्ञातयः पतिर्बन्धेषु बध्यते ॥ २८ ॥

nīlalohitaṃ bhavati kṛtyāsattirvyajyate |
edhante asyā jñātaya: patirbandheṣu badhyate || 28 ||

When she becomes blue and red, meaning becomes angree, then her destructive desire will increase, her kind of men increase, and the husband gets bounded. (28)

❍ ❍ ❍

परा देहि शामुल्यं ब्रह्मभ्यो वि भजा वसु ।
कृत्यैषा पद्वती भूत्व्या जाया विशते पतिम् ॥ २९ ॥

parā dehi śāmulyaṃ brahmabhyo vi bhajā vasu |
kṛtyaiṣā padvatī bhūtvyā jāyā viśate patim || 29 ||

Drop off clothes dirtied by the excreta of the body. Offer alms to the brahmins as atonements. The sorceress (कृत्या-the female evil spirit) has left, and now a wife is joining her husband. (29)

❍ ❍ ❍

अश्रीरा तनूर्भवति रुशती पापयामुया ।
पतिर्यद्वध्वो३ वाससा स्वमङ्गमभिधित्सते ॥ ३० ॥

aśrīrā tanūrbhavati ruśatī pāpayāmuyā |
patiryadvadhvo3 vāsasā svamaṅgamabhidhitsate || 30 ||

If the husband wants to cover his body with the clothes of the bride, the husband's body gets bereft of grandeur, and gets polluted by maladies. This bride full of sins, gives sufferings and pain. (30)

❍ ❍ ❍

ये वध्वश्चन्द्रं वहतुं यक्ष्मा यन्ति जनादनु ।
पुनस्तान् यज्ञिया देवा नयन्तु यत आगताः ॥ ३१ ॥

ye vadhvaścandraṃ vahatuṃ yakṣmā yanti janādanu |
punastān yajñiyā devā nayantu yata āgatā: || 31 ||

The maladies which are received by the husband's glorious body from the bride or her relatives, the worthier of Yajña (sacrifice) Indra!, Let those (maladies) be returned to their respective places, where they come from again and again. (31)

❍ ❍ ❍

मा विदन् परिपन्थिनो य आसीदन्ति दम्पती ।
सुगेभिर्दुर्गमतीतामप द्रान्त्वरातयः ॥ ३२ ॥

mā vidan paripanthino ya āsīdanti dampatī |
sugebhirdurgamatītāmapa drāntvarātaya: || 32 ||

May those adversaries, who oppose both husband-wife, not reach them. Let those adversaries go from comfortable places to difficult places. Let the enemies run away far-off. (32)

❍ ❍ ❍

सुमङ्गलीरियं वधूरिमां समेत पश्यत ।
सौभाग्यमस्यै दत्त्वायाऽथास्तं वि परेतन ॥ ३३ ॥

**sumaṅgalīriyaṃ vadhūrimāṃ sameta paśyata |
saubhāgyamasyai dattvāyā'thāstaṃ vi paretana || 33 ||**

May this bride be, brilliantly, propitious. May all the well-wishers come and bless her, wishing her to remain with husband, bless her and go back to their homes. (33)

❍ ❍ ❍

तृष्टमेतत् कटुकमेतदपाष्ठवद्विषवन्नैतदत्तवे ।
सूर्यां यो ब्रह्मा विद्यात् स इद्वाधूयमर्हति ॥ ३४ ॥

**tṛṣṭametat kaṭukametadapāṣṭhavadviṣavannaitadattave |
sūryāṃ yo brahmā vidyāt sa idvādhūyamarhati || 34 ||**

This robe is prone to burn, unacceptable, dirty and deadly, like poison. This is unuseable. The brahmin, who knows Sūrya well, alone can get the robe of the bride. (34)

❍ ❍ ❍

आशसनं विशसनमथो अधिविकर्तनम् ।
सूर्यायाः पश्य रूपाणि तानि ब्रह्मा तु शुन्धति ॥ ३५ ॥

**āśasanaṃ viśasanamatho adhivikartanam |
sūryāyā: paśya rūpāṇi tāni brahmā tu śundhati || 35 ||**

The form of Sūrya, in such robes having (अधिनिकर्तन) three parts, lustrous line (झालर-आश-सन) and the head ornament (विशसन), visualise Sūrya (in such form). The Vedic-brahmin (who knows the Vedas), alone purifies them. (35)

❍ ❍ ❍

गृभ्णामि ते सौभगत्वाय हस्तं मया पत्या जरदष्टिर्यथासः ।
भगो अर्यमा सविता पुरंधिर्मह्यं त्वादुर्गार्हपत्याय देवाः ॥ ३६ ॥

gṛbhṇāmi te saubhagatvāya hastaṃ mayā patyā jaradaṣṭiryathāsa: |
bhago aryamā savitā puraṃdhirmahyaṃ tvādurgārhapatyāya devā: || 36 ||

O bride! I take your hand for my waxing-good-fortune, so that you and I both reach and live through the old age together. The Gods—Bhaga, Aryamā, Savitā and Purandhi have given you to me to observe our household duties. (36)

❍ ❍ ❍

तां पूषञ्छिवतमामेरयस्व यस्यां बीजं मनुष्या३ वपन्ति ।
या न ऊरू उशती विश्रयाते यस्यामुशन्तः प्रहराम शेपम् ॥ ३७ ॥

tāṃ pūṣañchivatamāmerayasva yasyāṃ bījaṃ manuṣyā3 vapanti |
yā na ūrū uśatī viśrayāte yasyāmuśanta: praharāma śepam || 37 ||

O Pūṣā! In the womb of women, men sow seed of semen, meaning ejaculate, (women) who, desiring men, take support of both legs and men being lustful, penetrate their penis, Thou shalt impel her of great propititious qualities. (37)

❍ ❍ ❍

तुभ्यमग्रे पर्यवहन् त्सूर्यां वहतुना सह ।
पुनः पतिभ्यो जायां दा अग्ने प्रजया सह ॥ ३८ ॥

tubhyamagre paryavahan tsūryāṃ vahatunā saha |
puna: patibhyo jāyāṃ dā agne prajayā saha || 38 ||

O Agni (God of Fire)! The celestial musicians (Gandharvas) have given Thee Suryā alongwith first dowry, and Thou gaveth her to Soma with gifts, and Thou shalt give me (husband) best of progeny alongwith wife, meaning bless the married couple with best of progeny. (38)

❍ ❍ ❍

पुनः पत्नीमग्निरदादायुषा सह वर्चसा ।
दीर्घायुरस्या यः पतिर्जीवाति शरदः शतम् ॥ ३९ ॥

puna: patnīmagniradādāyuṣā saha varcasā |
dīrghāyurasyā ya: patirjīvāti śarada: śatam || 39 ||

Agni (The Fire-God) gave again wife blessed with long-life, lustre and enhanced beauty. May her husband live a long-life of a hundred years. (39)

❍ ❍ ❍

सोमः प्रथमो विविदे गन्धर्वो विविद उत्तरः ।
तृतीयो अग्निष्टे पतिस्तुरीयस्ते मनुष्यजाः ॥ ४० ॥

soma: prathamo vivide gandharvo vivida uttara: |
tṛtīyo agniṣṭe patisturīyaste manuṣyajā: || 40 ||

Firstly, Soma received Thee as wife, later on Gandharva got Thee. Thirdly, Agni is Thy husband. Fourthly, descendant of man is Thy husband. (40)

❍ ❍ ❍

सोमो ददद्गन्धर्वाय गन्धर्वो ददद‌ग्नये ।
रयिं च पुत्राँश्चादादग्निर्मह्यमथो इमाम् ॥ ४१ ॥

somo dadadgandharvāya gandharvo dadadagnaye |
rayiṃ ca putrāṁścādādagnirmahyamatho imām || 41 ||

Soma gave that woman to Gandharva. Gandharva gave her to Agni. Later on Agni gives her to me with affluence and progeny. (41)

❍ ❍ ❍

इहैव स्तं मा वि यौष्टं विश्वमायुर्व्यश्नुतम् ।
क्रीळन्तौ पुत्रैर्नप्तृभिर्मोदमानौ स्वे गृहे ॥ ४२ ॥

ihaiva staṃ mā vi yauṣṭaṃ viśvamāyurvyaśnutam |
krīḻantau putrairnaptṛbhirmodamānau sve gṛhe || 42 ||

O groom and bride! Both of you live here. Do not be ever separated, mutually. May ye have, especially, long life. May ye remain joyous, having joyous living with sons and grandsons. (42)

❍ ❍ ❍

आ नः प्रजां जनयतु प्रजापतिराजरसाय समनक्त्वर्यमा ।
अदुर्मङ्गलीः पतिलोकमा विश शं नो भव द्विपदे
शं चतुष्पदे ॥ ४३ ॥

ā na: prajāṃ janayatu prajāpatirājarasāya samanaktvaryamā|
adurmaṅgalī: patilokamā viśa śaṃ no bhava dvipade śaṃ catuṣpade || 43 ||

May Prajāpati (Brahmā) bless us with best of progeny. May Aryamā protect us till the end of old-age. Enter the household of husband, being propitious. May you be auspicious for our relatives, kinsmen and animals. (43)

❍ ❍ ❍

अघोरचक्षुरपतिघ्न्येधि शिवा पशुभ्यः सुमनाः सुवर्चाः ।
वीरसूर्देवकामा स्योना शं नो भव द्विपदे शं चतुष्पदे ॥ ४४ ॥

aghoracakṣurapatighnyedhi śivā paśubhya: sumanā: suvarcā: |
vīrasūrdevakāmā syonā śaṃ no bhava dvipade śaṃ catuṣpade || 44 ||

O Bride! May you be of peaceful aptitude and do not be a cause of pain to the husband. Be beneficent to the animals, be auspicious in your thoughts and mindset, be brilliant, beget braves and be devoted to Gods and be pleasant. May you be propitious to the two-footed and four-footed, meaning thereby, to men and animals. (44)

❍ ❍ ❍

इमां त्वमिन्द्र मीढ्वः सुपुत्रां सुभगां कृणु ।
दशास्यां पुत्राना धेहि पतिमेकादशं कृधि ॥ ४५ ॥

**imāṃ tvamindra mīḍhva: suputrāṃ subhagāṃ kṛṇu |
daśāsyāṃ putrānā dhehi patimekādaśaṃ kṛdhi || 45 ||**

O Indra! May Thou bless her have excellent sons and be auspicious. Bless her with ten sons, and alongwith the husband, may (she) have eleven persons in her family. (45)

❍ ❍ ❍

सम्राज्ञी श्वशुरे भव सम्राज्ञी श्वश्र्वां भव ।
ननान्दरि सम्राज्ञी भव सम्राज्ञी अधि देवृषु ॥ ४६ ॥

**samrājñī śvaśure bhava samrājñī śvaśravāṃ bhava |
nanāndari samrājñī bhava samrājñī adhi devṛṣu || 46 ||**

O Bride! May you be the queen of the father-in-law, mother-in-law, sisters-in-law and brothers-in-law — may you be like a queen, and exercise authority over all. (46)

❍ ❍ ❍

समञ्जन्तु विश्वे देवाः समापो हृदयानि नौ ।
सं मातरिश्वा सं धाता समु देष्ट्री दधातु नौ ॥ ४७ ॥
[ऋग्वेद १० । ४५]

**samañjantu viśve devā: samāpo hṛdayāni nau |
saṃ mātariśvā saṃ dhātā samu deṣṭrī dadhātu nau || 47 ||
[ṛgveda 10 | 45]**

May all the Gods create mutual understanding in our hearts. May (the elements) water, air, Dhāta (Brahmā, the creator) and Saraswatī join both of us together. (47)

❍ ❍ ❍

The Vital-breath Hymns

प्राण सूक्त

The fourth Sūkta (hymn) of the 11th Canto of the Atharvaveda is well known as 'the Prāṇa Sūkta' (The Life-breath Hymns). It comprises 26 mantrās. The vital-breath has been eulogised, depicting 'Prāṇa' as 'Paramātmā' (the Oversoul). The seer sage of this Sūkta, Bhārgava Vaidharbhi, eulogising 'Prāṇa', expresses his salutations to Prāṇa, which controls the world, pervading the entire world; and is the Lord:— 'Prāṇāya Namah' (प्राणाय-नमः). 'Prāṇa' is described as 'the life-energy' and is consecrated in the entire range of herbs. The rains are a form of 'Prāṇa', and it is 'Prāṇa', seated in the herbs as fire and Soma. Whatever flowing winds are there, i.e., 'Prāṇa, Apāna, Mātariśvā' and others, these are all expresed and unexpressed forms of 'Paramātmā' as 'Prāṇa'. The Sūkta goes as under:

प्राणाय नमो यस्य सर्वमिदं वशे ।
यो भूतः सर्वस्येश्वरो यस्मिन्त्सर्वं प्रतिष्ठितम् ॥ १ ॥

prāṇāya namo yasya sarvamidaṃ vaśe |
yo bhūta: sarvasyeśvaro yasmintsarvaṃ pratiṣṭhitam || 1 ||

Salutations to Prāṇa which has dominon over the universe. That Prāṇa is the Supreme Lord, and the entire universe lives in Thee. (1)

❍ ❍ ❍

नमस्ते प्राण क्रन्दाय नमस्ते स्तनयित्नवे ।
नमस्ते प्राण विद्युते नमस्ते प्राण वर्षते ॥ २ ॥

namaste prāṇa krandāya namaste stanayitnave |
namaste prāṇa vidyute namaste prāṇa varṣate || 2 ||

O Prāṇa! Salutations to Thy roar, salutations to Thy roar of thunder in the clouds. O Prāṇa! Salutations to lightning flashes, and O Prāṇa! Salutations to Thee, in the form of pouring rain. (2)

❍ ❍ ❍

यत् प्राण स्तनयित्नुनाभिक्रन्दत्योषधीः ।
प्र वीयन्ते गर्भान् दधतेऽथो बह्वीर्वि जायन्ते ॥ ३ ॥

yat prāṇa stanayitnunābhikrandatyoṣadhī: |
pra vīyante garbhān dadhate'tho bahvīrvi jāyante || 3 ||

O Prāṇa! When Thou dost roar through the clouds at the medicinal plants, they become potent and conceive, and spread over abundantly. (3)

❍ ❍ ❍

यत् प्राण ऋतावागतेऽभिक्रन्दत्योषधीः ।
सर्वं तदा प्र मोदते यत् किं च भूम्यामधि ॥ ४ ॥

yat prāṇa ṛtāvāgate'bhikrandatyoṣadhī: |
sarvaṃ tadā pra modate yat kiṃ ca bhūmyāmadhi || 4 ||

O Prāṇa! When the rainy-season arrives, Thou dost roar with the purpose of propagating herbal plants, then the entire world and all that exists on earth, becomes joyous. (4)

❍ ❍ ❍

यदा प्राणो अभ्यवर्षीद् वर्षेण पृथिवीं महीम् ।
पशवस्तत् प्र मोदन्ते महो वै नो भविष्यति ॥ ५ ॥

yadā prāṇo abhyavarṣīd varṣeṇa pṛthivīṃ mahīm |
paśavastat pra modante maho vai no bhaviṣyati || 5 ||

When Prāṇa doth bring rains on earth, cattle rejoice and feel that, surely, their strength will increase. (5)

❍ ❍ ❍

अभिवृष्टा ओषधयः प्राणेन समवादिरन् ।
आयुर्वै नः प्रातीतरः सर्वा नः सुरभीरकः ॥ ६ ॥

abhivṛṣṭā oṣadhaya: prāṇena samavādiran |
āyurvai na: prātītara: sarvā na: surabhīraka: || 6 ||

Enlivened by the rains, the herbal plants speak: O Prāṇa! Thou hast prolonged our age and given fragrance to us all. (6)

❍ ❍ ❍

नमस्ते अस्त्वायते नमो अस्तु परायते ।
नमस्ते प्राण तिष्ठत आसीनायोत ते नमः ॥ ७ ॥

namaste astvāyate namo astu parāyate |
namaste prāṇa tiṣṭhata āsīnāyota te nama: || 7 ||

Salutations to the advent of Prāṇa, salutations to the departing Prāṇa. O Prāṇa! Salutations to Thee when still and when getting seated. (7)

❍ ❍ ❍

नमस्ते प्राण प्राणते नमो अस्त्वपानते ।
पराचीनाय ते नमः प्रतीचीनाय ते नमः सर्वस्मै त इदं नमः ॥ ८ ॥

namaste prāṇa prāṇate namo astvapānate |
parācīnāya te nama: pratīcīnāya te nama: sarvasmai ta idaṃ nama: || 8 ||

O Prāṇa! Salutations to Thee, who is working for the existence of life, the inhaling of breath. Salutations to Thy exhaling of breath (अपान). Salutations to Prāṇa moving forward and withdrawing backwards. Salutations to Thee, doer of all acts. (8)

❍ ❍ ❍

या ते प्राण प्रिया तनूर्यो ते प्राण प्रेयसी ।
अथो यद् भेषजं तव तस्य नो धेहि जीवसे ॥ ९ ॥

yā te prāṇa priyā tanūryo te prāṇa preyasī |
atho yad bheṣajaṃ tava tasya no dhehi jīvase || 9 ||

O Prāṇa! Give us for our long life, my dear physical form, and Thy dear parts, and Thy medicinal (herbal) plants. (9)

❍ ❍ ❍

प्राणः प्रजा अनु वस्ते पिता पुत्रमिव प्रियम् ।
प्राणो ह सर्वस्येश्वरो यच्च प्राणति यच्च न ॥ १० ॥

prāṇa: prajā anu vaste pitā putramiva priyam |
prāṇo ha sarvasyeśvaro yacca prāṇati yacca na || 10 ||

Just as a father lives with his dear son, so does Prāṇa live with all the subjects. The Supreme Lord is the Prāṇa of all, whether animate or inanimate. (10).

❍ ❍ ❍

प्राणो मृत्युः प्राणस्तक्मा प्राणं देवा उपासते ।
प्राणो ह सत्यवादिनमुत्तमे लोक आ दधत् ॥ ११ ॥

prāṇo mṛtyu: prāṇastakmā prāṇaṃ devā upāsate |
prāṇo ha satyavādinamuttame loka ā dadhat || 11 ||

Prāṇa is death and Prāṇa is the life-force. Therefore, all the Gods, worship Prāṇa; it is Prāṇa who sends the truth speaking man, to the loftiest sphere, i.e. elevated Planets. (11)

❍ ❍ ❍

प्राणो विराट् प्राणो देष्ट्री प्राणं सर्व उपासते ।
प्राणो ह सूर्यश्चन्द्रमाः प्राणमाहुः प्रजापतिम् ॥ १२ ॥

prāṇo virāṭ prāṇo deṣṭrī prāṇaṃ sarva upāsate |
prāṇo ha sūryaścandramā: prāṇamāhu: prajāpatim || 12 ||

Prāṇa hath special power; and Prāṇa is the inspirator of all. Therefore, Prāṇa is worshipped by all. The Sun, the Moon and the Prajāpati are also Prāṇās. (12)

❍ ❍ ❍

प्राणापानौ व्रीहियवावनड्वान् प्राण उच्यते ।
यवे ह प्राण अहितोऽपानो व्रीहिरुच्यते ॥ १३ ॥

prāṇāpānau vrīhiyavāvanaḍvān prāṇa ucyate |
yave ha prāṇa ahito'pāno vrīhirucyate || 13 ||

Prāṇa and Apāna alone are rice and barley. The ox is the chief Prāṇa. In barley lies the Prāṇa; and rice is called Apāna (the exhaling wind). (13)

❍ ❍ ❍

अपानति प्राणति पुरुषो गर्भे अन्तरा ।
यदा त्वं प्राण जिन्वस्यथ स जायते पुनः ॥ १४ ॥

apānati prāṇati puruṣo garbhe antarā |
yadā tvaṃ prāṇa jinvasyatha sa jāyate puna: || 14 ||

The personal soul (Jīva) in the womb deals with Prāṇa and Apāna, meaning thereby inhales and exhales vital breath (Prāṇa) and (Apāna), respectively. O Prāṇa! when impelled by Thee, a child is born. (14)

❍ ❍ ❍

प्राणमाहुर्मातरिश्वानं वातो ह प्राण उच्यते ।
प्राणे ह भूतं भव्यं च प्राणे सर्वं प्रतिष्ठितम् ॥ १५ ॥

prāṇamāhurmātariśvānaṃ vāto ha prāṇa ucyate |
prāṇe ha bhūtaṃ bhavyaṃ ca prāṇe sarvaṃ pratiṣṭhitam || 15 ||

The Prāṇa is called 'Mātariśwā', and the name of the wind is Prāṇa. The past, the future and everything in present exists in Thyself, O Prāṇa! (15)

❍ ❍ ❍

आथर्वणीराङ्गिरसीर्दैवीर्मनुष्यजा उत ।
ओषधयः प्र जायन्ते यदा त्वं प्राण जिन्वसि ॥ १६ ॥

ātharvaṇīrāṅigarasīrdaivīrmanuṣyajā uta |
oṣadhaya: pra jāyante yadā tvaṃ prāṇa jinvasi || 16 ||

O Prāṇa! So far Ye inspireth the herbs and plants, Ātharvanī, Angirasī and the divine and man-made medicinal herbs spring forth, and fructify. (16)

❍ ❍ ❍

यदा प्राणो अभ्यवर्षीद् वर्षेण पृथिवीं महीम् ।
ओषधयः प्र जायन्तेऽथो याः काश्च वीरुधः ॥ १७ ॥

yadā prāṇo abhyavarṣīd varṣeṇa pṛthivīṃ mahīm |
oṣadhaya: pra jāyante'tho yā: kāśca vīrudha: || 17 ||

When Prāṇa bringeth rains on this vast earth, all the herbs and plants grow profusely. (17)

❍ ❍ ❍

यस्ते प्राणेदं वेद यस्मिंश्चासि प्रतिष्ठितः ।
सर्वे तस्मै बलिं हरानमुष्मिल्लोक उत्तमे ॥ १८ ॥

yaste prāṇedaṃ veda yasmiṃścāsi pratiṣṭhita: |
sarve tasmai baliṃ harānamuṣiṃmalloka uttame || 18 ||

O Prāṇa! The man who is aware of Thy (this) energy and the man in whom Ye exist, for such a man, in that most elevated world, everyone offers one's reverential tributes. (18)

❍ ❍ ❍

यथा प्राण बलिहृतस्तुभ्यं सर्वाः प्रजा इमाः ।
एवा तस्मै बलिं हरान् यस्त्वा शृणवत् सुश्रवः ॥ १९ ॥

yathā prāṇa balihṛtastubhyaṃ sarvā: prajā imā: |
evā tasmai baliṃ harān yastvāśṛṇavat suśrava: || 19 ||

O Prāṇa! As all the living creatures revere Thee; he, who is highly renowned and hears about Thy capability, for that also they offer sacifice. (19)

❍ ❍ ❍

अन्तर्गर्भश्चरति देवतास्वाभूतो भूतः स उ जायते पुनः ।
स भूतो भव्यं भविष्यत् पिता पुत्रं प्र विवेशा शचीभिः ॥ २० ॥

antargarbhaścarati devatāsvābhūto bhūta:
sa u jāyate puna: |
sa bhūto bhavyaṃ bhaviṣyat pitā putraṃ
pra viveśā śacībhi: || 20 ||

The Prāṇa, that pervades through the senses, the same moves in the womb also, and is born later. What was there earlier, is there now, and will be there onward also. The father enters into the son with all his powers.* (20)

* आत्मावै जायते पुत्रः।

❍ ❍ ❍

एकं पादं नोत्खिदति सलिलाद्धंस उच्चरन् ।
यदङ्ग स तमुत्खिदेन्नैवाद्य न श्वः स्यान्न रात्री
नाहः स्यान्न व्युच्छेत् कदा चन ॥ २१ ॥

ekaṃ pādaṃ notkhidati salilāddhaṃsa uccaran |
yadaṅga sa tamutkhidennaivādya na śva: syānna rātrī
nāha: syānna vyucchet kadā cana || 21 ||

While rising up in the waters, the Swan (हंस) does not lift one foot (one foot remains unmoved there). O Dear! There would be no today, tomorrow, night, daylight shine and darkness, if he were to lift the other foot also. (21)

❍ ❍ ❍

अष्टाचक्रं वर्तत एकनेमि सहस्त्राक्षरं प्र पुरो नि पश्चा ।
अर्धेन विश्वं भुवनं जजान यदस्यार्धं कतमः स केतुः ॥ २२ ॥

aṣṭācakraṃ vartata ekanemi sahasrākṣaraṃ pra puro
ni paścā |
ardhena viśvaṃ bhuvanaṃ jajāna yadasyārdhaṃ
katama: sa ketu: || 22 ||

This wheel of Prāṇa (प्राण-चक्र), comprises eight-wheels, as expressed in words, rolls on forward and backward. With one half, it procreated the worlds, and with the other half which remained, what sign does it tell us? (22)

❍ ❍ ❍

यो अस्य विश्वजन्मन ईशे विश्वस्य चेष्टतः ।
अन्येषु क्षिप्रधन्वने तस्मै प्राण नमोऽस्तु ते ॥ २३ ॥

yo asya viśvajanmana īśe viśvasya ceṣṭata: |
anyeṣu kṣipradhanvane tasmai prāṇa namo'stu te || 23 ||

O Prāṇa! The cause of all creation, and the Lord of the universe which stirs, and gives quick speed to others, we bow unto Thee. (23)

❍ ❍ ❍

यो अस्य सर्वजन्मन ईशे सर्वस्य चेष्टतः ।
अतन्द्रो ब्रह्मणा धीरः प्राणो मानु तिष्ठतु ॥ २४ ॥

yo asya sarvajanmana īśe sarvasya ceṣṭata: |
atandro brahmaṇā dhīra: prāṇo mānu tiṣṭhatu || 24 ||

May Prāṇa, the Lord of all (the entire creation), bearer of life and cause of activity, adorned with patience, without being slothful (indolent), infused with the soul-power, be near me forever (never shalt be estranged from me). (24)

❍ ❍ ❍

ऊर्ध्वः सुप्तेषु जागार ननु तिर्यङ् नि पद्यते ।
न सुप्तमस्य सुप्तेष्वनु शुश्राव कश्चन ॥ २५ ॥

ūrdhva: supteṣu jāgāra nanu tiryaṅ ni padyate |
na suptamasya supteṣvanu śuśrāva kaścana || 25 ||

Despite everyone being asleep, Prāṇa remains awake and erect, and is never laid aslant. No one has ever heard that Prāṇa hath been asleep, when others selpt. (25)

❍ ❍ ❍

प्राण मा मत् पर्यावृतो न मदन्यो भविष्यसि ।
अपां गर्भमिव जीवसे प्राण बध्नामि त्वा मयि ॥ २६ ॥
[अथर्ववेद ११ । ४]

**prāṇa mā mat paryāvṛto na madanyo bhaviṣyasi |
apāṃ garbhamiva jīvase prāṇa badhnāmi tvā mayi || 26 ||
[atharvaveda 11 | 4]**

O Prāṇa! Thou shalt never be separated from me, Thou shalt not get away from me. O Prāṇa! I bind Thee in myself for life, like the womb in the fluid (amniotic fluid). (26)

❍ ❍ ❍

Let there be no error in duties towards the gods and manes. Let your mother be a goddess unto you. Let your father be a god unto you. Let your guest and teacher be a god unto you. **(Taittriya Upan. XI|2)**

❍ ❍ ❍

Give with respect and faith[1], do not give without faith and respect. Give as per one's (financial) position[2] (not miserly). Give (even) with a sense of modesty[3]. Give (even) with fear[4]. Give with friendliness[5] and love. **(Taittriya Upan. XI|3)**

1. śraddhaya; 2. śriya; 3. hriyā; 4. bhiya; 5. saṁvidā

❍ ❍ ❍

Hymns On Achieving Fearlessness
अभयप्राप्ति सूक्त

What is dearest in life for one is one's own life 'Prāṇa'; and the greatest fear is losing one's life, i.e., the fear of death. The seer sage of the mantra, with this insight, prays to Prāṇa to be fearless by all means. The sage invokes 'Prāṇa' and says, as the heavens, the earth, the space, the Sun and the Moon etc. remain fearless, and never wane or become lean, O Prāṇa! Be Thee also fearless, and remain unbroken. This Sūkta teaches us to remain fearless and brave. The 15th sūkta of the second canto of the Atharvaveda comprises 13 mantrās. Brahmā is the sage of this Sūkta, the deities are 'Prāṇa'—'Apāna' etc., and the metre 'Trividgāyatrī'. This Sūkta can be greatly useful for the protection of 'Prāṇa' and for enhancing enthusiasm etc. in life. The text follows as under:

यथा द्यौश्च पृथिवी च न बिभीतो न रिष्यतः ।
एवा मे प्राण मा बिभेः एवा मे प्राण मा रिषः ॥ १ ॥

yathā dyauśca pṛthivī ca na bibhīto na riṣyata: |
evā me prāṇa mā bibhe: evā me prāṇa mā riṣa: || 1 ||

Just as the Heavens and the Earth neither fear nor wane, O my Prāṇa! Thou shalt also neither fear nor wane. (1)

❍ ❍ ❍

यथा वायुश्चान्तरिक्षं च न बिभीतो न रिष्यतः ।
एवा मे प्राण मा बिभेः एवा मे प्राण मा रिषः ॥ २ ॥

yathā vāyuścāntarikṣaṃ ca na bibhīto na riṣyata: |
evā me prāṇa mā bibhe: evā me prāṇa mā riṣa: || 2 ||

Just as the Air and the space neither fear nor wane, O My Prāṇa! Thou shalt also neither fear nor wane. (2)

❍ ❍ ❍

यथा सूर्यश्च चन्द्रश्च न बिभीतो न रिष्यतः ।
एवा मे प्राण मा बिभेः एवा मे प्राण मा रिषः ॥ ३ ॥

yathā sūryaśca candraśca na bibhīto na riṣyata: |
evā me prāṇa mā bibhe: evā me prāṇa mā riṣa: || 3 ||

Just as the sun and the moon neither fear nor wane, my Prāṇa! Thou shalt also neither fear nor wane. (3)

❍ ❍ ❍

यथाहश्च रात्री च न बिभीतो न रिष्यतः ।
एवा मे प्राण मा बिभेः एवा मे प्राण मा रिषः ॥ ४ ॥

yathāhaśca rātrī ca na bibhīto na riṣyata: |
evā me prāṇa mā bibhe: evā me prāṇa mā riṣa: || 4 ||

Just as the day and the night neither fear nor wane, O my Prāṇa! Thou shalt also neither fear nor wane. (4)

❍ ❍ ❍

यथा धेनुश्चानड्वांश्च न बिभीतो न रिष्यतः ।
एवा मे प्राण मा बिभेः एवा मे प्राण मा रिषः ॥ ५ ॥

yathā dhenuścānaḍvāṃśca na bibhīto na riṣyata: |
evā me prāṇa mā bibhe: evā me prāṇa mā riṣa: || 5 ||

Just as the cow and the bull neither fear nor wane, O my Prāṇa! Thou shalt also neither fear nor wane. (5)

❍ ❍ ❍

यथा मित्रश्च वरुणश्च न बिभीतो न रिष्यतः ।
एवा मे प्राण मा बिभेः एवा मे प्राण मा रिषः ॥ ६ ॥

yathā mitraśca varuṇaśca na bibhīto na riṣyata: |
evā me prāṇa mā bibhe: evā me prāṇa mā riṣa: || 6 ||

Just as Mitra* and Varuṇa** neither fear nor wane, O my Prāṇa! Thou shalt also neither fear nor wane. (6)

* Presiding God of Day and vital-breath.

** Presiding God of Night and passing out-wind, and the regent of the ocean and of the western quarter.

❍ ❍ ❍

यथा ब्रह्म च क्षत्रं च न बिभीतो न रिष्यतः ।
एवा मे प्राण मा बिभेः एवा मे प्राण मा रिषः ॥ ७ ॥

yathā brahma ca kṣatraṃ ca na bibhīto na riṣyata: |
evā me prāṇa mā bibhe: evā me prāṇa mā riṣa: || 7 ||

Just as the Brahm* and the Kśatra** neither fear nor wane, O my Prāṇa! Thou shalt also neither fear nor wane. (7)

* The Supreme Spirit
** Dominion

❍ ❍ ❍

यथेन्द्रश्चेन्द्रियं च न बिभीतो न रिष्यतः ।
एवा मे प्राण मा बिभेः एवा मे प्राण मा रिषः ॥ ८ ॥

yathendraścendriyaṃ ca na bibhīto na riṣyata: |
evā me prāṇa mā bibhe: evā me prāṇa mā riṣa: || 8 ||

Just as Indra and the senses neither fear nor wane, O my Prāṇa! Thou shalt also neither fear nor wane. (8)

❍ ❍ ❍

यथा वीरश्च वीर्यं च न बिभीतो न रिष्यतः ।
एवा मे प्राण मा बिभेः एवा मे प्राण मा रिषः ॥ ९ ॥

yathā vīraśca vīryaṃ ca na bibhīto na riṣyata: |
evā me prāṇa mā bibhe: evā me prāṇa mā riṣa: || 9 ||

Just as the brave and the prowess neither fear nor wane, O my Prāṇa! Thou shalt also neither fear nor wane. (9)

❍ ❍ ❍

यथा प्राणश्चापानश्च न बिभीतो न रिष्यतः ।
एवा मे प्राण मा बिभेः एवा मे प्राण मा रिषः ॥ १० ॥

yathā prāṇaścāpānaśca na bibhīto na riṣyata: |
evā me prāṇa mā bibhe: evā me prāṇa mā riṣa: || 10 ||

Just as 'Prāṇa' and 'Apāna' neither fear nor wane, O my Prāṇa! Thou shalt also neither fear nor wane. (10)

❍ ❍ ❍

यथा मृत्युश्चामृतं च न बिभीतो न रिष्यतः ।
एवा मे प्राण मा बिभेः एवा मे प्राण मा रिषः ॥ ११ ॥

yathā mṛtyuścāmṛtaṃ ca na bibhīto na riṣyata: |
evā me prāṇa mā bibhe: evā me prāṇa mā riṣa: || 11 ||

Just as death and immortality neither fear nor wane, O my Prāṇa! Thou shalt also neither fear nor wane. (11)

❍ ❍ ❍

यथा सत्यं चानृतं च न बिभीतो न रिष्यतः ।
एवा मे प्राण मा बिभेः एवा मे प्राण मा रिषः ॥ १२ ॥

yathā satyaṃ cānṛtaṃ ca na bibhīto na riṣyata: |
evā me prāṇa mā bibhe: evā me prāṇa mā riṣa: || 12 ||

Just as truth and untruth neither fear nor wane, O my Prāṇa! Thou shalt also neither fear nor wane. (12)

❍ ❍ ❍

यथा भूतं च भव्यं च न बिभीतो न रिष्यतः ।
एवा मे प्राण मा बिभे एवा मे प्राण मा रिषः ॥ १३ ॥
[अथर्ववेद, पैप्पलादशाखा २/१५]

yathā bhūtaṃ ca bhavyaṃ ca na bibhīto na riṣyata: |
evā me prāṇa mā bibhe evā me prāṇa mā riṣa: || 13 ||
[Atharvaved, Paippalādśākhā 2.15]

Just as past and future neither fear nor wane, O My Prāṇa! Thou shalt also neither fear nor wane. (13)

❍ ❍ ❍

The invocation for Peace

शान्त्यध्याय

ऋचं वाचं प्र पद्ये मनो यजुः प्र पद्ये साम
प्राणं प्र पद्ये चक्षुः श्रोत्रं प्र पद्ये ।
वागोजः सहौजो मयि प्राणापानौ ॥ १ ॥

ṛcaṃ vācaṃ pra padye mano yaju: pra padye sāma
prāṇaṃ pra padye cakṣu: śrotraṃ pra padye |
vāgoja: sahaujo mayi prāṇāpānau || 1 ||

I take the refuge of 'speech', in the form of 'Rigveda', the 'mind' in the form of 'Yajurveda', the 'Prāṇa' in the form of 'Sāmaveda' and that of 'Eye' and 'Ear', in order to have the strength of speech, the physical-strength, and that of 'Prāṇa' and 'Apāna' to remain in stable form within me. (1)

❍ ❍ ❍

यन्मे छिद्रं चक्षुषो हृदयस्य मनसो वातितृण्णं बृहस्पतिर्मे तद्दधातु ।
शं नो भवतु भुवनस्य यस्पतिः ॥ २ ॥

yanme chidraṃ cakṣuṣo hṛdayasya manaso vātitṛṇṇaṃ
bṛhaspatirme taddadhātu |
śaṃ no bhavatu bhuvanasya yaspati: || 2 ||

May Brihaspati, the preceptor (Guru) of Gods, eliminate the flaws of my eyes, heart and the mind. May the Oversoul, the Lord of the universe be propitious for me. (2)

❍ ❍ ❍

भूर्भुवः स्वः तत्सवितुर्वरेण्यं भर्गो देवस्य धीमहि ।
धियो यो नः प्रचोदयात् ॥ ३ ॥

bhūrbhuva: sva: tatsaviturvareṇyaṃ bhargo
devasya dhīmahi |
dhiyo yo na: pracodayāt || 3 ||

We engage in meditation of the Omniscient Supreme Being in the form of the Sun-God, appropriately adoptable and located in the solar-sphere, who inspires our intelligence toward noble-deeds. (3)

❍ ❍ ❍

कया नश्चित्रऽ आ भुवदूती सदावृधः सखा ।
कया शचिष्ठया वृता ॥ ४ ॥

kayā naścitra' ā bhuvadūtī sadāvṛdha: sakhā |
kayā śaciṣṭhayā vṛtā || 4 ||

O Indra, the ever evolving and astonishing! With which kind of oblation (तर्पणं), gratification or the sacrifice (यज्ञ) can Thou be gracious on us. (4)

❍ ❍ ❍

कस्त्वा सत्यो मदानां मꣳहिष्ठो मत्सदन्धसः ।
दृढा चिदारुजे वसु ॥ ५ ॥

kastvā satyo madānāṃ maꣳhiṣṭho matsadandhasa: |
dṛḍhā cidāruje vasu || 5 ||

O Supreme Being! Which is the most intoxicating of oblations; and which portion is the best of 'Soma' like food that pleases Thee most. Thou doth bestow wealth (in portions) upon devotees, who are happy in Thy happiness, whatever pleases Thee. (5)

❍ ❍ ❍

अभी षु णः सखीनामविता जरितॄणाम् ।
शतं भवास्यूतिभिः ॥ ६ ॥

abhī ṣu ṇa: sakhīnāmavitā jaritṝṇām |
śataṃ bhavāsyūtibhi: || 6 ||

O Indra! Thou doth assume numerous forms, in order to protect devotees, who eulogise Thee as friend. (6)

❍ ❍ ❍

कया त्वं न ऊत्याभि प्र मन्दसे वृषन् ।
कया स्तोतृभ्य आ भर ॥ ७ ॥

kayā tvaṃ na ūtyābhi pra mandase vr̥ṣan |
kayā stotr̥bhya ā bhara || 7 ||

O Indra! Satiated by which eulogising oblation, Thou doth please us, and impart wealth to which praying patron (यजमान)?

❍ ❍ ❍

इन्द्रो विश्वस्य राजति ।
शं नो अस्तु द्विपदे शं चतुष्पदे ॥ ८ ॥

indro viśvasya rājati |
śaṃ no astu dvipade śaṃ catuṣpade || 8 ||

May the Supreme Being, the Lord of the universe or the Sun, the illuminator of the universe, be propitious to our two-footed (meaning sons etc.), and four footed (meaning cows etc.). (8)

❍ ❍ ❍

शं नो मित्रः शं वरुणः शं नो भवत्वर्यमा ।
शं न इन्द्रो बृहस्पतिः शं नो विष्णुरुरुक्रमः ॥ ९ ॥

śaṃ no mitra: śaṃ varuṇa: śaṃ no bhavatvaryamā |
śaṃ na indro br̥haspati: śaṃ no viṣṇururukrama: || 9 ||

May Mitra, Varuṇa, Aryamā, Indra, Brihaspati and Viṣṇu (all the Gods) be propitious for us. (9)

❍ ❍ ❍

शं नो वातः पवताꣳ शं नस्तपतु सूर्यः ।
शं नः कनिक्रदद्देवः पर्जन्यो अभि वर्षतु ॥ १० ॥

śaṃ no vāta: pavatāꣳ śaṃ nastapatu sūrya: |
śaṃ na: kanikradaddeva: parjanyo abhi varṣatu || 10 ||

May Vāyu (God of winds), Sun and Varuṇa be propitious, meaning thereby, may the winds flow pleasantly, may the Sun rays spread over comfortably, and may Varuṇa shower useful rains. (10)

❍ ❍ ❍

अहानि शं भवन्तु नः शꣳ रात्रीः प्रति धीयताम् ।
शं न इन्द्राग्नी भवतामवोभिः शं न इन्द्रावरुणा रातहव्या ।
शं न इन्द्रापूषणा वाजसातौ शमिन्द्रासोमा सुविताय शं योः ॥ ११ ॥

ahāni śaṃ bhavantu na: śaꣳ rātrī: prati dhīyatām |
śaṃ na indrāgnī bhavatāmavobhi: śaṃ
na indrāvaruṇā rātahavyā |
śaṃ na indrāpūṣaṇā vājasātau śamindrāsomā suvitāya
śaṃ yo: || 11 ||

May the day and the night be pleasant and the Gods, Indrāgnī, Indravaruṇa, Indrapūṣā and Indrasoma be propitious for us, by eliminating our maladies and fear and be pleasurable for us. (11)

❍ ❍ ❍

शं नो देवीरभिष्टय आपो भवन्तु पीतये ।
शं योरभि स्रवन्तु नः ॥ १२ ॥

śaṃ no devīrabhiṣṭaya āpo bhavantu pītaye |
śaṃ yorabhi sravantu na: || 12 ||

May the brilliantly shining waters be propitious for us for sprinkling (on deities, Abhiśekam) or for accomplishing the desired goals and may it be, the eliminator of our diseases. (12)

❍ ❍ ❍

स्योना पृथिवि नो भवानृक्षरा निवेशनी ।
यच्छा नः शर्म सप्रथाः ॥ १३ ॥

syonā pṛthivi no bhavānṛkśarā niveśanī |
yacchā na: śarma sapratha: || 13 ||

O Earth! Be Thee bereft of thorns, meaning thereby, take us in Thy shelter, being thornless for our home on earth. (13)

❍ ❍ ❍

आपो हि ष्ठा मयोभुवस्ता न ऊर्जे दधातन ।
महे रणाय चक्षसे ॥ १४ ॥

āpo hi ṣṭhā mayobhuvastā na ūrje dadhātana |
mahe raṇāya cakśase || 14 ||

O Pool of water! Thou art the (source of drinking water and water to bathe) Thou art the establisher of joy in our lives and Thou art extremely delightful and a pleasure to watch and observe. (14)

❍ ❍ ❍

यो वः शिवतमो रसस्तस्य भाजयतेह नः ।
उशतीरिव मातरः ॥ १५ ॥

yo va: śivatamo rasastasya bhājayateha na: |
uśatīriva mātara: || 15 ||

O Pool of water! Share with us that nectar "Rasa', which is pleasing and tranquil. Just as a mother breast-feeds her son, so do Thee also feed us with nectar-like sweet-rasa, by giving us water. (15)

❍ ❍ ❍

तस्मा अरं गमाम वो यस्य क्षयाय जिन्वथ ।
आपो जनयथा च नः ॥ १६ ॥

tasmā araṃ gamāma vo yasya kṣayāya jinvatha |
āpo janayathā ca na: || 16 ||

O Pool of water! Thou art always reachable in all the worlds, as the entire universe upto Brahma live because of Thy existence. Thou shalt, therefore, enable us to generate offsprings by providing us sweet water. (16)

❍ ❍ ❍

द्यौः शान्तिरन्तरिक्षꣳ शान्तिः पृथिवी
शान्तिरापः शान्तिरोषधयः शान्तिः ।
वनस्पतयः शान्तिर्विश्वे देवाः शान्तिर्ब्रह्म शान्तिः सर्वꣳ
शान्तिः शान्तिरेव शान्तिः सा मा शान्तिरेधि ॥ १७ ॥

dyau: śāntirantarikṣaꣳ śānti: pṛthivī
śāntirāpa: śāntiroṣadhaya: śānti: |
vanaspataya: śāntirviśve devā: śāntirbrahma
śānti: sarvaꣳ
śānti: śāntireva śānti: sā mā śāntiredhi || 17 ||

The tranquility in heaven, the tranquility in space (the physical universe beyond the earth's atmosphere), the tranquility on earth, the tranquility in oceans (water, as an element), the tranquility in herbs (with their efficacy) and that in vegetation, the tranquility in Gods (overseeing the entire creation), the tranquility in Brahm (the causal super-energy), the tranquility in the entire universe, and the natural tranquility pervading the whole universe, O Parmātmā (the Oversoul)! Let Thy grace bestow upon me that tranquility. (17)

❍ ❍ ❍

दृते दृꣳह मा मित्रस्य मा चक्षुषा सर्वाणि समीक्षन्ताम् ।
मित्रस्याहं चक्षुषा सर्वाणि भूतानि समीक्षे ।
मित्रस्य चक्षुषा समीक्षामहे ॥ १८ ॥

dṛte dṛꣳha mā mitrasya mā cakṣuṣā sarvāṇi
samīkśantām |
mitrasyāhaṃ cakṣuṣā sarvāṇi bhūtāni samīkṣe |
mitrasya cakṣuṣā samīkṣāmahe || 18 ||

O Overlord (Omnipotent)! Make us strong when our oldage

weakens our body. May all the beings view us as their friends, and we also view them as our friends. Having friendly feeling, mutually, we view all as friends. (18)

❍ ❍ ❍

दृते दृꣳह मा ।

ज्योक्ते सन्दृशि जीव्यासं ज्योक्ते सन्दृशि जीव्यासम् ॥ १९ ॥

dṛte dṛꣳha mā |
jyotte sandṛśi jīvyāsaṃ jyotte sandṛśi jīvyāsam || 19 ||

O Lord (O Mighty)! Strengthen us. We shall be long-living by viewing Thee; we shall be long-living by viewing Thee. (19)

❍ ❍ ❍

नमस्ते हरसे शोचिषे नमस्ते अस्त्वर्चिषे ।

अन्याँस्ते अस्मत्तपन्तु हेतयः पावको अस्मभ्यꣳ शिवो भव ॥ २० ॥

namaste harase śociṣe namaste astvarciṣe |
anyāṁste asmattapantu hetaya: pāvako asmabhyaꣳ
śivo bhava || 20 ||

O Fire (Agne, God of Fire)! Salutations to Thy brilliant lustre (Teja). Salutation to Thy brilliant lustre, causing purification of all the matter. May Thy flames be the cause of sufferings to our adversaries and for us be quiet (calm), meaning, thereby, be propitious. (20)

❍ ❍ ❍

नमस्ते अस्तु विद्युते नमस्ते स्तनयित्नवे ।

नमस्ते भगवन्नस्तु यतः स्वः समीहसे ॥ २१ ॥

namaste astu vidyute namaste stanayitnave |
namaste bhagavannastu yata: sva: samīhase || 21 ||

O Lord (O Mighty)! Salutations to Thy thunerbolt-form. Salutations to Thy form of clouds. Salutations to the cause, which leads thee trying to reach heaven. (21)

❍ ❍ ❍

यतो यतः समीहसे ततो नो अभयं कुरु ।
शं नः कुरु प्रजाभ्योऽभयं नः पशुभ्यः ॥ २२ ॥

yato yata: samīhase tato no abhayaṃ kuru |
śaṃ na: kuru prajābhyo'bhayaṃ na: paśubhya: || 22 ||

O Overlord (Omnipotent)! Thou doth always let us have Thy grace by driving the misconducts away from us; let us be fearless from them. Let our descendants be happy, and let our animals also be fearless. (22)

❍ ❍ ❍

सुमित्रिया न आप ओषधयः सन्तु दुर्मित्रियास्तस्मै ।
सन्तु योऽस्मान् द्वेष्टि यं च वयं द्विष्मः ॥ २३ ॥

sumitriyā na āpa oṣadhaya: santu durmitriyāstasmai |
santu yo'smān dveṣṭi yaṃ ca vayaṃ dviṣma: || 23 ||

O Overlord! May water and herbs be placed for us as good friends. Those who are our opponents or to whom we treat as enemies, may water and herbs be, pleasantly, placed for both of us. (23)

❍ ❍ ❍

तच्चक्षुर्देवहितं पुरस्ताच्छुक्रमुच्चरत् ।
पश्येम शरदः शतं जीवेम शरदः शतꣳ शृणुयाम
शरदः शतं प्र ब्रवाम शरदः शतमदीनाः स्याम
शरदः शतं भूयश्च शरदः शतात् ॥ २४ ॥
[शुक्लयजुर्वेद ३६]

taccakṣurdevahitaṃ purastācchukramuccarat |
paśyema śarada: śataṃ jīvema śarada: śataꣳśṛṇuyāma
śarada: śataṃ pra bravāma śarada: śatamadīnā: syāma
śarada: śataṃ bhūyaśca śarada: śatāt || 24 ||
[śuklayajurveda 36]

Propitious for Gods or the fostered eyes of the loving Overlord, who in the form of Sun, rises brilliantly, in the direction of the East, May that Sun bless us to have unobstructed sight (vision) to enable us to behold Him very well throughout life. May (the Sun) bless us live through a hundred years, hear and speak through a hundred years. May (the Sun) bless us not to be wretched through this hundred years, meaning thereby, we never have to beg through a hundred years. May (the Sun) bless us live longer than a hundred years. (24)

❍ ❍ ❍

O Gods! Let our ears hear auspicious and beneficial thoughts while engaged in our worship services and prayers. Let our eyes see all good and auspicious; and with our stout body and sound limbs with our son etc., may we keep on hearing beneficial talks. May we enjoy such an age as dedicated to worshipping Gods.

(Ṛg. Swasti. 8)

❍ ❍ ❍

The syllable Om is all this. The past, present, or future is verily Om. And all that is beyond the entirety is also Om. **(Mundak Up. Ch. 1|1)**

❍ ❍ ❍

As a caterpillar reaches out for the next blade of grass,
As a goldsmith fashions an old ornament into a new and more beautiful one, so does the self.
As a person acts, so does he become in life.

(Brih. Up.)

❍ ❍ ❍

Perrenial joy or passing pleasure? Choice is yours.

(Kathopaniṣad)

❍ ❍ ❍

Can there be anything not known to That who is the One in all? Know One, know all. **(Kathopaniṣad)**

❍ ❍ ❍

Hymns on Donation of Wealth and Food

धनान्नदान सूक्त

The 117th Sūkta of the 10th Section of the Rigveda is famous with the name of 'Dhanānnadān Sūkta', i.e., the Sūkta on 'Donation of Wealth and Food'. The significance of donation has been beautifully enunciated in the Sūkta. The mantrās are didactic in nature and give us a moral lesson. The donor and the donation carry a special glory in the world. The richness of the wealthy man becomes meaningful in his nature of sharing his riches, not in his being miserly.

The seer sage of this mantra is 'Bhikśurāngirasa'. The metre used in the first and the second mantra is 'Jagatī', and in the rest of the metre is 'Anuṣtupa'.

The text follows here-under:

न वा उ देवाः क्षुधमिद्वधं ददुरुताशितमुप गच्छन्ति मृत्यवः ।
उतो रयिः पृणतो नोप दस्यत्युतापृणन् मर्डितारं न विन्दते ॥ १ ॥

na vā u devā: kṣudhamidvadhaṃ dadurutāśitamupa gacchanti mṛtyava: |
uto rayi: pṛṇato nopa dasyatyutāpṛṇan marḍitāraṃ na vindate || 1 ||

The Gods have almost killed living beings by inculcating appetite in them. He is a donor, who satisfies the flames of hunger by giving food in charity. One who does not give food to the hungry, and eats himself, one day, death takes away his life-breath. The donor's wealth never decreases, God blesses him with more, whereas, the miser, who never gives, does not get pleasure from anyone. (1)

❍ ❍ ❍

य आध्राय चकमानाय पित्वो ऽन्नवान्त्सन् रफितायोपजग्मुषे ।
स्थिरं मनः कृणुते सेवते पुरोतो चित् स मर्डितारं न विन्दते ॥ २ ॥

ya ādhrāya cakamānāya pitvo 'nnavāntsan raphitāyoepajagmuṣe |
sthiraṃ mana: kṛṇute sevate puroto cit sa marḍitāraṃ na vindate || 2 ||

The extremely cruel man who eats in front of a hungry man, standing at the door, spreading hands, desiring food; and he becomes so hard-hearted as not to extend his hands to give, despite having abundant of grains, that cruel man never gets happiness in life. (2)

❍ ❍ ❍

स इद् भोजो यो गृहवे ददात्यन्नकामाय चरते कृशाय ।
अरमस्मै भवति यामहूता उतापरीषु कृणुते सखायम् ॥ ३ ॥

sa id bhojo yo gṛhave dadātyannakāmāya carate kṛśāya |
aramasmai bhavati yāmahūtā utāparīṣu kṛṇute sakhāyam || 3 ||

He, who gives food to an extremely feeble man coming to his home, is blessed with all the fruits of a sacrifice (yajña), and he turns his enemies into friends. (3)

❍ ❍ ❍

न स सखा यो न ददाति सख्ये सचाभुवे सचमानाय पित्वः ।
अपास्मात् प्रेयान्न तदोको अस्ति पृणन्तमन्यमरणं चिदिच्छेत् ॥ ४ ॥

na sa sakhā yo na dadāti sakhye sacābhuve sacamānāya pitva: |
apāsmāt preyānna tadoko asti pṛṇantamanyamaraṇaṃ cidicchet || 4 ||

A friend is like one's own limb (of body). He is not a friend, who refuses to give to his friend, when asking (for help). One should go away far-off, abandoning him. It is not his home. One should take refuge of some other person, who is ready to give (and help). (4)

❍ ❍ ❍

पृणीयादिन्नाधमानाय तव्यान् द्राघीयांसमनु पश्येत पन्थाम् ।
ओ हि वर्तन्ते रथ्येव चक्रा ऽन्यमन्यमुप तिष्ठन्त रायः ॥ ५ ॥

pṛṇīyādinnādhamānāya tavyān drāghīyāṃsamanu paśyeta panthām |
o hi vartante rathyeva cakrā 'nyamanyamupa tiṣṭhanta rāya: || 5 ||

He alone is rich who gives food to a mendicant (याचक). He views clearly the auspicious path (ahead). The riches and luxury are like wheels of a chariot, moving back and forth. It remains with one at one time and with the other at other time. (5)

❍ ❍ ❍

मोघमन्नं विन्दते अप्रचेताः सत्यं ब्रवीमि वध इत् स तस्य ।
नार्यमणं पुष्यति नो सखायं केवलाघो भवति केवलादी ॥ ६ ॥

moghamannaṃ vindate apracetā: satyaṃ bravīmi vadha it sa tasya |
nāryamaṇaṃ puṣyati no sakhāyaṃ kevalāgho bhavati kevalādī || 6 ||

If one is not generous-minded, his producing food (grains) is futile. Accumulation becomes the cause of his death. One who does not gratify Gods and friends, he consumes nothing but sins in reality. (6)

❍ ❍ ❍

कृषन्नित् फाल आशितं कृणोति यन्नध्वानमप वृङ्क्ते चरित्रैः ।
वदन् ब्रह्मावदतो वनीयान् पृणन्नापिरपृणन्तमभि ष्यात् ॥ ७ ॥

kṛṣannit phāla āśitaṃ kṛṇoti yannadhvānamapa vṛṅtte caritrai: |
vadan brahmāvadato vanīyān pṛṇannāpiraprṇantamabhi ṣyāt || 7 ||

The gratifying plough-share, ploughs the field in order to

give food to the famers. The treading man paves the way with the marks of his footsteps. A brahmin, who speaks is better than a non-speaking one. (7)

❍ ❍ ❍

एकपाद् भूयो द्विपदो वि चक्रमे द्विपात् त्रिपादमभ्येति पश्चात् ।
चतुष्पादेति द्विपदामभिस्वरे संपश्यन् पङ्क्तीरुपतिष्ठमानः ॥ ८ ॥

ekapād bhūyo dvipado vi cakrame dvipāt tripādamabhyeti paścāt |
catuṣpādeti dvipadāmabhisvare saṃpaśyan paṅttīrupatiṣṭhamāna: || 8 ||

A rich man having one part follows a rich man having two parts. A rich man having two parts follows another having three. And the one, having four, leads in the line looking behind him all others. Therefore, one should donate without having false pride of one's riches. (8)

❍ ❍ ❍

समौ चिद्धस्तौ न समं विविष्टः संमातरा चिन्न समं दुहाते ।
यमयोश्चिन्न समा वीर्याणि ज्ञाती चित् संतौ न समं पृणीतः ॥ ९ ॥
[ऋक० १० । ११७]

samau ciddhastau na samaṃ viviṣṭa: saṃmātarā cinna samaṃ duhāte |
yamayościnna samā vīryāṇi jñātī cit saṃtau na samaṃ pṛṇīta: || 9 ||
[ṛka. 10 | 117]

The two hands are similar, but cannot perform equal work. The two cows, even being similar, do not yield equal amount of milk. The twins, being equal, are different in their prowess. So do the two men, born in one clan, despite being euqal—are not equal in granting donations. (9)

❍ ❍ ❍

Hymns on Warding-Off Diseases
रोग मुक्ति सूक्त

The 13th Sūkta of the 4th Section of the Atharvaveda and the 137th Sūkta of the 10th Section of the Rigveda are known with the name of 'रोग निवारण सूक्त' (The Sūkta on Warding off Diseases). The metre used in the Atharvaveda is 'Anuṣtupa' and the sage is 'śantāti', and the Gods are 'the Moon' (चन्द्रमा) and the 'Group of Gods' (विश्वेदेवा). Whereas, the seers in the 'Rigveda' are Bharadvāja of the first mantra, Kaśyap of the second, Gautam of the third, Atri of the fourth, Viśwāmitra of the fifth, Jamadagni of the sixth mantrās, respectively, and Vasiṣth that of the seventh mantra; and the God is 'Group of Gods' (विश्वेदेवा). Recitation of this Sūkta, as per the Vedas, wards-off maladies, meaning thereby, brings wellness. The sages pray to the Gods for liberation from diseases.

The text of the Sūkta follows as under:

उत देवा अवहितं देवा उन्नयथा पुनः ।
उतागश्चक्रुषं देवा देवा जीवयथा पुनः ॥ १ ॥
uta devā avahitaṃ devā unnayathā puna: |
utāgaścakruṣaṃ devā devā jīvayathā puna: || 1 ||

O Gods! O Gods, Lift upward the fallen one with determination. O Gods! Let the sinners be brought back to life again, brought back to life again (1)

❍ ❍ ❍

द्वाविमौ वातौ वात आ सिन्धोरा परावतः ।
दक्षं ते अन्य आवातु व्यन्यो वातु यद्रपः ॥ २ ॥
dvāvimau vātau vāta ā sindhorā parāvata: |
dakṣaṃ te anya āvātu vyanyo vātu yadrapa: || 2 ||

There are two kinds of winds. The first of winds comes from the oceans and the other from the plains far-off the earth. May one of the winds bring energy for you, and the other drive away far-off the disease*. (2)

* disease of gas formation

❍ ❍ ❍

आ वात वाहि भेषजं वि वात वाहि यद्रपः ।
त्वं हि विश्वभेषज देवानां दूत ईयसे ॥ ३ ॥

ā vāta vāhi bheṣajaṃ vi vāta vāhi yadrapa: |
tvaṃ hi viśvabheṣaja devānāṃ dūta īyase || 3 ||

O Wind (God of Winds)! Bring the herbs over here. O Wind! Ward-off the cause of disease. O Wind, the keeper of the entire lot of herbs! no doubt, Thou doth blow as the messenger of Gods goes on blowing on and on. (3)

❍ ❍ ❍

त्रायन्तामिमं देवास्त्रायन्तां मरुतां गणाः ।
त्रायन्तां विश्वा भूतानि यथायमरपा असत् ॥ ४ ॥

trāyantāmimaṃ devāstrāyantāṃ marutāṃ gaṇā: |
trāyantāṃ viśvā bhūtāni yathāyamarapā asat || 4 ||

O Gods! Protect this patient. O Group of Maruts (Winds)! Protect this patient. All the beings protect this patient (guard) in order to let free this patient from the disease. (4)

❍ ❍ ❍

आ त्वागमं शंतातिभिरथो अरिष्टतातिभिः ।
दक्षं त उग्रमाभारिषं परा यक्ष्मं सुवामि ते ॥ ५ ॥

ā tvāgamaṃ śaṃtātibhiratho ariṣṭatātibhi: |
dakṣaṃ ta ugramābhāriṣaṃ parā yakṣmaṃ suvāmi te || 5 ||

With the means of expansion of peace and imperishable means I approach Thee. (I) Fill Thee with vehement valour and Drive away Thy diseases faraway. (5)

❍ ❍ ❍

अयं मे हस्तो भगवानयं मे भगवत्तरः ।
अयं मे विश्वभेषजोऽयं शिवाभिमर्शनः* ॥ ६ ॥

ayaṃ me hasto bhagavānayaṃ me bhagavattara: |
ayaṃ me viśvabheṣajo'yaṃ śivābhimarśana: || 6 ||

My hands are fortunate. My this hand is more fortunate. My this hand is full of herbs (medicines) and the other one provides auspicious touch. (6)

* The Rigveda mantra is different from this and goes as under:

आप इद्वा उ भेषजीरापो अमीवचातनीः ।
आपः सर्वस्य भेषजीस्तास्ते कृण्वन्तु भेषजम् ॥

Water eliminates diseases. Water is the medicine of all diseases. May that water create medicine (औषधि) for you. (The Rigveda)

❍ ❍ ❍

हस्ताभ्यां दशशाखाभ्यां जिह्वा वाचः पुरोगवी ।
अनामयित्नुभ्यां हस्ताभ्यां ताभ्यां त्वाभि मृशामसि ॥ ७ ॥
[अथर्व० ४ । १३]

hastābhyāṃ daśaśākhābhyāṃ jihvā vāca: purogavī |
anāmayitnubhyāṃ hastābhyāṃ tābhyāṃ tvābhi mṛśāmasi || 7 ||
[atharva. 4 | 13]

My tongue initiates my speech alongwith my hands, that have ten branches. We touch you with our two hands, causing elimination of diseases. (7)

(Atharvaveda 4/13)

❍ ❍ ❍

Hymns on Medicines (Herbal Plants)
औषधि सूक्त

The 97th Sūkta of the 10th section of the Rigveda is known as 'Auśadhi Sūkta', i.e., 'The Sūkta on medicines' (Herbal plants). The sage of this Sūkta is 'Ātharvaṇ Bhiṣag' and the Deity 'Auśadhi'. The metre is 'Anuṣtupa' and the Sūkta comprises 23 mantrās in number. In the beginning of the Sūkta itself, the sage regards 'Auṣadhi' as a Deity and prays for elimination of diseaes, in order to achieve long life. The Sūkta enunciates that the herbal plants (ओषधियाँ) appeared earlier than the Gods — **'या ओषधीः पूर्वा जाता देवेभ्यः'**। The herbal palnts have been depicted as a mother, a protector and nourisher, and also adorned with limitless power. the Sūkta is regarded as immensely important from the point of view of achieving wellness.

The text of the Sūkta follows as under:

या ओषधीः पूर्वा जाता देवेभ्यस्त्रियुगं पुरा ।
मनै नु बभ्रूणामहं शतं धामानि सप्त च ॥ १ ॥

yā oṣadhī: pūrvā jātā devebhyastriyugaṃ purā |
manai nu babhrūṇāmahaṃ śataṃ dhāmāni sapta ca || 1 ||

I cogitate on yellow-complexioned (ancient) herbal plants, prosperous with one hundred and seven powers, which appeared earlier than the Gods, i.e., three generations before the Gods (Devās). (1)

❍ ❍ ❍

शतं वो अम्ब धामानि सहस्त्रमुत वो रुहः ।
अधा शतक्रत्वो यूयमिमं मे अगदं कृत ॥ २ ॥

śataṃ vo amba dhāmāni sahasramuta vo ruha: |
adhā śatakratvo yūyamimaṃ me agadaṃ kṛta || 2 ||

O Mothers (The herbal plants)! Thou art endowed with hundreds of powers and Thy growth is profuse (of a thousand kinds). O Herbal plants (medicinal plants), bearing hundreds of powers! Let this patient be free from ailment, definitely. (2)

❍ ❍ ❍

ओषधीः प्रति मोदध्वं पुष्पवतीः प्रसूवरीः ।
अश्वा इव सजित्वरीर्वीरुधः पारयिष्ण्वः ॥ ३ ॥

oṣadhī: prati modadhvaṃ puṣpavatī: prasūvarī: |
aśvā iva sajitvarīrvīrudha: pārayiṣṇva: || 3 ||

O Herbs! Rejoice (in my company). Thou doth blossom and beget fruits. Like mares winning in pairs (in a competition or a battle), these creepers will help reach across (in misfortune). (3)

❍ ❍ ❍

ओषधीरिति मातरस्तद्वो देवीरुप ब्रुवे ।
सनेयमश्वं गां वास आत्मानं तव पूरुष ॥ ४ ॥

oṣadhīriti mātarastadvo devīrupa bruve |
saneyamaśvaṃ gāṃ vāsa ātmānaṃ tava pūruṣa || 4 ||

O Herbs, Mothers, Goddesses! I pray Ye as to get horse, cow and clothe as a donation for my services (as gifts) and O Man (suffering from diseases)! May your spirit (set free from the clutches of diseases) be under my control. (4)

❍ ❍ ❍

अश्वत्थे वो निषदनं पर्णे वो वसतिष्कृता ।
गोभाज इत् किलासथ यत् सनवथ पूरुषम् ॥ ५ ॥

aśvatthe vo niṣadanaṃ parṇe vo vasatiṣkṛtā |
gobhāja it kilāsatha yat sanavatha pūruṣam || 5 ||

O Herbs! The place for Thy repose is the holy fig tree, and the 'Palāśa' tree is arranged for Thy abode. If Thou shalt bring this suffering patient (setting him free from the clutches of diseases) near me, Thou shalt be getting many cows (as reward). (5)

❍ ❍ ❍

यत्रौषधीः समग्मत राजानः समिताविव ।
विप्रः स उच्यते भिषग् रक्षोहामीवचातनः ॥ ६ ॥

yatrauṣadhī: samagmata rājāna: samitāviva |
vipra: sa ucyate bhiṣag rakṣohāmivacātana: || 6 ||

As the Kings participate in the royal-assemblies, so do the herbs reside in Brahmins' company (विप्रः) (in the company of Brahmins), people call him a physician (भिषक् – Doctor). Eliminating devils, he drives away diseases. (6)

❍ ❍ ❍

अश्वावतीं सोमावतीमूर्जयन्तीमुदोजसम् ।
आवित्सि सर्वा ओषधीरस्मा अरिष्टतातये ॥ ७ ॥

aśvāvatīm somāvatīmūrjayantīmudojasam |
āvitsi sarvā oṣadhīrasmā ariṣṭatātaye || 7 ||

In order to eliminate the sufferings of this (ailing) man, I have achieved soma-mixed (juice of a special plant), energising and invigorating all herbs, which fetches horse in the form of reward. (7)

❍ ❍ ❍

उच्छुष्मा ओषधीनां गावो गोष्ठादिवेरते ।
धनं सनिष्यन्तीनामात्मानं तव पूरुष ॥ ८ ॥

ucchuṣmā oṣadhīnāṃ gāvo goṣṭhādiverate |
dhanaṃ saniṣyantīnāmātmānaṃ tava pūruṣa || 8 ||

O ailing man! Desiring money, and capable of keeping under

their control, the powers of these herbs are getting emitted from me, just as the cows from the cowshed. (8)

❍ ❍ ❍

इष्कृतिर्नाम वो माता ऽथो यूयं स्थ निष्कृतीः ।
सीराः पतत्रिणीः स्थन यदामयति निष्कृथ ॥ ९ ॥

iṣkṛtirnāma vo mātā 'tho yūyaṃ stha niṣkṛtī: |
sīrā: patatriṇī: sthana yadāmayati niṣkṛtha || 9 ||

O Medicinal Herbs, enricher of healthy components! Thy mother is ('इष्कृति') healer (healingpower) and Thou art 'निष्कृति' (Nishkriti) curer (of diseases). Thou doth posses wings, despite having the nature of flowing. Thou doth drive out the causes of disease (from the body of the patient). (9)

❍ ❍ ❍

अति विश्वाः परिष्ठाः स्तेन इव व्रजमक्रमुः ।
ओषधीः प्राचुच्यवुर्यत् किं च तन्वो३ रपः ॥ १० ॥

ati viśvā: pariṣṭhā: stena iva vrajamakramu: |
oṣadhī: prācucyavuryat kiṃ ca tanvo3 rapa: || 10 ||

Just as a proficient thief, discarding all prohibitives as trivial, enters a cow-shed and drives away cows, so have our herbal-medicines entered into the body of the patient, and have driven away whatever (pain) sufferings were there in the body. (10)

❍ ❍ ❍

यदिमा वाजयन्नहमोषधीर्हस्त आदधे ।
आत्मा यक्ष्मस्य नश्यति पुरा जीवगृभो यथा ॥ ११ ॥

yadimā vājayannahamoṣadhīrhasta ādadhe |
ātmā yakṣmasya naśyati purā jīvagṛbho yathā || 11 ||

The time, I bear herbal medicines in my hand, instilling strength in them, the same moment, the core of the diseases is destroyed, just as 'the deer' etc. run away (saving life) before being caught alive by the tiger. (11)

❍ ❍ ❍

यस्यौषधीः प्रसर्पथाङ्गमङ्गं परुष्परुः ।
ततो यक्ष्मं वि बाधध्व उग्रो मध्यमशीरिव ॥ १२ ॥

yasyauṣadhī: prasarpathāṅgamaṅgaṃ paruṣparu: |
tato yakṣmaṃ vi bādhadhva ugro madhyamaśīriva || 12 ||

O Medicinal Herbs! Thou dost spread extensively on the limbs, severally, in each base and all the joints of the ailing man, as the fierce, mischievous wild animal in the midst of its preys. Thou doth eliminate that disease like the fireceness of that animal. (12)

❍ ❍ ❍

साकं यक्ष्म प्र पत चाषेण किकिदीविना ।
साकं वातस्य ध्राज्या साकं नश्य निहाकया ॥ १३ ॥

sākaṃ yakṣma pra pata cāṣeṇa kikidīvinā |
sākaṃ vātasya dhrājyā sākaṃ naśya nihākayā || 13 ||

O Pulmonary disease*! Fly you far off alongwith the birds 'Cāṣ' (चाष), the 'blue jay**' and 'Kikidivin' (किकिदीविन) 'Cātak' (चातक) or get destroyed by blinding winds and fog. (13)

* fawn coloured old world bird

** यक्ष्मा (Tuberculosis)

❍ ❍ ❍

अन्या वो अन्यामवत्वन्यान्यस्या उपावत ।
ताः सर्वाः संविदाना इदं मे प्रावता वचः ॥ १४ ॥

anyā vo anyāmavatvanyānyasyā upāvata |
tā: sarvā: saṃvidānā idaṃ me prāvatā vaca: || 14 ||

You help and talk with each other mutually and then with one intention, protect (guard) my (that) pledge. (14)

❍ ❍ ❍

याः फलिनीर्या अफला अपुष्पा याश्च पुष्पिणीः ।
बृहस्पतिप्रसूतास्ता नो मुञ्चन्त्वंहसः ॥ १५ ॥

yā: phalinīryā aphalā apuṣpā yāśca puṣpiṇī: |
bṛhaspatiprasūtāstā no muñcantvaṃhasa: || 15 ||

All those herbal plants, which fructify or do not (fructify), in which flowers appear or in which no flowers appear, all those medicinal herbs must let us liberate from misery by the command of 'Brihaspati' (Guru of Gods). (15)

❍ ❍ ❍

मुञ्चन्तु मा शपथ्या३दथो वरुण्यादुत ।
अथो यमस्य पड्वीशात् सर्वस्माद्देवकिल्बिषात् ॥ १६ ॥

muñcantu mā śapathyā3datho varuṇyāduta |
atho yamasya paḍvīśāt sarvasmāddevakilbiṣāt || 16 ||

Let me be freed (by the herbal medicines) from the calamity, built by the pledges of the enemies or objections set behind me by Varuṇa. Similarly, may they also redeem me from the bonds of Yama (God of death) and offences done against the Gods. (16)

❍ ❍ ❍

अवपतन्तीरवदन् दिव ओषधयस्परि ।
यं जीवमश्नवामहै न स रिष्याति पूरुषः ॥ १७ ॥

avapatantīravadan diva oṣadhayaspari |
yaṃ jīvamaśnavāmahai na sa riṣyāti pūruṣa: || 17 ||

Descending on earth from heaven, hither and thither, these herbs pledged that if they accept any man during his life span, he will never get ruined. (17)

❍ ❍ ❍

या ओषधीः सोमराज्ञीर्बह्वीः शतविचक्षणाः ।
तासां त्वमस्युत्तमारं कामाय शं हृदे ॥ १८ ॥

yā oṣadhī: somarājñīrbahvī: śatavicakṣaṇā: |
tāsāṃ tvamasyuttamāraṃ kāmāya śaṃ hṛde || 18 ||

Being in multitude, endowed with hundreds of efficacies, 'Soma' the king of herbs, Thou art excellent in the midst of all herbs, and art competent in fulfilling our wishes, providing happiness to our hearts. (18)

❍ ❍ ❍

या ओषधीः सोमराज्ञीर्विष्ठिताः पृथिवीमनु ।
बृहस्पतिप्रसूता अस्यै सं दत्त वीर्यम् ॥ १९ ॥

yā oṣadhī: somarājñīrviṣṭhitā: pṛthivīmanu |
bṛhaspatiprasūtā asyai saṃ datta vīryam || 19 ||

The Herbs (medicinal plants), which are scattered over the backside of the earth, hither and thither, whose king is 'Soma', and all of Ye (others), dedicate Thy respective energy to the herbs (in my hand) at the command of Brihaspati. (19)

❍ ❍ ❍

मा वो रिषत् खनिता यस्मै चाहं खनामि वः ।
द्विपच्चतुष्पदस्माकं सर्वमस्त्वनातुरम् ॥ २० ॥

mā vo riṣat khanitā yasmai cāhaṃ khanāmi va: |
dvipaccatuṣpadasmākaṃ sarvamastvanāturam || 20 ||

(O Herbs!) I dig Thee out from the womb of the earth, and the patient (the ailing man) for whom I do so, let there be no disruption (upsetness) in their life (the two of them). So do all our two-footed and four-footed beings (men and animals) and other beings—let all of them be healthy (free from diseases). (20)

❍ ❍ ❍

याश्चेदमुपशृण्वान्ते याश्च दूरं परागताः ।
सर्वाः संगत्य वीरुधो ऽस्यै सं दत्त वीर्यम् ॥ २१ ॥

yāścedamupaśṛṇvānte yāśca dūraṃ parāgatā: |
sarvā: saṃgatya vīrudho 'syai saṃ datta vīryam || 21 ||

O Herbal creepers! Those among Thee who hear me and those of Ye who are out away on their respective act, all of Ye, together, dedicate Thy energy to the herbs (that I have in hand). (21)

❍ ❍ ❍

ओषधयः सं वदन्ते सोमेन सह राज्ञा ।
यस्मै कृणोति ब्राह्मणस्तं राजन् पारयामसि ॥ २२ ॥

oṣadhaya: saṃ vadante somena saha rājñā |
yasmai kṛṇoti brāhmaṇastaṃ rājan pārayāmasi || 22 ||

The entire (group of) herbs pledge in agreement before their King, Soma, O King! For whom this Brahmin (Kavirāj) consecrates us, we redeem him beyond diseases. (22)

❍ ❍ ❍

त्वमुत्तमास्योषधे तव वृक्षा उपस्तयः ।
उपस्तिरस्तु सोऽस्माकं यो अस्माँ अभिदासति ॥ २३ ॥
[ऋक्० १० । १७]

tvamuttamāsyoṣadhe tava vṛkṣā upastaya: |
upastirastu so'smākaṃ yo asmāṁ abhidāsati || 23 ||
[ṛk. 10 | 17]

O Herbs! Thou art the best. All the trees are subservient, obeying Thee. (Likewise) One, who wants to torment us, has to remain under our control (as a slave). (23)

❍ ❍ ❍

Hymns on Longevity of Life
दीर्घायुष्य सूक्त

This Sūkta 'Dīrghāyu Sūkta' (The Longevity of Life Sūktam) belongs to the 'Pippalād' (पिप्पलाद) branch of the 'Atharvaveda'. This provides longevity, equally, to all the beings. The seer of the mantra, sage 'Pippalād' prays to Gods, sages, demi-gods, planets, directions, herbs and rivers and oceans etc. for longevity. Longevity is desired, almost, by all, hence it is important as a prayer.

The text follows hereunder:

सं मा सिञ्चन्तु मरुतः सं पूषा सं बृहस्पतिः ।
सं मायमग्निः सिञ्चन्तु प्रजया च धनेन च ।
दीर्घमायुः कृणोतु मे ॥ १ ॥

**saṃ mā siñcantu maruta: saṃ pūṣā saṃ bṛhaspati: |
saṃ māyamagni: siñcantu prajayā ca dhanena ca |
dīrghamāyu: kṛṇotu me || 1 ||**

May the hosts of God, Maruta (Gods of winds), Pūṣā (The Sun), Brihaspati (Guru of Gods) and Fire (God of Fire) pour out on me progeny and wealth, and bless me with longevity. (1)

❍ ❍ ❍

सं मा सिञ्चन्त्वादित्याः सं मा सिञ्चन्त्वग्नयः ।
इन्द्रः समस्मान् सिञ्चतु प्रजया च धनेन च ।
दीर्घमायुः कृणोतु मे ॥ २ ॥

**saṃ mā siñcantvādityā: saṃ mā siñcantvagnaya: |
indra: samasmān siñcatu prajayā ca dhanena ca |
dīrghamāyu: kṛṇotu me || 2 ||**

May Āditya (The Sun God) (a son of Aditi, Agni (The Fire-God) and Indra (King of Gods) pour out on me progeny and wealth and bless me with longevity. (2)

❍ ❍ ❍

सं मा सिञ्चन्त्वरुषः समर्का ऋषयश्च ये ।
पूषा समस्मान् सिञ्चतु प्रजया च धनेन च ।
दीर्घमायुः कृणोतु मे ॥ ३ ॥

saṃ mā siñcantvaruṣa: samarkā ṛṣayaśca ye |
pūṣā samasmān siñcatu prajayā ca dhanena ca |
dīrghamāyu: kṛṇotu me || 3 ||

May the flames of fire, Prāṇa (vital-breath), group of sages and Pūṣā pour out on me progeny and wealth and bless me with longevity. (3)

❍ ❍ ❍

सं मा सिञ्चन्तु गन्धर्वाप्सरसः सं मा सिञ्चन्तु देवताः ।
भगः समस्मान् सिञ्चतु प्रजया च धनेन च ।
दीर्घमायुः कृणोतु मे ॥ ४ ॥

saṃ mā siñcantu gandharvāpsarasa: saṃ mā siñcantu devatā: |
bhaga: samasmān siñcatu prajayā ca dhanena ca |
dīrghamāyu: kṛṇotu me || 4 ||

May the demigods* and nymphs (Gandharva and Apsarās), Gods and good fortune pour out on me progeny and wealth and bless me with longevity. (4)

* celestial musicians

❍ ❍ ❍

सं मा सिञ्चतु पृथिवी सं मा सिञ्चन्तु या दिवः ।
अन्तरिक्षं समस्मान् सिञ्चतु प्रजया च धनेन च ।
दीर्घमायुः कृणोतु मे ॥ ५ ॥

saṃ mā siñcatu pṛthivī saṃ mā siñcantu yā diva: |
antarikṣaṃ samasmān siñcatu prajayā ca dhanena ca |
dīrghamāyu: kṛṇotu me || 5 ||

May the earth, heaven and space (atmosphere between heaven and earth) pour out on me progeny and wealth and bless me with longevity. (5)

❍ ❍ ❍

सं मा सिञ्चन्तु प्रदिशः सं मा सिञ्चन्तु या दिशः ।
आशाः समस्मान् सिञ्चन्तु प्रजया च धनेन च ।
दीर्घमायुः कृणोतु मे ॥ ६ ॥

saṃ mā siñcantu pradiśa: saṃ mā siñcantu yā diśa: |
āśā: samasmān siñcantu prajayā ca dhanena ca |
dīrghamāyu: kṛṇotu me || 6 ||

May the four directions and the intermediary directions (Ten directions),—the intermediate points of quarters and the upper and lower regions pour out on me progeny and wealth and bless me with longevity. (6)

❍ ❍ ❍

सं मा सिञ्चन्तु कृषयः सं मा सिञ्चन्त्वोषधीः ।
सोमः समस्मान् सिञ्चतु प्रजया च धनेन च ।
दीर्घमायुः कृणोतु मे ॥ ७ ॥

saṃ mā siñcantu kṛṣaya: saṃ mā siñcantvoṣadhī: |
soma: samasmān siñcatu prajayā ca dhanena ca |
dīrghamāyu: kṛṇotu me || 7 ||

May the produces of farming—grains, herbs and soma* pour out on me progeny and wealth, and bless me with longevity. (7)

* Soma plant—provides kind of juice. (सोमरस)

❍ ❍ ❍

सं मा सिञ्चन्तु नद्यः सं मा सिञ्चन्तु सिन्धवः ।
समुद्रः समस्मान् सिञ्चतु प्रजया च धनेन च ।
दीर्घमायुः कृणोतु मे ॥ ८ ॥

saṃ mā siñcantu nadya: saṃ mā siñcantu sindhava: |
samudra: samasmān siñcatu prajayā ca dhanena ca |
dīrghamāyu: kṛṇotu me || 8 ||

May the rivers, Sindhu (great-river) and oceans pour out on me progeny and wealth and bless me with longevity. (8)

❍ ❍ ❍

सं मा सिञ्चन्त्वापः सं मा सिञ्चन्तु कृष्टयः ।
सत्यं समस्मान् सिञ्चतु प्रजया च धनेन च ।
दीर्घमायुः कृणोतु मे ॥ ९ ॥
[अथर्व० पैप्पलाद]

saṃ mā siñcantvāpa: saṃ mā siñcantu kṛṣṭaya: |
satyaṃ samasmān siñcatu prajayā ca dhanena ca |
dīrghamāyu: kṛṇotu me || 9 ||
[atharva. paippalāda]

May the water, cultivated-herbs (कृष्ट औषधियाँ) and reality (truth) pour out on me progeny and wealth and bless me with longevity. (9)

❍ ❍ ❍

Hymns on Existence (Truth or Reality)

ऋत सूक्त

The 190th Sūkta of 10th Section (Mandal) of the Rigveda is 'Ṛta Sūkta' (ऋत सूक्त) (The Sūkta on Truth-Existence). The sage of the Sūkta is 'Mādhuccchanda Aghamarṣaṇa', the deity 'Bhāvavritta' and the metre is 'anuṣtupa'. The Sūkta enunciates about the creation (existence). Praying to the Supreme Father, the Over Lord, the sage says: Firstly, 'Ṛta' (Divine Law) and 'Truth' (in general) appeared as a result of great austerity (physical – Tapa (penance) (तप). Thereafter, with the grace of the Supreme Being were created the night of annihilation, oceans, samvatsar (year), day-night, Sun, Moon, Heavens and Earth, respectively. This Sūkta is also applied during daily 'Sandhyā' for the purpose of elimination of sins. It comprises three mantrās only

The text follows as under:

ऋतं च सत्यं चाभीद्धात् तपसोऽध्यजायत ।
ततो रात्र्यजायत ततः समुद्रो अर्णवः ॥ १ ॥

ṛtaṃ ca satyaṃ cābhīddhāt tapaso'dhyajāyata |
tato rātryajāyata tata: samudro arṇava: || 1 ||

With the severe penance (Tapa) of the Oversoul (Paramātmā), there appeared 'Ṛta' (Divine Law) and 'Truth' (reality – existence) (firstly). Thereafter, were created night of annihilation and the great ocean, filled with water. (1)

❍ ❍ ❍

समुद्रादर्णवादधि संवत्सरो अजायत ।
अहोरात्राणि विदधद् विश्वस्य मिषतो वशी ॥ २ ॥

samudrādarṇavādadhi saṃvatsaro ajāyata |
ahorātrāṇi vidadhad viśvasya miṣato vaśī || 2 ||

It is after the oceans filled with water, 'samvatsar' (year) was created; later, within wink of eye, the controller of the universe, the Supreme Father created day and night. (2)

❍ ❍ ❍

सूर्याचन्द्रमसौ धाता यथापूर्वमकल्पयत् ।
दिवं च पृथिवीं चाऽन्तरिक्षमथो स्वः ॥ ३ ॥
[ऋग्वेद १० । १९०]

sūryācandramasau dhātā yathāpūrvamakalpayat |
divaṃ ca pṛthivīṃ cā'ntarikṣamatho sva: || 3 ||
[ṛgveda 10 | 190]

Thereafter, the bearer of entire creation, the Oversoul (Paramātmā) created the Sun, Moon, Heavens, Earth, Space (atmosphere) and joyous heaven and surface of the ground and sky as they were created earlier. (3)

❍ ❍ ❍

A Clarion Call of Baba Neeb Karori Maharaj

- ***Love All***
- ***Serve All***
- ***Feed All***

Hymns on (Divine) Faith

श्रद्धा सूक्त

The 151st Sūkta in the 10th section (Mandal) of the Rigveda is known as 'Śraddhā Sūkta' (श्रद्धा – Divine Faith). The sage of this Sūkta is 'Śraddhā Kāmāyani' (a female-sage), the deity is 'Śraddhā', and the metre used is 'Anuṣṭupa'. The Sūkta depicts the greatness (power) of (divine) faith. The Sūkta also enunciates that there is no difference between the God having great names, like Agni, Indra, Varuṇa and the other deities, having scanty mention. Faith carries paramount importance in all the sacrificial Karmās (activities) and in worshipping etc. The sage invokes 'Śraddha' as a Goddess and prays Her to initiate firm faith in our hearts. The Sūkta comprises five mantrās in all.

The text follows as under:

श्रद्धयाग्निः समिध्यते श्रद्धया हूयते हविः ।
श्रद्धां भगस्य मूर्धनि वचसा वेदयामसि ॥ १ ॥

śraddhayāgni: samidhyate śraddhayā hūyate havi: |
śraddhāṃ bhagasya mūrdhani vacasā vedayāmasi || 1 ||

The sacrificial fire is iginted through the faith (श्रद्धा) alone. The oblations are offered in yajña with faith. We eulogise 'Śraddhā' which is above wealth or opulence. (1)

❍ ❍ ❍

प्रियं श्रद्धे ददतः प्रियं श्रद्धे दिदासतः ।
प्रियं भोजेषु यज्वस्विदं म उदितं कृधि ॥ २ ॥

priyaṃ śraddhe dadata: priyaṃ śraddhe didāsata: |
priyaṃ bhojeṣu yajvasvidaṃ ma uditaṃ kṛdhi || 2 ||

O Śraddhā (Goddess of Faith)! Bless the donor with the

desired fruits (wishes). O Śraddhā! (with Thy grace) Grant aspired wishes of the donor. Grant wishes of those having thirst for worldly enjoyments. (2)

❍ ❍ ❍

यथा देवा असुरेषु श्रद्धामुग्रेषु चक्रिरे ।
एवं भोजेषु यज्वस्वस्माकमुदितं कृधि ॥ ३ ॥

yathā devā asureṣu śraddhāmugreṣu cakrire |
evaṃ bhojeṣu yajvasvasmākamuditaṃ kṛdhi || 3 ||

Just as the Gods resolved to destroy the demons, in order to defeat them, so do grant, and provide with aspired enjoyments to our faithful performers of sacrifices (याज्ञिक). (3)

❍ ❍ ❍

श्रद्धां देवा यजमाना वायुगोपा उपासते ।
श्रद्धां हृदय्य३ याकूत्या श्रद्धया विन्दते वसु ॥ ४ ॥

śraddhāṃ devā yajamānā vāyugopā upāsate |
śraddhāṃ hṛdayya3 yākūtyā śraddhayā vindate vasu || 4 ||

Getting secured from the strong winds, Gods and men engage in worshipping 'Śraddhā'; with resolution in mind (अंतः करण) or heart, they worship 'Śraddhā' (The Goddess of Faith). Faith brings prosperity and wealth. (4)

❍ ❍ ❍

श्रद्धा प्रातर्हवामहे श्रद्धां मध्यंदिनं परि ।
श्रद्धां सूर्यस्य निम्रुचि श्रद्धे श्रद्धापयेह नः ॥ ५ ॥
[ऋग्वेद १० । १५१]

śraddhā prātarhavāmahe śraddhāṃ
madhyaṃdinaṃ pari |
śraddhāṃ sūryasya nimruci śraddhe
śraddhāpayeha na: || 5 ||
[ṛgveda 10 | 151]

We pray to (Goddess) Śraddhā in the morning. We worship 'Śraddhā' during noon-time. We also pray to 'Śraddhā' at the sun-set time. O Goddess Śraddhā! Grace us to be faithful (श्रद्धावान्) in the world. (5)

❍ ❍ ❍

Chaitanya Mahaprabhu's Cardinal Lesson

"Be more humble than a blade of grass, more tolerant than a tree, always offering respect on to others and never expecting any in return."

The Rigvedic Nectar of Maxims
ऋग्वेदीय सूक्ति-सुधा

१-न स सखा यो न ददाति सख्ये । (१० । ११७ । ४)

1. na sa sakhā yo na dadāti sakhye | (10 | 117 | 4)

'वह मित्र ही क्या, जो अपने मित्र को सहायता नहीं देता।'
(१० । ११७ । ४)

One is not a friend, who does not assist his friend.
(10 | 117 | 4)

❍ ❍ ❍

२-सत्यस्य नावः सुकृतमपीपरन् ॥ (९ । ७३ । १)

2. satyasya nāva: sukṛtamapīparan || (9 | 73 | 1)

'धर्मात्मा को सत्य की नाव पार लगाती है।' (९ । ७३ । १)
The boat of truth takes the righteous across. (9 | 73 | 1)

❍ ❍ ❍

३-स्वस्ति पन्थामनु चरेम । (५ । ५१ । १५)

3. svasti panthāmanu carema | (5 | 51 | 15)

'हे प्रभो! हम कल्याण-मार्ग के पथिक बनें।' (५ । ५१ । १५)
a **(5 | 51 | 15)**
O Paramātmā! May we tread on the path of welfare (righteousness). (5 | 51 | 15)

❍ ❍ ❍

४-अग्ने सख्ये मा रिषामा वयं तव ॥ (१ । ९४ । ४)

4. agne sakhye mā riṣāmā vayaṃ tava || (1 | 94 | 4)

'परमेश्वर! हम तेरे मित्र भाव में दुःखी और विनष्ट न हों।'
(१ । ९४ । ४)

O Agni (Fire God)! May we not suffer or get destroyed in befriending Thee. (1 | 94 | 4)

❍ ❍ ❍

५-शुद्धाः पूता भवत यज्ञियासः ॥ (१० । १८ । २)

5-śuddhā: pūtā bhavata yajñiyāsa: || (10 | 18 | 2)

'शुद्ध और पवित्र बनो तथा परोपकारमय जीवनवाले हो।'
(१० । १८ । २)

Be purged and pious and be philanthropic in life. (10 | 18 | 2)

❍ ❍ ❍

६-सत्यमूचुर्नर एवा हि चक्रुः । (४ । ३३ । ६)

6. satyamūcurnara evā hi cakru: | (4 | 33 | 6)

'पुरुषों ने सत्य का ही प्रतिपादन किया है और वैसा ही आचरण किया है।' (४ । ३३ । ६)

The righteous men establish truthfulness and observe it in conduct. (4 | 33 | 6)

❍ ❍ ❍

७-सुगा ऋतस्य पन्थाः ॥ (८ । ३१ । १३)

7. sugā ṛtasya panthā: || (8 | 31 | 13)

'सत्य का मार्ग सुख से गमन करने योग्य है, सरल है।'
(८ । ३१ । १३)

The path of righteousness is comfortable to tread on, and is simple. (8 | 31 | 13)

❍ ❍ ❍

८-ऋतस्य पन्थां न तरन्ति दुष्कृतः ॥ (९ । ७६ । ६)

8. ṛtasya panthāṃ na taranti duṣkṛta: || (9 | 76 | 6)

'सत्य के मार्ग को दुष्कर्मी पार नहीं कर पाते।' (९ । ७६ । ६)
The unchaste and faithless fail to cross over the path of truthfulness. (9 | 76 | 6)

❍ ❍ ❍

९-दक्षिणावन्तो अमृतं भजन्ते । (१ । १२५ । ६)

9. dakṣiṇāvanto amṛtaṃ bhajante | (1 | 125 | 6)

'दानी अमरपद प्राप्त करते हैं।' (१ । १२५ । ६)
Munificents attain immortal-state. (1 | 125 | 6)

❍ ❍ ❍

१०-समाना हृदयानि वः । (१० । १९१ । ४)

10. samānā hṛdayāni va: | (10 | 191 | 4)

'तुम्हारे हृदय (मन) एक-से हों।' (१० । १९१ । ४)
May your hearts be harmonious with one another.
(10 | 191 | 4)

❍ ❍ ❍

११-सरस्वतीं देवयन्तो हवन्ते । (१० । १७ । ७)

11. sarasvatīṃ devayanto havante | (10 | 17 | 7)

'देवपदके अभिलाषी सरस्वती का आह्वान करते है।'
(१० । १७ । ७)
Aspirants of divinity invoke Goddess Saraswati. (10 | 17 | 7)

❍ ❍ ❍

१२-उद्बुध्यध्वं समनसः सखायः । (१० । १०१ । १)

12. udbudhyadhvaṃ samanasa: sakhāya: | (10 | 101 | 1)

'एक विचार और एक प्रकार के ज्ञान से युक्त मित्र जनो उठो। जागो।।' (१० । १०१ । १)
Friends having one kind of thought and knowledge! Rise! Awake!! (10 | 101 | 1)

❍ ❍ ❍

१३-इच्छन्ति देवाः सुन्वन्तं न स्वप्नाय स्पृहयन्ति ।

(८ । २ । १८)

13. icchanti devā: sunvantaṃ na svapnāya spṛhayanti || (8 | 2 | 18)

'देवता यज्ञकर्ता, पुरुषार्थी तथा भक्त को चाहते हैं, आलसी से प्रेम नहीं करते।' (८ । २ । १८)

Gods like sacrifice-performers, industrious people and devotees. They do not love the lazy (bereft of activity). (8 | 2 | 18)

❍ ❍ ❍

14-यच्छा नः शर्म सप्रथः ॥ (१ । २२ । १५)

14. yacchā na: śarma sapratha: || (1 | 22 | 15)

'भगवन्! तुम हमें अनन्त अखण्डैकरसपरिपूर्ण सुखों को प्रदान करो।' (१ । २२ । १५)

Bhagvān (The Oversoul)! Bless us with imperishable pleasurable-joyousness. (1 | 22 | 15)

❍ ❍ ❍

१५-सुम्नमस्मे ते अस्तु । (१ । ११४ । १०)

15. sumnamasme te astu | (1 | 114 | 10)

'हे परमात्मन्! हमारे अंदर तुम्हारा महान् (कल्याणकारी) सुख प्रकट हो।' (१ । ११४ । १०)

O Overlord! Let Thy great propitious joy appear within us. (1 | 114 | 10)

❍ ❍ ❍

१६-अस्य प्रियासः सख्ये स्याम ॥ (४ । १७ । ९)

16. asya priyāsa: sakhye syāma || (4 | 17 | 9)

'हम देवताओं से प्रीति युक्त मैत्री करें।' (४ । १७ । ९)

May we have loving friendship with Gods. (4 | 17 | 9)

❍ ❍ ❍

१७-पुनर्ददताघ्नता जानता सं गमेमहि ॥ (५ । ५१ । १५)

17. punardadatāghnatā jānatā saṃ gamemahi || (5 | 51 | 15)

'हम दानशील पुरुष से, विश्वासघातादि न करनेवाले से और विवेक-विचार-ज्ञानवान्‌से सत्संग करते रहें।' (५ । ५१ । १५)

May we associate with alms-givers, untreacherous and wise-reflective-knowledgeable men.

(5 | 51 | 15)

❍ ❍ ❍

१८-जीवा ज्योतिरशीमहि ॥ (७ । ३२ । २६)

18. jīvā jyotiraśīmahi || (7 | 32 | 26)

'हम जीवगण प्रभु की कल्याणमयी ज्योति को प्रतिदिन प्राप्त करें।' (७ । ३२ । २६)

'May we, the living beings (Jīvās –जीवगण), receive the propitious brilliant light of Paramātmā every day.' (7 | 32 | 26)

❍ ❍ ❍

१९-भद्रं नो अपि वातय मनो दक्षमुत क्रतुम् । (१० । २५ । १)

19. bhadraṃ no api vātaya mano dakṣamuta kratum | (10 | 25 | 1)

'हे परमेश्वर! हम सबको कल्याणकारक मन, कल्याणकारक बल और कल्याणकारक कर्म प्रदान करो।' (१० । २५ । १)

O Paramātmā Oversoul! Bless us with propitious mind, propitious energy and propitious Karmās (actions).

(10 | 25 | 1)

❍ ❍ ❍

The Yajurvedic Nectar of Maxims
यजुर्वेदीय सूक्ति-सुधा

१-तस्मिन् ह तस्थुर्भुवनानि विश्वा । (३१ । १९)

1. tasmin ha tasthurbhuvanāni viśvā | (31 | 19)

'उस परमात्मामें ही सम्पूर्ण लोक स्थित हैं।' (३१ । १९)
The entire universe exists in That Paramātmā (The Oversoul).' (31 | 19)

❍ ❍ ❍

२-अस्माकꣳ सन्त्वाशिषः सत्याः । (२ । १०)

2. asmākaꣳ santvāśiṣa: satyā: | (2 | 10)

'हमारी कामनाएँ सच्ची हों।' (२ । १०)
'Let our aspirations be truthful.' (2 | 10)

❍ ❍ ❍

३-भूत्यै जागरणमभूत्यै स्वपनम् (३० । १७)

3. bhūtyai jāgaraṇamabhūtyai svapanam (30 | 17)

'जागना (ज्ञान) ऐश्वर्यप्रद है। सोना (आलस्य) दरिद्रताका मूल है।' (३० । १७)
Wakefulness (enlightenment) is divinity. Sleepiness (lethargy) is the root of wretchedness (extreme poverty). (30 | 17)

❍ ❍ ❍

४-सं ज्योतिषाभूम ॥ (२ । २५)

4. saṃ jyotiṣābhūma || (2 | 25)

'हम ब्रह्मज्ञानसे संयुक्त हों।' (२ । २५)

May we be in unison with the 'Absolute Enlightenment' (ब्रह्मज्ञान). (2 | 25)

❍ ❍ ❍

५-अगन्म ज्योतिरमृता अभूम । (८ । ५२)

5. aganma jyotiramṛtā abhūma | (8 | 52)

'हम तुम्हारी ज्योति को प्राप्त कर मृत्यु के भय से मुक्त हों।' (८ । ५२)

'May we be free from the fear of death, attaining Thy Light.' (8 | 52)

❍ ❍ ❍

६-वैश्वानरज्योतिर्भूयासम् । (२० । २३)

6-vaiśvānarajyotirbhūyāsam | (20 | 23)

'मैं परमात्मा की महिमामयी ज्योति को प्राप्त करूँ।' (२० । २३)

'May we attain the magnificient Light of Paramātmā (The Supreme Soul)'. **(20 | 23)**

❍ ❍ ❍

७-सुमृडीको भवतु विश्ववेदाः । (२० । ५१)

7. sumṛḍīko bhavatu viśvavedā: | (20 | 51)

'सर्वज्ञ प्रभु हमारे लिए सुखकारी हों।' (२० । ५१)

'May the Omniscient Lord be propitious for us.' **(20 | 51)**

❍ ❍ ❍

८-अप नः शोशुचदघम् (३५ । ६)

8-apa na: śośucadagham (35 | 6)

'देवगण हमारे पापों को भली भाँति नष्ट कर दें।' (३५ । ६)

'May Gods, completely, erase our sins.' (35 | 6)

❍ ❍ ❍

९-स्योना पृथिवि नः । (३५ । २१)

9. syonā pṛthivi na: | (35 | 21)

'हे पृथिवी! तुम हमारे लिए सुख देने वाली हो।' (३५ । २१)
'O Earth! Be Thou auspicious for us.'

❍ ❍ ❍

१०-इहैव रातयः सन्तु ॥ (३८ । १३)

10. ihaiva rātaya: santu || (38 | 13)

'हमें अपने ही स्थान में अनेक प्रकार के ऐश्वर्य प्राप्त हों।'
(३८ । १३)
'May all kinds of opulences become available to us at our own place.' (38 | 13)

❍ ❍ ❍

११-ब्रह्मणस्तन्वं पाहि । (३८ । १९)

11. brahmaṇastanvaṃ pāhi | (38 | 19)

'हे भगवन्! तुम ब्राह्मण के शरीर का पालन (रक्षण) करो।'
(३८ । १९)
'O Bhagwān (Paramātmā)! Nourish (Protect) the body of Brahmin.' (38 | 19)

❍ ❍ ❍

The Sāmvedic Nectar of Maxims

सामवेदीय सूक्ति-सुधा

१-भद्रा उत प्रशस्तयः (१११)

1. bhadrā uta praśastaya: (111)

'हमें कल्याणकारिणी स्तुतियाँ प्राप्त हों।' (१११)
'Let us receive propitious hymns.' (111)

❍ ❍ ❍

२-वि रक्षो वि मृधो जहि । (१८६७)

2. vi rakśo vi mṛdho jahi | (1867)

'राक्षसों और हिंसक शत्रुओं का नाश करो।' (१८६७)
'Let the demons and violent enemies be eliminated.' (1867)

❍ ❍ ❍

३-जीवा ज्योतिरशीमहि । (२५९)

3. jīvā jyotiraśīmahi | (259)

'हम शरीरधारी प्राणी विशिष्ट ज्योति को प्राप्त करें।' (२५९)
'May we, the body-bearing-beings (शरीरधारी प्राणी), receive distinctly brilliant light.' (249)

❍ ❍ ❍

४-नः सन्तु सनिषन्तु नो धियः ॥ (५५५)

4. na: santu saniṣantu no dhiya: || (555)

'हमारी देवविषयक स्तुतियाँ देवताओं को प्राप्त हों।' (५५५)
'May the Gods receive our divine eulogies.' (555)

❍ ❍ ❍

५-विश्वे देवा मम शृण्वन्तु यज्ञम् । (६१०)

5. viśve devā mamaśṛṇvantu yajñam | (610)

'सम्पूर्ण देवगण मेरे मान करने योग्य पूजन को स्वीकार करें।' (६१०)

'May the entire group of Gods accept our adorable worship. (610)

❍ ❍ ❍

६-अहं प्रवदिता स्याम् ॥ (६११)

6. ahaṃ pravaditā syām || (611)

'मैं सर्वत्र प्रगल्भतासे बोलने वाला बनूँ।' (६११)
'May I be blessed to speak boldly, everywhere.' (611)

❍ ❍ ❍

७-यः सपर्यति तस्य प्राविता भव । (८५४)

7. ya: saparyati tasya prāvitā bhava | (854)

'जो तेरी पूजा करता है, उसका तू रक्षक हो।' (८५४)
Thou shalt be his protector, who worships Thee. (845)

❍ ❍ ❍

८-मनौ अधि पवमानः राजा मेधाभिः अन्तरिक्षेण यातवे ईयते । (८३३)

8. manau adhi pavamāna: rājā medhābhi: antarikṣeṇa yātave īyate | (833)

'मनुष्यों में शुद्ध होने वाला अपनी बुद्धि से उच्च मार्ग से जाने की कोशिश करता है।' (८३३)
The upright (undefiled by his own selfhood) among men, by his wisdom, ventures to tread on the elevated path (in life). (833)

❍ ❍ ❍

९-जनाय उर्जं वरिवः कृधि । (८४२)

9. janāya urjaṃ variva: kṛdhi | (842)

'लोगों में श्रेष्ठ बल पैदा करो।' (८४२)
'Inculcate excellent strength in the people.' (842)

❍ ❍ ❍

१०-पुरन्धिं जनय । (८६१)

10. purandhiṃ janaya | (861)

'बहुत से उत्तम कर्म करने में समर्थ बुद्धि को उत्पन्न करो।' (८६१)
Beget intellect, competent in performing many distinguished feats. (861)

❍ ❍ ❍

११-विचर्षणिः, अभिष्टिकृत्, इन्द्रियं हिन्वानः, ज्यायः, महित्वं आनशे । (८३९)

11. vicarṣaṇi:, abhiṣṭikṛt, indriyaṃ hinvāna:, jyāya:, mahitvaṃ ānaśe | (839)

'विशेष ज्ञानी और इष्ट की सिद्धि करनेवाला अपनी शक्ति को प्रयोग में लाकर श्रेष्ठत्व प्राप्त करता है।' (८३९)
'A distinctly wise man and accomplisher of pious desires achieves excellence by the application of his powers. (839)

❍ ❍ ❍

१२-ऋतावृधौ ऋतस्पशौ बृहन्तं क्रतुं ऋतेन आशाथे । (८४८)

12-ṛtāvṛdhau ṛtaspaśau bṛhantaṃ kratuṃ ṛtena āśāthe | (848)

'सत्य बढ़ाने वाले, सत्य को स्पर्श करने वाले सत्य से ही महान् कार्य करते हैं।' (८४८)

'Those who expand truth, contact truth, accomplish great tasks by the truth itself.' (848)

❍ ❍ ❍

१३-यः सखा सुशेवः अद्वयुः । (६४९)

13. ya: sakhā suśeva: advayu: | (649)

'जो उत्तम मित्र, उत्तम प्रकार से सेवा के योग्य तथा अच्छा व्यवहार करने वाला है, वह उत्तम होता है।' (६४९)

He, who is an excellent friend, highly serviceable with excellent conduct, is superb. (649)

❍ ❍ ❍

१४-ईडेन्यः नमस्यः तमांसि तिरः दर्शतः वृषा अग्निः सं इध्यते । (१५३८)

14. īḍenya: namasya: tamāṃsi tira: darśata: vṛṣā agni: saṃ idhyate | (1538)

'जो प्रशंसनीय, नमस्कार करने योग्य, अन्धकार को दूर करनेवाला दर्शनीय और बलवान् है; उसका तेज बढ़ता है।' (१५३८)

The man, who is appreciable, reverend, dispeller of darkness (ignorance), charming and stout, his aura increases.

❍ ❍ ❍

The Atharv-Vedic Nectar of Maxims

अथर्ववेदीय सूक्ति-सुधा

१-स एष एक एकवृदेक एव। (१३ । ५ । २०)

1. sa eṣa eka ekavṛdeka eva | (13 | 5 | 20)

'वह ईश्वर एक और सचमुच एक ही है।' (१३ । ५ । २०)
That Supreme is one, and, verily, one. (13 | 5 | 20)

❍ ❍ ❍

२-एक एव नमस्यो विक्ष्वीड्यः। (२ । २ । १)

2. eka eva namasyo vikṣvīḍya: | (2 | 2 | 1)

'एक परमेश्वर ही पूजा के योग्य और प्रजाओं में स्तुत्य है।'
(२ । २ । १)

The one Oversoul (Paramātmā) alone is worthy of worship and hallowed among progenies. (2 | 2 | 1)

❍ ❍ ❍

३-तमेव विद्वान् न बिभाय मृत्योः। (१० । ८ । ४४)

3. tameva vidvān na bibhāya mṛtyo: | (10 | 8 | 44)

'उस आत्मा को ही जान लेने पर मनुष्य मृत्यु से नहीं डरता।'
(१० । ८ । ४४)

Man is not scared of death, when he knows that Supreme (Soul). (10 | 8 | 44)

❍ ❍ ❍

४-रमन्तां पुण्या लक्ष्मीर्याः पापीस्ता अनीनशम्॥
(७ । ११५ । ४)

4-ramantāṃ puṇyā lakṣmīryā: pāpīstā anīnaśam ||
(7 | 115 | 4)

'पुण्य की कमाई मेरे घर की शोभा बढ़ाये, पाप की कमाई को मैंने नष्ट कर दिया है।' (७ । ११५ । ४)

May the wealth of my rightful earnings increase the splendour of my home; the sinful earnings have been destroyed by me. (7 | 115 | 4)

❍ ❍ ❍

५-मा जीवेभ्यः प्र मदः । (८ । १ । ७)

5-mā jīvebhya: pra mada: | (8 | 1 | 7)

'प्राणियों की ओर से बेपरवाह मत हो।' (८ । १ । ७)

Do not be uncaring towards all living beings. (8 | 1 | 7)

❍ ❍ ❍

६-वयं सर्वेषु यशसः स्याम ॥ (६ । ५८ । २)

6. vayaṃ sarveṣu yaśasa: syāma || (6 | 58 | 2)

'हम समस्त जीवों में यशस्वी होवें।' (६ । ५८ । २)

May we be renowned amongst all living beings. (6 | 58 | 2)

❍ ❍ ❍

७-उद्यानं ते पुरुष नावयानम् । (८ । १ । ६)

7. udyānaṃ te puruṣa nāvayānam | (8 | 1 | 6)

'पुरुष! तुम्हें तेरे लिए ऊपर उठना चाहिये, न कि नीचे गिरना।' (८ । १ । ६)

'Man! Rise up for your own sake, not that you fall down. (8 | 1 | 6)

❍ ❍ ❍

८-मा नो द्विक्षत कश्चन । (१२ । १ । २४)

8-mā no dvikṣata kaścana | (12 | 1 | 24)

'हमसे कोई भी द्वेष करनेवाला न हो।' (१२ । १ । २४)
Let none bear animosity against us. (12 | 1 | 24)

❍ ❍ ❍

९-सम्यञ्चः सव्रता भूत्वा वाचं वदत भद्रया । (३ । ३० । ३)

9. samyañca: savratā bhūtvā vācaṃ vadata bhadrayā | (3 | 30 | 3)

'समान गति, समान कर्म, समान ज्ञान और समान नियम वाले बनकर परस्पर कल्याणयुक्त वाणी से बोलो।' (३ । ३० । ३)
Observing similar rules with similar speed, similar deeds and similar knowledge, speak mutually, propitiously. (3 | 30 | 3)

❍ ❍ ❍

१०-मा मा प्रापत् पाप्मा मोत मृत्युः । (१७ । १ । २९)

10. mā mā prāpat pāppā mota mṛtyu: | (17 | 1 | 29)

'मुझे पाप और मौत न व्यापे।' (१७ । १ । २९)
Do not let sins and death pervade me. (17 | 1 | 29)

❍ ❍ ❍

११-अभि वर्धतां पयसाभि राष्ट्रेण वर्धताम् । (६ । ७८ । २)

11. abhi vardhatāṃ payasābhi rāṣṭreṇa vardhatām | (6 | 78 | 2)

'मनुष्य दुग्धादि पदार्थों से बढ़े और राज्य से बढ़े।' (६ । ७८ । २)
May men prosper with milk-products and nation. (6 | 78 | 2)

❍ ❍ ❍

१२-अरिष्टाः स्याम तन्वा सुवीराः ॥ (५ । ३ । ५)

12. ariṣṭā: syāma tanvā suvīrā: || (5 | 3 | 5)

'हम शरीर से निरोग हों और उत्तम वीर बनें।' (५ । ३ । ५)
May we be healthy (without diseases), physically, and be brave, superbly. (5 | 3 | 5)

❍ ❍ ❍

१३-सर्वान् पथो अनृणा आ क्षियेम ॥ (६ । ११७ । ३)

13. sarvān patho anṛṇā ā kṣiyema || (6 | 117 | 3)

'हम लोग ऋणरहित होकर परलोक के सभी मार्गों पर चलें।'
(६ । ११७ । ३)
May we tread on all the paths of the next world, being (completely) debtless. (6 | 117 | 3)

❍ ❍ ❍

१४-वाचा वदामि मधुमद् । (१ । ३४ । ३)

14. vācā vadāmi madhumad | (1 | 34 | 3)

'वाणी से माधुर्ययुक्त ही बोलता हूँ।' (१ । ३४ । ३)
Speak sweetly spoken words alone. (1 | 34 | 3)

❍ ❍ ❍

१५-ज्योगेव दृशेम सूर्यम् ॥ (१ । ३१ । ४)

15. jyogeva dṛśema sūryam || (1 | 31 | 4)

'हम सूर्य को बहुत काल तक देखते रहें।' (१ । ३१ । ४)
May we watch the Sun for a very long period of time.
(1 | 31 | 4)

❍ ❍ ❍

१६-मा पुरा जरसो मृथाः ॥ (५ । ३० । १७)

16-mā purā jaraso mṛthā: || (5 | 30 | 17)

'हे मनुष्य! तू बुढ़ापे से पहले मत मर।' (५ । ३० । १७)
O Man! You do not die before old age. (5 | 30 | 17)

❍ ❍ ❍

१७-शतहस्त समाहर सहस्त्रहस्त सं किर । (३ । २४ । ५)

17. śatahasta samāhara sahasrahasta saṃ kira | (3 | 24 | 5)

'सैकड़ों हाथों से इकठ्टा करो और हजारों हाथों से बाँटों' (३ । २४ । ५)

Accumulate with hundreds of hands, and spend with thousands of hands. (3 | 24 | 5)

❍ ❍ ❍

१८-शिवं मह्यं मधुमदस्त्वन्नम् ॥ (६ । ७१ । ३)

18. śivaṃ mahyaṃ madhumadastvannam || (6 | 71 | 3)

'मेरे लिए अन्न कल्याणकारी और स्वादिष्ट हो।' (६ । ७१ । ३)
May the food be propitious and tasteful for me. (6 | 71 | 3)

❍ ❍ ❍

१९-शिवा नः सन्तु वार्षिकीः ॥ (१ । ६ । ४)

19. śivā na: santu vārṣikī: || (1 | 6 | 4)

'हमें वर्षा द्वारा प्राप्त जल सुख दे।' (१ । ६ । ४)
May the water available in rains jubilate us. (1 | 6 | 4)

❍ ❍ ❍

20-पितेव पुत्रानभि रक्षतादिमम् ॥ (२ । १३ । १)

20. piteva putrānabhi rakṣatādimam || (2 | 13 | 1)

'हे भगवन्! जिस प्रकार पिता अपने अपराधी पुत्र की रक्षा करता है, उसी प्रकार आप भी इस (हमारे) बालककी रक्षा करें।' (२ । १३ । १)

O Bhagwān (The Oversoul)! Protect this (our) boy, as a father protects his son, even being an outlaw. (2 | 13 | 1)

❍ ❍ ❍

२१-विश्वकर्मन् नमस्ते पह्य१स्मान् । (२ । ३५ । ४)

21-viśvakarman namaste pahya1smān | (2 | 35 | 4)

'हे विश्वकर्मन्! तुमको नमस्कार है, तुम हमारी रक्षा करो।' (२ । ३५ । ४)

'O Viśwakarman (all-creator) obeisances to Thee. Thou shalt protect us.' (2 | 35 | 4)

❍ ❍ ❍

२२-शतं जीवेम शरदः सर्ववीराः ॥ (३ । १२ । ६)

22-śataṃ jīvema śarada: sarvavīrā: || (3 | 12 | 6)

'हम स्वभिलषित पुत्र-पौत्रादिसे परिपूर्ण होकर सौ वर्ष तक जीवित रहें।' (३ । १२ । ६)

'Bless us live for a hundred years with our self-desired sons and grandsons.' (3 | 12 | 6)

❍ ❍ ❍

२३-निर्दुरर्मण्य ऊर्जा मधुमती वाक् । (१६ । २ । १)

23-nirdurarmaṇya ūrjā madhumatī vāk | (16 | 2 | 1)

'हमारी शक्तिशालिनी मीठी वाणी कभी भी दुष्ट स्वभाव वाली न हो।' (१६ । २ । १)

May our powerful sweet speech, never be of wicked nature. (16 | 2 | 1)

❍ ❍ ❍

The Rigvedic Nectar of Mantrās
ऋग्वेदीय मन्त्र सुधा

ॐ वाङ् मे मनसि प्रतिष्ठिता मनो मे वाचि प्रतिष्ठितमाविरावीर्म एधि। वेदस्य म आणीस्थः श्रुतं मे मा प्रहासीः। अनेनाधीते-नाहोरात्रान्संदधाम्यृतं वदिष्यामि। सत्यं वदिष्यामि तन्मामवतु। तद् वक्तारमवतु। अवतु मामवतु वक्तारमवतु वक्तारम्। ॐ शान्तिः! शान्तिः!! शान्तिः!!!

(ऋग्वेद, शान्तिपाठ)

oṃ vāṅ me manasi pratiṣṭhitā mano me vāci pratiṣṭhitamāvirāvīrma edhi| vedasya ma āṇīstha: śrutaṃ me mā prahāsī:| anenādhīte-nāhorātrānsaṃdadhāmyṛtaṃ vadiṣyāmi| satyaṃ vadiṣyāmi tanmāmavatu| tad vaktāramavatu| avatu māmavatu vaktāramavatu vaktāram| oṃ śānti:! śānti:!! śānti:!!!

(ṛgveda, śāntipāṭha)

This is Rigvedic mantra, invoking Paramātmā with a prayer for peace against all kinds of impediments, which may, likely arise in the midst of their vedic studies of scriptures.

O Paramātmā! (The unified form of Existence – Consciousness – Bliss). Let my speech be established in my mind, and the mind be established in my speech in order to have unison of both of them. Speech is to be similar to the thoughts, and the thoughts, the same as the speech. The speech and the thought should follow each other, mutually. O self-radiant Oversoul! Manifest Thyself for me, remove the veil of illusion lying before me. In such a state of things, the seeker asks the speech and the mind, in unison to fetch the vedic-enlightenment to be able to acquire deep vedic-knowledge. Whatever I have heard from the Guru and what I have experienced personally, let that not forsake me. May I keep that remembering forever, and I never forget that I desire ardently to bring day and night together, in this endeavour for studies. This is like, studying and contempleting over Brahma-enlightenment*, day and night; and no time ends up, futilely.

I shall always give utterance to noble and elevated words, devoid of blemishes (ऋतम्). I shall speak nothing but truth. Resolving this way, firmly, I pray, O Paramātmā (Oversoul)! Protect me. Protect my Guru, protect me. Protect my preceptor, enlightening me; O Lord! Protect my preceptor. This is followed by the prayer for peace in order to prevent the possible onslaughts of the three kinds of sufferings (tapās), if any, arising in future. Om Peace! Om Peace!! Om Peace!!!

* ब्रह्मज्ञान

❍ ❍ ❍

मनस्येकं वचस्येकं कर्मण्येकं महात्मनाम् ।
मनस्यन्यत वचस्यन्यत कर्मण्यऽन्यत दुरात्मनाम् ॥

manasyekaṃ vacasyekaṃ karmaṇyekaṃ mahātmanām |
manasyanyata vacasyanyata karmaṇya'nyata durātmanām ||

One observing oneness of mind, speech and action is a great-soul, i.e., Mahātmā. Behaving otherwise than this, one is none else but a wicked-soul, i.e., Durātmā. This is like a whetstone in order to test the goodness of a man.

❍ ❍ ❍

जानन्ति वृष्णो अरुषस्य शेवमुत ब्रध्नस्य शासने रणन्ति ।
दिवोरुचः सुरुचो रोचमाना इळा येषां गण्या माहिना गीः ।
(ऋग्वेद ३ । ७ । ५)

jānanti vṛṣṇo aruṣasya śevamuta bradhnasya śāsane raṇanti |
divoruca: suruco rocamānā iḻā yeṣāṃ gaṇyā māhinā gī: |
(ṛgveda 3 | 7 | 5)

Whose speech is acceptable and appreciable because of (their) dignity, they alone know the wealth of nonviolence, causing rains of happiness; and (they) enjoy delightfulness in the realms of vastness (महत), and emblaze with divine grace. Rigveda 3 | 7 | 5

❍ ❍ ❍

जातो जायते सुदिनत्वे अह्नां समर्य आ विदथे वर्धमानः ।
पुनन्ति धीरा अपसो मनीषा देवया विप्र उदियर्ति वाचम् ॥
(ऋग्वेद ३ । ८ । ५)

jāto jāyate sudinatve ahnāṃ samarya ā vidathe vardhamāna: |
punanti dhīrā apaso manīṣā devayā vipra udiyarti vācam ||
(ṛgveda 3 | 8 | 5)

A man is born to make life beautiful. He toils to achieve his goal during the struggle of life. A composed man purges his deeds (Karmās) through introspection-power; and the wisemen with divine concept, give utterance to speech.

Rigveda 3|8|5

❍ ❍ ❍

स हि सत्यो यं पूर्वे चिद् देवासश्चिद् यमीधिरे ।
होतारं मन्द्रजिह्वमित् सुदीतिभिर्विभावसुम् ॥
(ऋग्वेद ५ । २५ । २)

sa hi satyo yaṃ pūrve cid devāsaścid yamīdhire |
hotāraṃ mandrajihvamit sudītibhirvibhāvasum ||
(ṛgveda 5 | 25 | 2)

That which is true is brilliant, delights the speech; and in the yesteryears, scholars have highlighted that with bright light.

Rigveda 5 | 25 | 2

❍ ❍ ❍

सुविज्ञानं चिकितुषे जनाय सच्चासच्च वचसी पस्पृधाते ।
तयोर्यत् सत्यं यतरदृजीयस्तदित् सोमोऽवति हन्त्यासत् ॥

(ऋग्वेद ७ । १०४ । १२)

suvijñānaṃ cikituṣe janāya saccāsacca vacasī paspṛdhāte |
tayoryat satyaṃ yataradṛjīyastadit somo'vati hantyāsat ||

(ṛgveda 7 | 104 | 12)

For a man aspiring for the research of excellent knowledge, the true and the untrue statements stand competing one another. What is true in them is more simple. One, desiring peace, chooses it and forsakes the untrue.

(Rigveda 10 | 37 | 2)

❍ ❍ ❍

सा मा सत्योक्तिः परि पातु विश्वतो द्यावा च यत्र ततनन्नहानि च ।
विश्वमन्यन्नि विशते यदेजति विश्वाहापो विश्वाहोदेति सूर्यः ॥

(ऋग्वेद १० । ३७ । २)

sā mā satyokti: pari pātu viśvato dyāvāca yatra tatanannahāni ca |
viśvamanyanni viśate yadejati viśvāhāpo viśvāhodeti sūrya: ||

(ṛgveda 10 | 37 | 2)

May that true statement protect me from all corners which causes day and night to spread in all directions, and this world merges in another, which initiates the Sun to rise, and the water ever, keeps flowing.

(Rigveda 10 | 37 | 2)

❍ ❍ ❍

मन्त्रमखर्वं सुधितं सुपेशसं दधात यज्ञियेष्वा ।
पूर्वीश्चन प्रसितयस्तरन्ति तं य इन्द्रे कर्मणा भुवत् ॥
(ऋग्वेद ७ । ३२ । १३)

mantramakharvaṃ sudhitaṃ supeśasaṃ dadhāta yajñiyeṣvā |
pūrvīścana prasitayastaranti taṃ ya indre karmaṇā bhuvat ||
(ṛgveda 7 | 32 | 13)

Let an ever good-conduct-man, having beautiful facial-image, imbued with the sacrificial spirit, be given well considered high-prudence-mantra. The binding karmās (actions) of the previous lives set a man free, who performs his karmās dedicated to Lord Indra. (Rigveda 7 | 32 | 13)

❍ ❍ ❍

त्रिभिः पवित्रैरपुपोद्ध्य१ र्कं हृदा मतिं ज्योतिरनु प्रजानन् ।
वर्षिष्ठं रत्नमकृत स्वधाभिरादिद् द्यावापृथिवी पर्यपश्यत् ॥
(ऋग्वेद ३ । २६ । ८)

tribhi: pavitrairapupoddhya1 rkaṃ hṛdā matiṃ jyotiranu prajānan |
varṣiṣṭhaṃ ratnamakṛta svadhābhirādid dyāvāpṛthivī paryapaśyat ||
(ṛgveda 3 | 26 | 8)

A man or a seeker (साधक), understanding well, by heart, enlightenment and divine-light, purges his soul by three divine – means, i.e., sacrifice (yajña), donation and by observing asceticism (Tapa). He attains 'Supreme-enligthenment (ब्रह्मज्ञान) by his own entitlement (समार्थ्य), and then he looks upon this world as trivial.
(Rigveda 3 | 26 | 8)

❍ ❍ ❍

नकिर्देवा मिनीमसि नकिरा योपयामसि मन्त्रश्रुत्यं चरामसि ।
पक्षेभिरपिकक्षेभिरत्राभि सं रभामहे ॥
(ऋग्वेद १० । १३४ । ७)

nakirdevā minīmasi nakirā yopayāmasi mantraśrutyaṃ carāmasi |
pakṣebhirapikakṣebhiratrābhi saṃ rabhāmahe ||
(ṛgveda 10 | 134 | 7)

O Gods! May we do neither violence, nor do we cause ill will; on the other, may we follow the vedic way in our conduct. May we work together even with the weakest of beings, like particles. (Rigveda 10 | 134 | 7)

❍ ❍ ❍

यस्तित्याज सचिविदं सखायं न तस्य वाच्यपि भागो अस्ति ।
यदीं शृणोत्यलकं शृणोति नहि प्रवेद सुकृतस्य पन्थाम् ॥
(ऋग्वेद १० । ७१ । ६)

yastityāja sacividaṃ sakhāyaṃ na tasya vācyapi bhāgo asti |
yadīṃ śṛṇotyalakaṃ śṛṇoti nahi praveda sukṛtasya panthām ||
(ṛgveda 10 | 71 | 6)

A man who forsakes a friend, delivering instructions on truthful-knowledge, his words are not heeded. He hears nothing, but untruth. He is ignorant of the path of truthfulness. (Rigveda 10 | 71 | 6)

❍ ❍ ❍

स इद्भोजो यो गृहवे ददात्यन्नकामाय चरते कृशाय ।
अरमस्मै भवति यामहूता उतापरीषु कृणुते सखायम् ॥
(ऋग्वेद १० । ११७ । ३)

sa idbhojo yo gṛhave dadātyannakāmāya carate kṛśāya |
aramasmai bhavati yāmahūtā utāparīṣu kṛṇute sakhāyam ||

(ṛgveda 10 | 117 | 3)

One who gives food to a poor beggar desiring food, he alone eats food in reality. Such a man possesses plenty of food; and in time of need, many friends appear ready to help him. (Rigveda 10 | 117 | 3)

❍ ❍ ❍

पृणीयादिन्नाधमानाय तव्यान् द्राघीयांसमनु पश्येत पन्थाम् ।

(ऋग्वेद १० । ११७ । ५)

pṛṇīyādinnādhamānāya tavyān drāghīyāṃsamanu paśyeta panthām |

(ṛgveda 10 | 117 | 5)

May a man be blessed to see a long way in life, and make people happy, who are begging for alms. (Rigveda 10 | 117 | 5)

❍ ❍ ❍

ये अग्ने नेरयन्ति ते वृद्धा उग्रस्य शवसः ।
अप द्वेषो अप ह्वरो ऽन्यव्रतस्य सश्चिरे ॥

(ऋग्वेद ५ । २० । २)

ye agne nerayanti te vṛddhā ugrasya śavasa: |
apa dveṣo apa hvaro 'nyavratasya saścire ||

(ṛgveda 5 | 20 | 2)

The real elderly people are those who do not get upset or moved and set aside the jealousy and wickedness of staunch atheists. (Rigveda 5 | 20 | 2)

❍ ❍ ❍

श्रद्धयाग्निः समिध्यते श्रद्धया हूयते हविः ।
श्रद्धां भगस्य मूर्धनि वचसा वेदयामसि ॥

(ऋग्वेद १० । १५१ । १)

**śraddhayāgni: samidhyate śraddhayā hūyate havi: |
śraddhāṃ bhagasya mūrdhani vacasā vedayāmasi ||**

(ṛgveda 10 | 151 | 1)

The fire is ignited by faith, and the oblations are made in the sacrificial fire (Havan – हवन) by faith; we all regard faith as the best opulence, through our words of appreciation.

(Rigveda 10 | 151 | 1)

❍ ❍ ❍

स नः पितेव सूनवे ऽग्ने सूपायनो भव ।
सचस्वा नः स्वस्तये ॥

(ऋग्वेद १ । १ । ९)

**sa na: piteva sūnave 'gne sūpāyano bhava |
sacasvā na: svastaye ||**

(ṛgveda 1 | 1 | 9)

O Fire (God of Fire)! Be Thee available to us by pleasing means, just as a father wishing propitiousness for his son is accessible to him. Be Thee with us for our welfare.

(Rigveda 1 | 1 | 9)

❍ ❍ ❍

सुक्षेत्रिया सुगातुया वसूया च यजामहे ।
अप नः शोशुचदघम् ॥

(ऋग्वेद १ । ९७ । २)

**sukṣetriyā sugātuyā vasūyā ca yajāmahe |
apa na: śośucadagham ||**

(ṛgveda 1 | 97 | 2)

We adore Thee in order to achieve great splendour, righteous path and opulence. May our sins be eliminated.

(Rigveda 1 | 97 | 2)

❍ ❍ ❍

स नः सिन्धुमिव नावयाति पर्षा स्वस्तये ।
अप नः शोशुचदघम् ॥
(ऋग्वेद १ । ९७ । ८)

sa na: sindhumiva nāvayāti parṣā svastaye |
apa na: śośucadagham ||
(ṛgveda 1 | 97 | 8)

May the Oversoul*, for our propitiousness, help us cross over the ocean of the world, just as the ocean is crossed over by a boat. May our sins be eliminated.

(Rigveda 1 | 97 | 8)

* Parmeśwar

❍ ❍ ❍

स्वस्तये वायुमुप ब्रवामहै सोमं स्वस्ति भुवनस्य यस्पतिः ।
बृहस्पतिं सर्वगणं स्वस्तये स्वस्तय आदित्यासो भवन्तु नः ॥
(ऋग्वेद ५ । ५१ । १२)

svastaye vāyumupa bravāmahai somaṃ svasti bhuvanasya yaspati: |
bṛhaspatiṃ sarvagaṇaṃ svastaye svastaya ādityāso bhavantu na: ||
(ṛgveda 5 | 51 | 12)

We worship the God of Wind for our auspiciousness, eulogise Soma, the Supreme-Being of the universe, and we worship Brihaspati alongwith all the group of attendants. May Āditya (Sun God) also be propitious to us.

(Rigveda 5 | 51 | 12)

❍ ❍ ❍

अपि पन्थामगन्महि स्वस्तिगामनेहसम् ।
येन विश्वाः परि द्विषो वृणक्ति विन्दते वसु ।
(ऋग्वेद ६ । ५१ । १६)

**api panthāmaganmahi svastigāmanehasam |
yena viśvā: pari dviṣo vṛṇakti vindate vasu |
(ṛgveda 6 | 51 | 16)**

May we tread on that auspicious and sinless path, which helps man give up hatred and achieve wealth.
(Rigveda 6 | 51 | 16)

❍ ❍ ❍

शं नो अग्निर्ज्योतिरनीको अस्तु शं नो मित्रावरुणावश्विना शम् ।
शं नः सुकृतां सुकृतानि सन्तु शं न इषिरो अभि वातु वातः ॥
(ऋग्वेद ७ । ३५ । ४)

**śaṃ no agnirjyotiranīko astu śaṃ no
mitrāvaruṇāvaśvinā śam |
śaṃ na: sukṛtāṃ sukṛtāni santu śaṃ na iṣiro
abhi vātu vāta: ||
(ṛgveda 7 | 35 | 4)**

May that Agni (Fire-God), who has brightness itself on His face, be propitious for us, Varuṇa and Ashwini Kumar be propitious to us; the actions (Karmās) of the righteous men be pleasing to us; and may the wind also flow in order to provide us peace. (Rigveda 7 | 35 | 4)

❍ ❍ ❍

शं नो द्यावापृथिवी पूर्वहूतौ शमन्तरिक्षं दृशये नो अस्तु ।
शं न ओषधीर्वनिनो भवन्तु शं नो रजसस्पतिरस्तु जिष्णुः ॥
(ऋग्वेद ७ । ३५ । ५)

**śaṃ no dyāvāpṛthivī pūrvahūtau śamantarikṣaṃ
dṛśaye no astu |
śaṃ na oṣadhīrvanino bhavantu śaṃ no
rajasaspatirastu jiṣṇu: ||
(ṛgveda 7 | 35 | 5)**

May the heavens and the earth be pleasant for us, the space be propitious for our sight, the herbal plants and trees be beneficient for us, and may the Lord of the world, Indra give us peace. (Rigveda 7 | 35 | 5)

❍ ❍ ❍

शं नः सूर्य उरुचक्षा उदेतु शं नश्चतस्त्रः प्रदिशो भवन्तु ।
शं नः पर्वता ध्रुवयो भवन्तु शं नः सिन्धवः शमु सन्त्वापः ॥
(ऋग्वेद ७ । ३५ । ८)

śaṃ na: sūrya urucakṣā udetu śaṃ naścatasra: pradiśo bhavantu |
śaṃ na: parvatā dhruvayo bhavantu śaṃ na: sindhava: śamu santvāpa: ||
(ṛgveda 7 | 35 | 8)

May the Sun rise with wide-spread brilliance, rendering auspiciousness for all of us. May all the four quarters be auspicious to us. May the steady mountains be propitious for us, the rivers be beneficient and their water be propitious for us. (Rigveda 7 | 35 | 8)

❍ ❍ ❍

शं नो अदितिर्भवतु व्रतेभिः शं नो भवन्तु मरुतः स्वर्काः ।
शं नो विष्णुः शमु पूषा नो अस्तु शं नो भवित्रं शम्वस्तु वायुः ॥
(ऋग्वेद ७ । ३५ । ९)

śaṃ no aditirbhavatu vratebhi: śaṃ no bhavantu maruta: svarkā: |
śaṃ no viṣṇu: śamu pūṣā no astu śaṃ no bhavitraṃ śamvastu vāyu: ||
(ṛgveda 7 | 35 | 9)

May Aditi (The Goddess Aditi, the mother of Gods) be propitious for us, Marudgaṇās (the group of winds) be propitious for us. May God Viṣṇu and the nourishing Gods be auspicious for us, and the water and the wind be peace giving for us. (Rigveda 7 | 35 | 9)

❍ ❍ ❍

शं नो देवः सविता त्रायमाणः शं नो भवन्तूषसो विभातीः ।
शं नः पर्जन्यो भवतु प्रजाभ्यः शं नः क्षेत्रस्य पतिरस्तु शम्भुः ॥
(ऋग्वेद ७ । ३५ । १०)

śaṃ no deva: savitā trāyamāṇa: śaṃ no bhavantūṣaso vibhātī: |
śaṃ na: parjanyo bhavatu prajābhya: śaṃ na: kṣetrasya patirastu śambhu: ||
(ṛgveda 7 | 35 | 10)

May Savitā (The Sun), the protector, be auspicious for us, the very brilliant Goddess Ushā (The Goddess-Dawn) be pleasant for us; may Indra (The God of rains — Parjanya), who brings rains, be propitious for our people (subjects – प्रजा) and the Lord of the region, Śambhu also provide peace to all of us. (Rigveda 7 | 35 | 10)

❍ ❍ ❍

शं नो देवा विश्वेदेवा भवन्तु शं सरस्वती सह धीभिरस्तु ।
(ऋग्वेद ७ । ३५ । ११)

śaṃ no devā viśvedevā bhavantu śaṃ sarasvatī saha dhībhirastu |
(ṛgveda 7 | 35 | 11)

May all the Gods be propitious for us, the Goddess of Wisdom, Goddess Saraswatī, also be propitious for us.
(Rigveda 7 | 35 | 11)

❍ ❍ ❍

त्वं हि नः पिता वसो त्वं माता शतक्रतो बभूविथ ।
अधा ते सुम्नमीमहे ॥
(ऋग्वेद ८ । १८ । ११)

tvaṃ hi na: pitā vaso tvaṃ mātā śatakrato babhūvitha |
adhā te sumnamīmahe ||
(ṛgveda 8 | 18 | 11)

O Patron (the giver of shelter – आश्रयदाता)! Thou art our father. O Śatakratu (Indra)! Thou art our mother. We aspire for auspiciousness from Thee. (Rigveda 8 | 98 | 11)

❍ ❍ ❍

इमे जीवा वि मृतैराववृत्रन्नभूद्भद्रा देवहूतिर्नो अद्य ।
प्राञ्चो अगाम नृतये हसाय द्राघीय आयुः प्रतरं दधानाः ॥

(ऋग्वेद १० । १८ । ३)

ime jīvā vi mṛtairāvavṛtrannabhūdbhadrā devahūtirno adya |
prāñco agāma nṛtaye hasāya drāghīya āyu: prataraṃ dadhānā: ||

(ṛgveda 10 | 18 | 3)

These living beings are not surrounded by the dead men, therefore, we could complete our divine-sacrifice (देवयज्ञ) causing our wellness. Making our long life even longer in order to dance and rejoice. May we tread on the path of progress.

(Rigveda 10 | 18 | 3)

❍ ❍ ❍

भद्रं नो अपि वातय मनो दक्षमुत क्रतुम् ।

(ऋग्वेद १० । २५ । १)

bhadraṃ no api vātaya mano dakṣamuta kratum |

(ṛgveda 10 | 25 | 1)

O Oversoul! Inspire us to have an auspicious mind, and strength to do welfare work and deeds for wellness.

(Rigveda 10 | 25 | 1)

❍ ❍ ❍

The Yajurvedic Nectar of Mantrās
यजुर्वेदीय मन्त्र-सुधा

अग्ने व्रतपते व्रतं चरिष्यामि तच्छकेयं तन्मे राध्यताम् ।
इदमहमनृतात्सत्यमुपैमि ॥

(यजूर्वेद १ । ५)

agne vratapate vrataṃ cariṣyāmi tacchakeyaṃ tanme rādhyatām |
idamahamanṛtātsatyamupaimi ||
(yajūrveda 1 | 5)

O Agni (The Fire-God), the protector of vows (austerity)! I desire to be upholder of Truth. Bless me to takeup this vow, may this vow be accomplished. Giving up untruth, I accept truthfulness. (Yajurveda 1 | 5)

❍ ❍ ❍

व्रतेन दीक्षामाप्नोति दीक्षयाऽऽप्नोति दक्षिणाम् ।
दक्षिणा श्रद्धामाप्नोति श्रद्धया सत्यमाप्यते ॥

(यजुर्वेद १९ । ३०)

vratena dīkṣāmāpnoti dīkṣayā"pnoti dakṣiṇām |
dakṣiṇā śraddhāmāpnoti śraddhayā satyamāpyate ||
(yajurveda 19 | 30)

The vow (of truth) leads to initiation, initiation gives rise to dexterity, and dexterity, in turn, establishes faith, and faith helps accomplish truth. (Yajurveda 19 | 30)

❍ ❍ ❍

अग्ने नय सुपथा राये अस्मान्विश्वानि देव वयुनानि विद्वान ।
युयोध्यस्मज्जुहुराणमेनो भूयिष्ठां ते नम उक्तिं विधेभ ॥

(यजुर्वेद ५ । ३६)

agne naya supathā rāye asmānviśvāni deva vayunāni vidvāna |
yuyodhyasmajjuhurāṇameno bhūyiṣṭhāṃ te nama uktiṃ vidhema ||

(yajurveda 5 | 36)

O Agni (The Fire-God)! Lead us to the righteous path, in order to attain elevated soul. Thou knoweth well all our actions (Karmās). Protect us from the crooked, sinful pursuances. We bow again and again unto Thee.

(Yajurveda 5 | 36)

❍ ❍ ❍

दृते दृꣳह मा मित्रस्य मा चक्षुषा सर्वाणि भूतानि समीक्षन्ताम् ।
मित्रस्याहं चक्षुषा सर्वाणि भूतानि समीक्षे ।
मित्रस्य चक्षुषा समीक्षामहे ॥

(यजुर्वेद ३६ । १८)

dṛte dṛꣳha mā mitrasya mā cakṣuṣā sarvāṇi bhūtāni samīkṣantām |
mitrasyāhaṃ cakṣuṣā sarvāṇi bhūtāni samīkṣe |
mitrasya cakṣuṣā samīkṣāmahe ||

(yajurveda 36 | 18)

May my (inner) sight be strong; may all the beings view me as friends; may I also view all the beings as friends; may we, mutually, view each other as friends.

(Yajurveda 36 | 18)

❍ ❍ ❍

सह नाववतु । सह नौ भुनक्तु । सह वीर्यं करवावहै ।
तेजस्वि नावधीतमस्तु । मा विद्विषावहै ।
ॐ शान्तिः शान्तिः शान्तिः ।

(कृष्णयजुर्वेदीय शान्तिपाठ)

saha nāvavatu | saha nau bhunaktu | saha vīryaṃ karavāvahai |
tejasvi nāvadhītamastu | mā vidviṣāvahai |
oṃ śānti: śānti: śānti: |
(kṛṣṇayajurvedīya śāntipāṭha)

O Oversoul (the Absolute Reality)! Protect both of us, (the disciple and the preceptor, in all possible manner, from all harms). Nourish and bring up both of us. May we grow stronger and achieve strength, together. Let our acquired knowledge and studies be illuminating and enlightening. Let both of us, never be envious of each other or dislike each other. Om Peace! Om Peace!! Om Peace !!!

❍ ❍ ❍

स्योना पृथिवि नो भवानृक्षरा निवेशनी ।
यच्छा नः शर्म सप्रथाः । अप नः शोशुचदघम् ॥
(यजुर्वेद ३५ । २१)

syonā pṛthivi no bhavānṛkṣarā niveśanī |
yacchā na: śarma sapratha: | apa na: śośucadagham ||
(yajurveda 35 | 21)

O Earth! Be thee auspicious by providing us comfortable place, worth sitting, which is pleasant for us. Eradicate our sins. (Yajurveda 35 | 21)

❍ ❍ ❍

यन्मे छिद्रं चक्षुषो हृदयस्य मनसो वातितृण्णं बृहस्पतिर्मे तद्दधातु ।
शं नो भवतु भुवनस्य यस्पतिः ॥
(यजुर्वेद ३६ । २)

yanme chidraṃ cakṣuṣo hṛdayasya manaso vātitṛṇṇaṃ bṛhaspatirme taddadhātu |
śaṃ no bhavatu bhuvanasya yaspati: ||
(yajurveda 36 | 2)

O Brihaspati! Remove the flaws of my eyes and heart and

the big errors of my mind. May the Lord of the universe be propitious for us. (Yajurveda 36 | 2)

❍ ❍ ❍

भूर्भुवः स्वः तत्सवितुर्वरेण्यं भर्गो देवस्य धीमहि ।
धियो यो नः प्रचोदयात् ॥

(यजुर्वेद ३६ । ३)

bhūrbhuva: sva: tatsaviturvareṇyaṃ bhargo devasya dhīmahi |
dhiyo yo na: pracodayāt ||

(yajurveda 36 | 3)

May we meditate upon existence, consciousness, bliss and the excellent brilliance of the creator of the universe. May He initiate auspiciousness in our intellect. (Yajurveda 36 | 3)

❍ ❍ ❍

द्यौः शान्तिरन्तरिक्षꣳशान्तिः पृथिवी शान्तिरापः
शान्तिरोषधयः शान्तिः ।
वनस्पतयः शान्तिर्विश्वे देवाः शान्तिर्ब्रह्म शान्तिः सर्वꣳशान्तिः
शान्तिरेव शान्तिः सा मा शान्तिरेधि ॥

(यजुर्वेद ३६ । १७)

dyau: śāntirantarikṣaꣳśānti: pṛthivī śāntirāpa:
śāntiroṣadhaya: śānti: |
vanaspataya: śāntirviśve devā: śāntirbrahma śānti:
sarvaṃśānti: śāntireva śānti: sā mā śāntiredhi ||

(yajurveda 36 | 17)

The tranquility in heaven, the tranquility in space (the physical universe beyond the earth's atmosphere), the tranquility on earth, the tranquility in oceans (water, as an element), the tranquility in herbs (with their efficacy) and that in vegetation, the tranquility in Gods (overseeing the entire world), the tranquility in BRAHM (the Supreme energy), the tranquility in the entire universe, and the natural tranquility pervading the whole world, O Paramātmā (The Oversoul)! Let Thy grace bestow upon me that tranquility for ever.

(Yajurveda 36 | 17)

❍ ❍ ❍

यतो यतः समीहसे ततो नो अभयं कुरु ।
शं नः कुरु प्रजाभ्योऽभयं नः पशुभ्यः ॥

(यजुर्वेद ३६ । २२)

yato yata: samīhase tato no abhayaṃ kuru |
śaṃ na: kuru prajābhyo'bhayaṃ na: paśubhya: ||
(yajurveda 36 | 22)

Provide us fearlessness, from whichsoever corner it is needful. Let it be propitious for our people, and let our animals also have fearlessness. (Yajurveda 36 | 22)

❍ ❍ ❍

तच्चक्षुर्देवहितं पुरस्ताच्छुक्रमुच्चरत् ।
पश्येम शरदः शतं जीवेम शरदः शतं श्रृणुयाम शरदः
शतं प्र ब्रवाम शरदः शतमदीनाः स्याम शरदः
शतं भूयश्च शरदः शतात् ॥

(यजुर्वेद ३६ । २४)

taccakṣurdevahitaṃ purastācchukramuccarat |
paśyema śarada: śataṃ jīvema śarada:
śataṃśṛṇuyāma śarada:
śataṃ pra bravāma śarada: śatamadīnā: syāma śarada:
śataṃ bhūyaśca śarada: śatāt ||
(yajurveda 36 | 24)

The wisdom-eye like bright Sun is rising in (our) front for the wellness of the enlightened men*, let us see for a hundred years, let us live our lives for a hundred years, hear for a hundred years, speak for a hundred years, live for a hundred years without degradation or wretchedness, and live longer than even hundred years. (Yajurveda 36 | 24)

* with its power

❍ ❍ ❍

The Sāmvedic Nectar of Mantrās

सामवेदीय मन्त्र सुधा

शं नो देवीरभिष्टये शं नो भवन्तु पीतये ।
शं योरभि स्त्रवन्तु नः ॥
(सामवेद १ । ३ । १३)

śaṃ no devīrabhiṣṭaye śaṃ no bhavantu pītaye |
śaṃ yorabhi sravantu na: ||
(sāmaveda 1 | 3 | 13)

The waters with celestial quality which would enable us to achieve the desirable, and would also be potable for wellness, may it be auspicious from all corners.

(Samveda 1 | 3 | 13)

❍ ❍ ❍

स्वस्ति न इन्द्रो वृद्धश्रवाः स्वस्ति नः पूषा विश्ववेदाः ।
स्वस्ति नस्ताक्ष्र्यो अरिष्टनेमिः स्वस्ति नो बृहस्पतिर्दधातु ॥
(सामवेद २१ । ३ । ९)

svasti na indro vṛddhaśravā: svasti na: pūṣā viśvavedā: |
svasti nastārkṣyo ariṣṭanemi: svasti no bṛhaspatirdadhātu ||
(sāmaveda 21 | 3 | 9)

O highly renowned Indra (the King of the Gods)! Be propitious to us. O Omniscient Sun! Be propitious to us. O Garuḍa (Eagle)! The dissipator of all ill omens, be propitious to us; and O Brihaspati! The God of wisdom, be Thee propitious to us.

(Sāmveda 21 | 3 | 9)

❍ ❍ ❍

चन्द्रमा अप्स्वाऽ३न्तरा सुपर्णो धावते दिवि ।
न वो हिरण्यनेमयः पदं विन्दन्ति विद्युतो वित्तं में अस्य रोदसी ॥
(सामवेद पूर्वा० २ । ३१ । ९)

candramā apsvā'3ntarā suparṇo dhāvate divi |
na vo hiraṇyanemaya: padaṃ vindanti vidyuto vittaṃ memṃ asya rodasī ||

(sāmaveda pūrvā0 2 | 31 | 9)

The moon, the dweller of the space is dynamic in the sky with its excellent rays. O the excellent golden rays of the Sun, like lightning! Our senses are unable to catch up the front part of Thy feet. O heaven and earth! Accept my eulogies. The light of the Sun transmits in the sky during night also, but our senses do not experience it. The light is available through the moon only.

(Sāmveda Purva 2 | 31 | 9)

❍ ❍ ❍

ॐ

त्वमेव माता च पिता त्वमेव
त्वमेव बन्धुश्च सखा त्वमेव ।
त्वमेव विद्या द्रविणं त्वमेव
त्वमेव सर्वं मम देवदेव ॥

Om

Thou art verily our mother, and
Thou art verily our father,
Thou art verily our relation, and
Thou art verily an ever companion,
Thou art verily our wisdom,
Thou art verily our wealth,
Thou art verily Supreme,
O our Lord of Gods!

The Atharv-vedic Nectar of Mantrās

अथर्ववेदीय मन्त्र सुधा

जिह्वाया अग्रे मधु मे जिह्वामूले मधूलकम् ।
ममेदह क्रतावसो मम चित्तमुपायसि ॥

(अथर्ववेद १ । ३४ । २)

jahvāyā agre madhu me jihvāmūle madhūlakam |
mamedaha kratāvaso mama cittamupāyasi ||

(atharvaveda 1 | 34 | 2)

Let the front of my tongue be sweet. Let the root of my tongue be sweet. Let there exist sweetness in my deeds and O Sweetness! Reach the core of my heart.

(Atharvaveda 1 | 34 | 2)

❍ ❍ ❍

मधुमन्मे निक्रमणं मधुमन्मे परायणम् ।
वाचा वदामि मधुमद् भूयासं मधुसंदृशः ॥

(अथर्ववेद १ । ३४ । ३)

madhumanme nikramaṇaṃ madhumanme parāyaṇam |
vācā vadāmi madhumad bhūyāsaṃ madhusaṃdṛśa: ||

(atharvaveda 1 | 34 | 3)

Let my going be with sweetness. Let my arrival be with sweetness. Let my speech be sweet and let my features have sweet looks.

(Atharvaveda 1 | 34| 3)

❍ ❍ ❍

प्राणो ह सत्यवादिनमुत्तमे लोक आ दधत् ॥

(अथर्ववेद ११ । ४ । ११)

prāṇo ha satyavādinamuttama loka ā dadhat ||
(atharvaveda 11 | 4 | 11)

One, who speaks truthfully, is established in the excellent world by Prāṇa (vital air of life).

(Atharvaveda 11 | 4 | 11)

❍ ❍ ❍

सुश्रुतौ कर्णौ भद्रश्रुतौ कर्णौ भद्रं श्लोकं श्रूयासम् ॥
(अथर्ववेद १६ । २ । ४)

suśrutau karṇau bhadraśrutau karṇau bhadraṃ ślokaṃ śrūyāsam ||
(atharvaveda 16 | 2 | 4)

May my ears that hear lucky and auspicious words, hear only propitious words.

(Atharvaveda 16 | 2 | 4)

❍ ❍ ❍

ज्यायस्वन्तश्चित्तिनो मा वि यौष्ट संराधयन्तः सधुराश्चरन्तः ।
अन्यो अन्यस्मै वल्गु वदन्त एत सध्रीचीनान्वः संमनसस्कृणोमि ॥
(अथर्ववेद ३ । ३० । ५)

jyāyasvantaścittino mā vi yauṣṭa saṃrādhayanta: sadhurāścaranta: |
anyo anyasmai valgu vadanta eta sadhrīcīnānva: saṃmanasaskṛṇomi ||
(atharvaveda 3 | 30 | 5)

One should be respectful to the old, reflective, engaged in accomplishing desired work with one-mindedness. (Just as oxen), bearing the same yoke while moving, one should not get separated (from each other). Come along discoursing, sweetly, mutually, I (Parmātmā) bless you to have one-speed (harmonious speed) and one-mindedness (harmonious mindset).

(Atharvaveda 3 | 30 | 5)

❍ ❍ ❍

सध्रीचीनान्वः संमनसस्कृणोम्येकश्नुष्टीन्त्संवननेन सर्वान् ।
देवा इवामृतं रक्षमाणाः सायंप्रातः सौमनसो वो अस्तु ॥
(अथर्ववेद ३ । ३० । ७)

sadhrīcīnānva:
saṃmanasaskṛṇomyekaśnuṣṭīntsaṃvananena sarvān |
devā ivāmṛtaṃ rakṣamāṇā: sāyaṃprāta:
saumanaso vo astu ||
(atharvaveda 3 | 30 | 7)

All those who have the same harmonious speed and elevated mindset, I (Parmātmā) bless them with good heart to be of similar food habits. May their mornings and evenings be auspicious as those of the Gods, who protect nectar.

(Atharvaveda 3 | 30 | 7)

❍ ❍ ❍

शिवा भव पुरुषेभ्यो गोभ्यो अश्वेभ्यः शिवा ।
शिवास्मै सर्वस्मै क्षेत्राय शिवा न इहैधि ॥
(अथर्ववेद ३ । २८ । ३)

śivā bhava puruṣebhyo gobhyo aśvebhya: śivā |
śivāsmai sarvasmai kṣetrāya śivā na ihaidhi ||
(atharvaveda 3 | 28 | 3)

O New-bride! May you be auspicious for men, cows and steeds. May you be auspicious for all places, and being propitious for me also, come here.

(Atharvaveda 3 | 28 | 3)

❍ ❍ ❍

अनुव्रतः पितुः पुत्रो मात्रा भवतु संमनाः ।
जाया पत्ये मधुमतीं वाचं वदतु शन्तिवाम् ॥
(अथर्ववेद ३ । ३० । २)

anuvrata: pitu: putro mātrā bhavatu saṃmanā: |
jāyā patye madhumatīṃ vācaṃ vadatu śantivām ||
(atharvaveda 3 | 30 | 2)

May the son be in accord with the father in pursuit of aims. May the wife be sweet, soft-spoken and peace-giving.

(Atharvaveda 3 | 30 | 2)

❍ ❍ ❍

मा भ्राता भ्रातरं द्विक्षन्मा स्वसारमुत स्वसा ।
सम्यञ्चः सव्रता भूत्वा वाचं वदत भद्रया ॥

(अथर्ववेद ३ । ३० । ३)

mā bhrātā bhrātaraṃ dvikṣanmā svasāramuta svasā |
samyañca: savratā bhūtvā vācaṃ vadata bhadrayā ||

(atharvaveda 3 | 30 | 3)

May brothers bear no ill intention with each other, sisters bear no hatred with one another with uniform speed and uniformity in rules, may they speak auspiciously.

(Atharvaveda 3 | 30 | 3)

❍ ❍ ❍

यथा सिन्धुर्नदीनां साम्राज्यं सुषुवे वृषा ।
एवा त्वं सम्राज्ञ्येधि पत्युरस्तं परेत्य ॥

(अथर्ववेद १४ । १ । ४३)

yathā sindhurnadīnāṃ sāmrājyaṃ suṣuve vṛṣā |
evā tvaṃ samrāḍhayedhi patyurastaṃ paretya ||

(atharvaveda 14 | 1 | 43)

Just as powerful ocean creates an empire of rivers, so do you become the empress of the household of (your) husband, on reaching there.

(Atharvaveda 14 | 1| 43)

❍ ❍ ❍

सम्राज्ञ्येधि श्वशुरेषु सम्राज्ञ्युत देवृषु ।
ननान्दुः सम्राज्ञ्येधि सम्राज्ञ्युत श्वश्र्वाः ॥

(अथर्ववेद १४ । १ । ४४)

samrājñayedhi śvaśureṣu samrājñayuta devṛṣu |
nanāndu: samrājñayedhi samrājñayuta śvaśravā: ||
(atharvaveda 14 | 1 | 44)

May you be the empress of father-in-law, be the empress in the midst of brothers-in-law (देवर), be the empress of sisters-in-law (ननद) and the mother-in-law.

(Atharvaveda 14 | 1 | 44)

❍ ❍ ❍

सर्वो वा एषोऽजग्धपाप्मा यस्यान्नं नाश्नन्ति ॥
(अथर्ववेद ९ । ६ । २६)

sarvo vā eṣo'jagdhapāpmā yasyānnaṃ nāśnanti ||
(atharvaveda 9 | 6 | 26)

If the food of someone is not shared by other men, he is not liberated from all sins.

(Atharvaveda 9 | 6| 26)

❍ ❍ ❍

हिरण्यस्त्रगयं मणिः श्रद्धां यज्ञं महो दधत् ।
गृहे वसतु नोऽतिथिः ॥
(अथर्ववेद १० । ६ । ४)

hiraṇyasragayaṃ maṇi: śraddhāṃ yajñaṃ
maho dadhat |
gṛhe vasatu no'tithi: ||
(atharvaveda 10 | 6 | 4)

May this gem like guest, wearing a gold chain and bearing reverence, sacrifice and greatness, dwell in our home.

(Atharvaveda 10 | 6 | 4)

❍ ❍ ❍

तद् यस्यैवं विद्वान् व्रात्यो राज्ञोऽतिथिर्गृहानागच्छेत् ॥
श्रेयांसमेनमात्मनो मानयेत् .... ॥
(अथर्ववेद १५ । १० । १-२)

tad yasyaivaṃ vidvān vrātyo rājño'tithirgṛhānāgacchet ||
śreyāṃsamenamātmano mānayet .... ||

(atharvaveda 15 | 10 | 1-2)

If an enlightened and avowed guest comes to the palace of a king, he (king) must understand it as his fortune.

(Atharvaveda 15 | 10 |1-2)

❍ ❍ ❍

न ता नशन्ति न दभाति तस्करो नासामामित्रो व्यथिरा दधर्षति ।
देवांश्च याभिर्यजते ददाति च ज्योगित्ताभिः सचते गोपतिः सह ॥

(अथर्ववेद ४ । २१ । ३)

na tā naśanti na dabhāti taskaro nāsāmāmitro vyathirā dadharṣati |
devāṃśca yābhiryajate dadāti ca jyogittābhi: sacate gopati: saha ||

(atharvaveda 4 | 21 | 3)

Commodities, with which a man performs sacrifice (yajña), for the Gods or donates, he is joined with them; the reason being, those things neither get destroyed, nor can they be stolen by any enemy. (Atharvaveda 4 | 21 | 3)

❍ ❍ ❍

स्वस्ति मात्र उत पित्रे नो अस्तु स्वस्ति गोभ्यो जगते पुरुषेभ्यः ।
विश्वं सुभूतं सुविदत्रं नो अस्तु ज्योगेव दृशेम सूर्यम् ॥

(अथर्ववेद १ । ३१ । ४)

svasti mātra uta pitre no astu svasti gobhyo jagate puruṣebhya: |
viśvaṃ subhūtaṃ suvidatraṃ no astu jyogeva dṛśema sūryam ||

(atharvaveda 1 | 31 | 4)

May our parents be blessed. May the cows, the entire world and all men be blessed. May everything be blessed with firm reality (सूदृढ़ सत्ता) and auspicious knowledge; and may we see the Sun to eternity. (Atharvaveda 1 | 31 | 4)

❍ ❍ ❍

परोऽपेहि मनस्पाप किमशस्तानि शंससि ।
परेहि न त्वा कामये वृक्षां वनानि सं चर गृहेषु गोषु मे मनः ॥
(अथर्ववेद ६ । ४५ । १)

paro'pehi manaspāpa kimaśastāni śaṃsasi |
parehi na tvā kāmaye vṛkṣāṃ vanāni saṃ cara gṛheṣu goṣu me mana: ||
(atharvaveda 6 | 45 | 1)

O the bundle of sins of my mind! Get faraway. Why do you concieve of getting (me) unlauded, get faraway, I do not desire for you. Be there with trees and forests, may my mind be fixed in my home and cows. (Atharvaveda 6 | 45 | 1)

❍ ❍ ❍

इयं या परमेष्ठिनी वाग्देवी ब्रह्मसंशिता ।
ययैव ससृजे घोरं तयैव शान्तिरस्तु नः ॥
(अथर्ववेद १९ । ९ । ३)

iyaṃ yā parameṣṭhinī vāgdevī brahmasaṃśitā |
yayaiva sasṛje ghoraṃ tayaiva śāntirastu na: ||
(atharvaveda 19 | 9 | 3)

May the Goddess of speech, Saraswatī, who is adorned by Brahmā, and the speech which does fierce acts on its own, May She in Her speech form bestow peace on us.
(Atharvaveda 19 | 9 | 3)

❍ ❍ ❍

इदं यत् परमेष्ठिनं मनो वां ब्रह्मसंशितम् ।
येनैव ससृजे घोरं तेनैव शान्तिरस्तु नः ॥
(अथर्ववेद १९ । ९ । ४)

idaṃ yat parameṣṭhinaṃ mano vāṃ brahmasaṃśitam |
yenaiva sasṛje ghoraṃ tenaiva śāntirastu na: ||
(atharvaveda 19 | 9 | 4)

Sharpened by Parmeshthi* Brahmā, this mind commits horrible sins, may that mind (by His Grace) give us peace.
(Atharvaveda 19 | 9 | 4)

* an epithet of Brahm

❍ ❍ ❍

इमानि यानि पञ्चेन्द्रियाणि मनः षष्ठानि मे हृदि
ब्रह्मणा संशितानि ।
यैरेव ससृजे घोरं तैरेव शान्तिरस्तु नः ॥
(अथर्ववेद १९ । ९ । १५)

imāni yāni pañcendriyāṇi mana: ṣaṣṭhāni me hṛdi
brahmaṇā saṃśitāni |
yaireva sasṛje ghoraṃ taireva śāntirastu na: ||
(atharvaveda 19 | 9 | 15)

Well consecrated by Brahmā, these five senses and the mind, which commit horrible acts, may (तैरेव) they (themselves) give us peace (by His Grace).
(Atharvaveda 19 | 9 | 5)

❍ ❍ ❍

शं नो मित्रः शं वरुणः शं विवस्वांछमन्तकः ।
उत्पाताः पार्थिवान्तरिक्षाः शं नो दिविचरा ग्रहाः ॥
(अथर्ववेद १९ । ९ । ७)

śaṃ no mitra: śaṃ varuṇa: śaṃ vivasvāṃchamantaka: |
utpātā: pārthivāntarikṣā: śaṃ no divicarā grahā: ||
(atharvaveda 19 | 9 | 7)

May Mitra (The presiding God of Day and life-breath – प्राण) be propitious and bring joyousness for us; May the Sun God, and Yam be propitious for us. May Varuṇa (Presideing

God of Night and passing out-wind) (अपान) be propitious and bring joyousness for us; May the ominousness on the earth and the sky be propitious for us, and may the planets moving in heavens also provide us peace.

(Atharvaveda 19 | 9 | 7)

❍ ❍ ❍

पश्येम शरदः शतम् ॥ जीवेम शरदः शतम् ॥ बुध्येम शरदः शतम ॥ रोहेम शरदः शतम् ॥ पूषेम शरदः शतम् ॥ भवेम शरदः शतम् ॥ भूयेम शरदः शतम् ॥ भूयसीः शरदः शतात् ॥

(अथर्ववेद १९ । ६७ । १-८)

paśyema śarada: śatam || jīvema śarada: śatam || budhyema śarada: śatama || rohema śarada: śatam || pūṣema śarada: śatam || bhavema śarada: śatam || bhūyema śarada: śatam || bhūyasī: śarada: śatāt ||

(atharvaveda 19 | 67 | 1-8)

May we see for a hundred years, live for a hundred years, acquire knowledge for a hundred years, rise and prosper for a hundred years, remain healthy and strong for a hundred years, remain getting elegance and dignity for a hundred years, and may live longer than for an age of a hundred years.

(Atharvaveda 19 | 67 | 1–8)

❍ ❍ ❍

The Vedic Exhortation (Convocation)
वैदिक दीक्षान्त उपदेश

वेदमनूच्याचार्योऽन्तेवासिनमनुशास्ति।
सत्यं वद। धर्मं चर। स्वाध्यायान्मा प्रमदः। आचार्याय
प्रियं धनमाहृत्य प्रजातन्तुं मा व्यवच्छेत्सीः। सत्यान्न
प्रमदितव्यम्। धर्मान्न प्रमदितव्यम्। कुशलान्न प्रमदितव्यम्।
भूत्यै न प्रमदितव्यम्। स्वाध्यायप्रवचनाभ्यां न प्रमदितव्यम्।
देवपितृकार्याभ्यां न प्रमदितव्यम्।

vedamanūcyācāryo'ntevāsinamanuśāsti| satyaṃ vada| dharmaṃ cara| svādhyāyānmā pramada:| ācāryāya priyaṃ dhanamāhṛtya prajātantuṃ mā vyavacchetsī:| satyānna pramaditavyam| dharmānna pramaditavyam| kuśalānna pramaditavyam| bhūtyai na pramaditavyam| svādhyāyapravacanābhyāṃ na pramaditavyam| devapitṛkāryābhyāṃ na pramaditavyam|

This is a kind of most importaqnt exhortation to the departing pupils, having completed their studies in Gurukuls. Ācārya says:

Speak the truth. Practise righteousness (follow the path of duty). Let there be no idleness in regular studies. Gift, whatever pleases your teacher and enter into family-life without cutting off the thread of progeny. Let not truth get neglected. Let not the righteous path get neglected. Let not your welfare get ignored in idleness. Pursue ways to increase propserity without neglecting it. Pursuance of studies and teaching, let them not get ignored. So do our duties to our gods, and ancestors are not to be ignored.

❍ ❍ ❍

मातृदेवो भव। पितृदेवो भव। आचार्यदेवो भव। अतिथिदेवो भव। यान्यनवद्यानि कर्माणि। तानि सेवितव्यानि। नो इतराणि। यान्यस्माकꣳसुचरितानि। तानि त्वयोपास्यानि। नो इतराणि।

mātṛdevo bhava| pitṛdevo bhava| ācāryadevo bhava| atithidevo bhava| yānyanavadyāni karmāṇi| tāni sevitavyāni| no itarāṇi| yānyasmākaꣳsucaritāni| tāni tvyopāsyāni| no itarāṇi|

(Consider your mother, father and teacher as God. Consider your guest as God.) (You) Be one to whom the mother is a god, your father is a god (to you). Your teacher is a god (to you). Be one to whom the guest is a god. Deeds without blemishes be practised and remembered, not others. Whatever is good needs to be adopted by you, nothing other than this.

❍ ❍ ❍

ये के चास्मच्छ्रेयाꣳसो ब्राह्मणाः। तेषां त्वयाऽऽसनेन प्रश्वसितव्यम्। श्रद्धया देयम! अश्रद्धयादेयम्। श्रिया देयम्। ह्रिया देयम्। भिया देयम्। संविदा देयम्।

ye ke cāsmaccherayāꣳso brāhmaṇā:| teṣāṃ tvayā”sanena praśvasitavyam| śraddhayā deyama! aśraddhayādeyam| śriyā deyam| hriyā deyam| bhiyā deyam| saṃvidā deyam|

Wherever Brahmaṇās, superior to us, are there, their discourses should be heard sincerely, and they should be greeted with respect. Whatever is to be given to others, be given with faith. Nothing should be given without faith. Give with happiness and with humility. Give even with fear and with love.

❍ ❍ ❍

अथ यदि ते कर्मविचिकित्सा वा वृत्तविचिकित्सा वा स्यात्। ये तत्र ब्राह्मणाः सम्मर्शिनः। युक्ता आयुक्ताः। अलूक्षा धर्मकामाः स्युः। यथा ते तत्र वर्तेरन्। तथा तत्र वर्तेथाः।

ha yadi te karmavicikitsā vā vṛttavicikitsā vā syāt| ye tatra brāhmaṇā: sammarśina:| yuktā āyuktā:| alūkṣā dharmakāmā: sya:| yathā te tatra varteran| tathā tatra vartethā:|

While doing so, if you have some doubt in understanding, as to what is ethical and what is unehtical, and are quite uncertain about the right course to adopt, then behave yourself following the wise and competent, devoted to the good deeds, who are quiet, simple and virtuous by nature, and do as they would do in such circumstances.

❍ ❍ ❍

अथाभ्याख्यातेषु। ये तत्र ब्राह्मणाः सम्मर्शिनः। युक्ता आयुक्ताः। अलूक्षा धर्मकामाः स्युः। यथा ते तेषु वर्तेरन्। तथा तेषु वर्तेथाः।

athābhyākhyāteṣu| ye tatra brāhmaṇā: sammarśina:| yuktā āyuktā:| alūkṣā dharmakāmā: syu:| yathā te teṣu varteran| tathā teṣu vartethā:|

In regards to the persons with blemished conduct, behave with them in the same manner as the Brahmaṇās, who are competent to judge, virtuous in behaviour, not harsh or rude, righteous and wise, would behave with them.

❍ ❍ ❍

एष आदेशः। एष उपदेशः। एषा वेदोपनिषत्। एतदनुशासनम्। एवमुपासितव्यम्। एवमु चैतदुपास्यम्।

[कृष्णयजुर्वेदीय तैत्तिरीयोपनिषद्]

eṣa ādeśa:| eṣa upadeśa:| eṣā vedopaniṣat| etadanuśāsanam| evamupāsitavyam| evamu caitadupāsyam|

[kṛṣṇayajurvedīya taittirīyopaniṣad]

This is the command. This is exhortation. This is the quintessence (secret doctrine) of the Vedas and Upaniṣads. This is the instruction. Live your life according to these instructions.

❍ ❍ ❍

Vedic National Prayer
वैदिक राष्ट्रप्रार्थना

आ ब्रह्मन् ब्राह्मणो ब्रह्मवर्चसी जायतामा राष्ट्रे राजन्यः शूर इषव्योऽतिव्याधी महारथो जायतां दोग्ध्री धेनुर्वोढानड्वानाशुः सप्तिः पुरन्धिर्योषा जिष्णू रथेष्ठाः सभेयो युवास्य यजमानस्य वीरो जायतां निकामे निकामे नः पर्जन्यो वर्षतु फलवत्यो न ओषधयः पच्यन्तां योगक्षेमो नः कल्पताम्॥

(यजु० सं० २२ । २२)

ā brahman brāhmaṇo brahmavarcasī jāyatāmā rāṣṭre rājanya: śūra iṣavyo'tivyādhī mahāratho jāyatāṃ dogdhrī dhenurvoḍhānaḍvānāśu: sapti: purandhiryoṣā jiṣṇū ratheṣṭhā: sabheyo yuvāsya yajamānasya vīro jāyatāṃ nikāme nikāma na: parjanyo varṣatu phalavatyo na oṣadhaya: pacyantāṃ yogakṣemo na: kalpatām||

(yaju. saṃ0 22 | 22)

O Paramātmā! Let our nation be enriched with all means; the learned BRAHMINS, knowledgeable class wear divine grace, the brave soldiers be enabled to shoot the target, the cows go on fulfilling the nation, by their sweet milk, the bulls bearing burden be strong to carry big loads, the steed be well speedy, treading on uneven paths, women be beautiful, wise and virtuous, welcoming the national heroes, returning homes, their tales of bravery echoing from all directions, the sons of the nation be engaged in sacrifices (Yajña and Service of the people) being brave, cultured and educated, humble and simple, performing righteous deeds, becoming and proving to be reliable support of the nation, the seasons of the year be friendly, the clouds bringing rains in plenty wherever and whenever needed, grains, herbs and ripened fruits have growth in abundance, and O PARAMĀTMĀ! fetch for us the needed, and save for us what we have. (YOGAKŚEMAM VAHĀMYAHAM)

❍ ❍ ❍

Vedic Peace – Invocation
वैदिक शान्तिपाठ

ॐ शं नो मित्रः शं वरुणः । शं नो भवत्वर्यमा । शं न इन्द्रो बृहस्पतिः । शं नो विष्णुरुरुक्रमः । नमो ब्रह्मणे । नमस्ते वायो । त्वमेव प्रत्यक्षं ब्रह्मासि । त्वामेव प्रत्यक्षं ब्रह्म वदिष्यामि । ऋतं वदिष्यामि । सत्यं वदिष्यामि । तन्मामवतु । तद्वक्तारमवतु । अवतु माम् । अवतु वक्तारम् । ॐ शान्तिः शान्तिः शान्तिः ॥ 1 ॥

(कृष्णयजुर्वेदीय)

oṃ śaṃ no mitra: śaṃ varuṇa: | śaṃ no bhavatvaryamā | śaṃ na indro bṛhaspati | śaṃ no viṣṇururukrama: | namo brahmaṇe | namaste vāyo | tvameva pratyakṣaṃ brahmāsi | tvāmeva pratyakṣaṃ brahma vadiṣyāmi | ṛtaṃ vadiṣyāmi | satyaṃ vadiṣyāmi tanmāmavatu | tadvaktāramavatu | avatu mām | avatu vaktāram | oṃ śānti: śānti: śānti: || 1 ||

(kṛṣṇayajurvedīya)

Om! May Mitra, (Presiding God of Day (दिन) and life-breath (प्राण)) be propitious and bring joyousness for us.

May Varuṇa, (presiding God of night (रात्रि) and passing wind (अपान), be propitious and bring joyousness for us.

May Aryamā (the chief God of eyes and the solar-sphere) be propitious and bring joyousness for us.

May Indra (King of Gods) and Brihaspati (presiding chief of power and arms, also Guru of Gods), together, be propitious and bring joyousness for us.

May Viṣṇu, the Supreme Being, with a very long one-foot-step, (त्रिविक्रम) (presideing God of feet), be propitious and bring joyousness for us.

O Brahm! (The Supreme Being) obeisances to Thee. O Vāyu! (God of winds, apparent as life-breath in all beings)

I offer obeisances to Thee. Thou art the apparent Brahm. Thou, alone shalt I call the apparent Brahm.

Thou, alone, shalt I call ṛta (scriptrual definitive meaning and perfect rhythm, as in entire nature. ऋदत् Thou shalt I call absolute reality (Truth). May that (Brahm) protect me. Let that (Brahm) protect the preceptor. Let me be protected. Let preceptor be protected. Om Peace! Peace!! Peace!!!

* * * * * * * * *

The Detailed Explanation: This is Krishna-Yajurvedic prayer offered, to the various Gods and to the Supreme Reality, Viṣṇu, before commencing vedic-studies, by the disciples and the preceptor, together. They pray, together, to the Sun (Mitra), the chief life-source of energy, light and enlightenment, and all produces; and above all life-breath (प्राण), to bring joyousness and be propitious to them. To Varuṇ, the presiding God of night and passing out wind from body (अपान) to bring joyousness and be propitious to them. To Aryamā, the chief God of eyes, and solar-sphere, which enable us to see the world around us and pursue our studies, to bring joyousness and be propitious to them.

To Indra and Brihaspati, together, the presiding deity, of strength and arms, and the deity of speech and intellect, respectively, to bring joyousness and be propitious to them.

And to Viṣṇu, the Supreme, the Over-Soul, with a very long one foot-step (त्रिविक्रम) and the God of feet, to bring joyousness and be propitious to them. O Almighty, the absolute Reality (ब्रह्म), obeisances to Thee.

O Vāyu! Obeisances to Thee. Thou (Vāyu, the life-breath in all beings) art the apparent Brahm (Reality).

Thou alone, shalt we call the apparent Brahm (Reality).

Thou alone, shalt we call Ṛta (ऋत्), (the scriptural definitive meaning and perfect rythm in nature).

Thou shalt we call Absolute Reality (सत्य) (Truth).

That (Oversoul) (परमात्मा) protect me.

Let That protect the preceptor.

Let me be protected. Let preceptor be protected.

And at the end of their prayer, they repeat, together, thrice.

Om Peace! Peace!! Peace!!!

Three categories of afflictions torment all mankind. They are known as 'Tṛtāp' (त्रिताप). These are 'Daihik' (दैहिक), 'Daivik' (दैविक), and 'Bhautik' (भौतिक) sufferings, we undergo in life, at one time or the other. 'Daihik' sufferings are also known as "ādhidaihik' or 'ādhyatmik'. These are physical sufferings. Inner desire and lustful thoughts, anger, greed, attachment, envy and hatred. Many times these are not visible in a person. Physical ailments, like cardiac-problems, cancer, lung-diseases and accidents causing physical injuries, apparent ones are all covered within 'daihik' or ādhyātmic sufferings.

The second category covers up the natural calamities over which one has no control. The strongest and most sound administration, any where, becomes altogether, helpless in the face of earthquakes, tsunami, hurricanes and floods. Sometimes, epidemics cause lot of havoc bringing confusion and loss of life.

And the third category of afflictions are caused to humanity by pesonal enemies of one another, warring nations or belligerent neighbours. And thus, three times repetition of 'Om Peace' (ॐ शान्ति) is offered in prayers, in order to ward off the three categories of all sufferings.

❍ ❍ ❍

ॐ सह नाववतु । सह नौ भुनक्तु । सह वीर्यं करवावहै ।
तेजस्वि नावधीतमस्तु मा विद्विषावहै ।
ॐ शान्तिः शान्तिः शान्तिः ॥ २ ॥

[कृष्णयजुर्वेदीय]

oṃ saha nāvavatu | saha nau bhunaktu | saha vīryaṃ karavāvahai | tejasvi nāvadhītamastu mā vidviṣāvahai | oṃ śānti: śānti: śānti: || 2 ||

[kṛṣṇayajurvedīya]

Om! O Oversoul (the absolute reality) save both of us, the disciple and the preceptor, in all possible manner, from all harm, make both of us, partake the fruits of knowledge together. May we (both of us) grow stronger and achieve strength, together. Let our acquired knowledge and studies be illuminating and enlightening for others as well. Let both of us, never be envious of each other or dislike each other.

Om Peace! Peace!! Peace!!! (Kṛṣṇayajurveda)

Om is a single syllable Brahm, the Supreme Reality. It is called 'Nād Brahm' also (नाद् ब्रह्म), when pronounced. It comprises three syllables, i.e. A U M. The Bhagavat Gita also says, "ॐ इत्येकाक्षर ब्रह्म।" The Vedic prayers and mantrās begin with pronouncing OM. Before commencing Vedic studies, the Guru and his students pray to the Oversoul (Paramātmā) to protect both of them from any possible harms, if any ever, during this course of their acquiring spiritual knowledge. They pray to the Almighty to nourish and raise them well, both of them. They make an earnest prayer to become stronger and get strengthened, together. If they ail, either the Guru or the disciples, their studies will get affected. They also pray to Paramātmā that no animosity arises among them at any point of time, which may cause interference in their studies and later on. Om Peace! Peace!! Peace!!!

The Guru (preceptor) and the disciples pray to the Oversoul for peace also, in order to ward off the three kinds of sufferings (Tritāpās) afflicting all mankind, daihik (physical), daivik (natural) and bhautik (wordly). A remarkable feature in the Vedic-prayer is repetition of urges. It is not to be taken without meaning. It works like a force or an impulse that urges. It is like a continuing impulse toward an activity or goal to attain. The two above Kṛṣṇa-yajurvedic mantrās discussed here, throw ample light on this feature. They pray for the well-being and to be taken care of, before initiation of studies, together, for enlightenment in onward life.

❍ ❍ ❍

ॐ यश्छन्दसामृषभो विश्वरूपः छन्दोभ्योऽध्यमृतात्संबभूव । स मेन्द्रो मेधया स्पृणोतु । अमृतस्य देव धारणो भूयासम् । शरीरं मे विचर्षणम् । जिह्वा मे मधुमत्तमा । कर्णाभ्यां भूरि विश्रुवम् । ब्रह्मणः कोशोऽसि मेधया पिहितः । श्रुतं मे गोपाय ।
ॐ शान्तिः शान्तिः शान्तिः ॥ ३ ॥

[कृष्णयजुर्वेदीय]

oṃ yaśchandasāmṛṣabho viśvarūpa: chandobhyo'dhyamṛtātsaṃbabhūva | sa mendro medhayā spṛṇotu | amṛtasya deva dhāraṇo bhūyāsam | śarīraṃ me vicarṣaṇam | jihvā me madhumattamā | karṇābhyāṃ bhūri viśruvam | brahmaṇa: kośo'si medhaya pihita: | śrutaṃ me gopāya |
oṃ śānti: śānti: śānti: || 10 ||

[kṛṣṇayajurvedīya]

Om is the highest and purest nectar derived mainly as the Supreme element from the Vedas. It is the most prominent of the 'Prāṇav rhythms', comprising all forms. This mantra is a prayer to the Prāṇav form Om (Oversoul Indra) to provide and bless us with the power of wisdom in order to imbibe the nectar of ultimate reality (Truth). It is a prayer to remain physically fit in all respects. The body should be free from any disease and illness of any kind, as in order to digest this purest nectar, the fitness of body is essential. The urger goes on to urge Paramātmā in the Om form (the one syllable Brahm) to make his tongue speak, softly and sweetly. He also prays to be able to hear more from the sense organs of hearing (intact ears). Our ears are the treasure-house of all assimilated knowledge of the Absolute Reality (Brahm). This treasure is hidden from our mundane intellect. O Paramātmā! whatever I have assimilated through my ears from my preceptors, protect it. Let it be kept intact. As the nectar of Truth, the Absolute Reality (Om), reaches as unmixed, unadulterated, in pure and real form because of the Guru. Let it remain intact in the treasure-house of ears, O Paramātmā!

And, as usual, there is a prayer for peace from the three 'Tritāpās' (त्रिताप), the physical, the natural and the mundane causes of sufferings in our life. The 'tritāpās' have already been discussed with the first mantra.

❍ ❍ ❍

ॐ अहं वृक्षस्य रेरिवा । कीर्तिः पृष्ठं गिरेरिव । ऊर्ध्वपवित्रो
वाजिनीव स्वमृतमस्मि । द्रविणꣳसवर्चसम् । सुमेधा अमृतोक्षितः ।
इति त्रिशङ्कोर्वेदानुवचनम् । ॐ शान्तिः शान्तिः शान्तिः ॥ ४ ॥
[कृष्णयजुर्वेदीय]

**oṃ ahaṃ vṛkṣasya rerivā | kīrti: pṛṣṭhaṃ
gireriva | ūrdhvapavitro vājinīva svamṛtamasmi |
draviṇa꞉savarcasam | sumedhā amṛtokṣita:| iti
triśaṅkorvedānuvacanam | oṃ śānti: śānti: śānti: || 4 ||
[kṛṣṇayajurvedīya]**

This mantra is an utterance by Triśanku*, who speaks this Kṛṣṇayajurvedic mantra after acquiring Vedic-knowledge. He says that he is the innermost initiator of the world in the tree-form, whose nature is to get cut or destroyed. This is true of the nature of a tree either to get cut or destroyed. This is how it comes to end, and this is true for the tree of this world also. He speaks of his glory and fame as high as the pinnacle of a mountain. He is utter-sacrosanct, which means that the sacrosanct Oversoul is the cause of his utter-position. He calls himself as purely immortal as the Sun is immortal with all the treasure of food in the world. He is the wealth with all its grandeur. He is the one with beautiful wisdom. He is deathless and imperishable also. This is followed by the prayer for peace made to Paramātmā in order to remain free from the three kinds of sufferings in the world as described in earlier mantrās. Om Peace! Peace!! Peace!!!

* Triśanku was a member of the Ikśvaku clan of kings. He was seized with an inordinate ambition to reach heaven in his physical frame. He went from place to place in order to accomplish this goal. He approached

Vasiṣtha, who laughed him out of his request. Trishanku went away haughtily. He sought Vasiṣtha's sons, when he wanted to command to peform huge sacrificial rituals as needed. They asked him not to attempt in this ridiculous aspiration. Triśanku was a king. He became aggressive and mendacious. The priests cursed him to become a 'candāla' for this sin. Viśwāmitra, the life-long arch rival of Vasiṣtha, accosted Triśanku and promised to help him. With intense concentration and great sacrifice, Viśwāmitra helped him to levitate, soar skyward and was soon out of sight. Viśwāmitra brags and boasts. No sooner had Viśwamitra said this than Triśanku started coming back. Many times Viśwamitra tried and sent him up, but he was pushed off by Indra, calling him a 'candāla'. At last Viśwamitra created a special heaven amidst the galaxies and sent Triśanku there. Triśanku lived there in his own heaven with his feet upward and head down. This position could not be changed by Viśwamitra.

❍ ❍ ❍

ॐ पूर्णमदः पूर्णमिदं पूर्णात्पूर्णमुदच्यते ।
पूर्णस्य पूर्णमादाय पूर्णमेवावशिष्यते ॥
ॐ शान्तिः शान्तिः शान्तिः ॥ ५ ॥

[शुक्लयजुर्वेदीय]

oṃ pūrṇamada: pūrṇamidaṃ pūrṇātpūrṇamudacyate |
pūrṇasya pūrṇamādāya pūrṇamevāvaśiṣyate ||
oṃ śānti: śānti: śānti: || 5 ||

[śuklayajurvedīya]

This mantra is a salutation to the absolute perfection of the Supreme Being. It is an invocation of the grace of the Om form of the Oversoul. Om is 'Sat-Cit-Ānand', the nature of Existence – Consciousness – Bliss. That Oversoul is perfect, wholly, in all respects, eternally. He is Existence – Consciousness – Bliss unified. These are aspects of the one Oversoul, Om. These aspects are non-different from each other. The Oversoul is an integrated whole of these three aspects — Existence – Consciousness – Bliss, which points out to the nature of the Supreme Being in His one form. This universe (Jagat) is also wholly perfect with Him, as the universe emanates from the Oversoul. A wholly perfect form of the universe is born out of the Perfect-Whole Paramātmā. The universe, being a derivative form of the Whole, does not affect the fullness of the wholly Perfect, Oversoul, and the perfection of the Oversoul remains, entirely, intact.

This mantra is also followed by invoking the grace of Paramātmā to maintain peace, warding off three kinds of sufferings, afflicting mankind. The three tāpās are the physical (Daihik) or (Ādhyātimic), the natural and the worldly (Bhautik) ones.

In the beginning and at the end of an Upaniṣad, a prayer for peace and well-being is recited. This is Śuklayajurvedic mantra in the beginning of 'Iśopaniṣad'. It describes about the grandeur and the fullness of the absolute Reality. It is a peace-recital by the Guru (Āchārya) and his disciples before commencing spiritual studies for enlightenment.

O O O

ॐ आप्यायन्तु ममाङ्गानि वाक् प्राणश्चक्षुः श्रोत्रमथो बलमिन्द्रियाणि च सर्वाणि । सर्वं ब्रह्मौपनिषदं माहं ब्रह्म निराकुर्यां मा मा ब्रह्म निराकरोदनिराकरणमस्त्वनिराकरणं मेऽस्तु । तदात्मनि निरते य उपनिषत्सु धर्मास्ते मयि सन्तु ते मयि सन्तु । ॐ शान्तिः शान्तिः शान्तिः ॥ ६ ॥

[सामवेदीय]

oṃ āpyāyantu mamāṅni vāk prāṇaścakṣu: śrotramatho balamindriyāṇi ca sarvāṇi | sarvaṃ brahmaupaniṣadaṃ māhaṃ brahma nirākuryāṃ mā mā brahma nirākarodanirākaraṇamastvanirākaraṇaṃ me'stu | tadātmani nirate ya upaniṣatsu dharmāste mayi santu te mayi santu | oṃ śānti: śānti: śānti: || 6 ||

[sāmavedīya]

It is a Sāmvedic prayer to the absolute Reality (Paramātmā) Om, for the fitness of the body. O Oversoul! Let all the limbs of man's body, speech, vital breath, eyes, ears and all the sense organs may be fully sound and energetic, comprising life-breath-group of 'panć Paramātmā' physical and mental energy and the inner glow. May all these be sound. Let me never be indifferent toward Brahm, and let that Brahm also not be indifferent toward me, and accept me forever. Let us have amicable relations forever, my relations with Him and His relations with me. Also whatever tenets of righteousness, as elucidated in all the Upaniṣads, let them always remain illuminated in me, may I be engaged endlessly, in the one chief-goal, knowledge of the Oversoul-enlightenment. Let those who are constantly in love with Brahm, reside in me, reside in me. This prayer is followed by the peace-recital of Om Peace! Peace!! Peace!!! The three tāpās, afflicting mankind do not spare even the seekers of Truth, hence this prayer to ward off the physical, the natural and the mundane kinds of sufferings, is repeatedly offered.

It is a special beauty of our Vedic-approach. While seeking enlightenment, one has to have all round alertness, so that no impdeiments can come in our way. A prayer is a very powerful medium toward physical or natural onslaughts. And as such, the physical fitness of a seeker is of paramount importance **'शरीर माद्यं खलु धर्म साधनम्'।** Body is the vehicle to reach the destination (Realisation of God), hence this prayer is for the soundness of various limbs of the body of the seeker. **'सोइ जानइ जेहि देहु जनाई'** He, alone, can know Him, whom He, so desires. It is, therefore, entreated that the Oversoul accepts the humble petitions of the seeker in order to achieve the desired goal of enlightenment.

❍ ❍ ❍

ॐ वाङ् मे मनसि प्रतिष्ठिता । मनो मे वाचि प्रतिष्ठितमाविरावीर्म एधि । वेदस्य म आणीस्थः श्रुतं मे मा प्रहासीः । अनेनाधीतेनाहोरात्रान्सन्दधाम्यृतं वदिष्यामि । सत्यं वदिष्यामि । तन्मामवतु । तद्वक्तारमवतु । अवतु मामवतु वक्तारमवतु वक्तारम् । ॐ शान्तिः शान्तिः शान्तिः ॥ ७ ॥

[ऋग्वेदीय]

oṃ vāṅ me manasi pratiṣṭhitā | mano me vāci pratiṣṭhitamāvirāvīrma edhi | vedasya ma āṇīstha: śrutaṃ me mā prahāsī: | anenādhītenāhorātrānsandadhāmyṛtaṃ vadiṣyāmi | satyaṃ vadiṣyāmi | tanmāmavatu | tadvaktāramavatu | avatu māmavatu vaktāramavatu vaktāram | oṃ śānti: śānti: śānti: || 7 ||

[ṛgvedīya]

It is a Rigvedic mantra invoking Paramātmā with a prayer for peace against all kinds of impediment which may likely arise in the midst of their vedic studies of scripture.

O Paramātmā! (the unified form of Existence–Consciousness – Bliss) Let my speech be established in my mind, and my mind be established in my speech, in order to have unison of both of them. Speech is to be similar to the thoughts, and the thoughts, the same as the speech. The speech and the thought should follow each other, mutually. O Self-radiant Oversoul! Manifest Thyself for me, remove the veil of illusion hanging before me. In such a state of things, the seeker asks the speech and the mind, in unison, to fetch the vedic-enlightenment which would enable to acquire deep vedic-knowledge. Whatever I have heard from the Guru and what I have experienced personally, let that not forsake me. May I keep that remembering forever, and I never forget that. I desire, ardently, to bring day and night together in this endeavour for studies. Studying and contemplating over Brahma-Enlightenment (ब्रह्मज्ञान), day and night; and no time ends up, futilely*.

* I shall always give utterence to noble and elevated words, devoid of blemish (महतम्). I shall speak, nothing but truth. Resolving this way, firmly, I pray, O Paramātmā (Oversoul)! Protect me. Protect my Guru. Protect me. Protect my preceptor, enlightening me, O Lord protect my preceptor.

This is followed by the prayer for peace in order to prevent the possible onslaughts of the three kinds of (tāpās) sufferings, if any, arising in future. (Om Peace! Peace!! Peace!!!)

मनस्येकं वचस्येकं कर्मण्येकं महात्मनाम् ।
मनस्यन्यत वचस्यन्यत कर्मण्य्ऽन्यत दुरात्मनाम् ॥

One, observing oneness of the mind, speech and action is a great-soul, i.e., Mahātmā; behaving otherwise, than this, one is nonthing else but a wicked-soul. This is like a whetstone, in order to test the goodness of a man.

❍ ❍ ❍

ॐ भद्रं नो अपि वातय मनः ॥
ॐ शान्तिः शान्तिः शान्तिः ॥ ८ ॥

[ऋग्वेदीय]

oṃ bhadraṃ no api vātaya mana: ||
oṃ śānti: śānti: śānti: || 8 ||

[ṛgvedīya]

O Paramātmā! Bless me for my well-being, purge my mind of ignoble thoughts and sins. Om Peace! Peace!! Peace!!!

It is a Rigvedic maxim, a prayer in brevity, beseeching the Ovesoul to take care of the welfare, i.e., health, happiness and prosperity of the seeker. It is impotant to have the purity of thoughts arising in our mind, hence the prayer is for the purgation of thoughts. It is also followed by entreatment for peace for obtaining freedom from the physical, the natural and the mundane suffering faced by all mankind.

❍ ❍ ❍

ॐ भद्रं कर्णेभिः शृणुयाम देवा भद्रं पश्येमाक्षभिर्यजत्राः ।
स्थिरैरङ्गैस्तुष्टुवाꣳसस्तनूभिर्व्यशेम देवहितं यदायुः ॥ स्वस्ति न
इन्द्रो वृद्धश्रवाः । स्वस्ति नः पूषा विश्ववेदाः । स्वस्ति नस्तार्क्ष्यो
अरिष्टनेमिः स्वस्ति नो बृहस्पतिर्दधातु ॥
ॐ शान्तिः शान्तिः शान्तिः ॥ ९ ॥

[अथर्ववेदीय]

oṃ bhadraṃ karṇebhi:śṛṇuyāma devā bhadraṃ paśyemākṣabhiryajatrā: | sthirairaṅgaistuṣṭuvā꞉sastanūbhirvyaśema devahitaṃ yadāyu: || svasti na indro vṛddhaśravā: | svasti na: pūṣā viśvavedā: | svasti nastārkṣyo ariṣṭanemi: svasti no bṛhaspatirdadhātu || oṃ śānti: śānti: śānti: || 9 ||

[atharvavedīya]

In the vedic-culture, it was a given practice of the scholars and their disciples to pray for the welfare of all humanity and that of their ownselves, in the Gurukuls, the seats of higher learning named after their Guru's names. In this mantra, they pray together. O Gods! (the presiding deities in different spheres) Let our ears hear auspicious and beneficial thoughts. Let our eyes also see all good and auspicious, and with our stout body and sound limbs, we keep entreating, as beneficent to Gods; such an age in life, may we enjoy, O Gods! The prayer is made, then, to the individual Gods. O highly renowned Indra! Be propitious to us. O Omniscient Sun! Be propitious to us. O Eagle! (Garuḍ) the dissipater of all bad omens, be propitious to us; and Brihaspati! The God of wisdom, Thou be propitious to us. Om Peace! Peace!! Peace!!! The three kinds of afflictions inflict all mankinds. These are very well known as the Daihik (the physical), the Daivik (the natural), and the Bhautik (the worldly) tāpās (त्रिताप). It is a prayer to the ultimate Reality (Om) to dissipate fully these three tāps, so that their studies in these seats of higher learning do not get affected in any manner.

It is a unique vedic-mantra. The prayer is a powerful and very popular one. In the known popular upaniṣads, this mantra appears in seventeen of them, all these being Atharv-vedic upaniṣads. The special kind of powerful vibrations arise in the recitation of this mantra by a group of scholars. Not only this, this is true of all Vedic treatises. The Vedas are the treatises on a systematic exposition of one's life's chief goal, seeking liberation, enjoying and living a fruitful and meaningful life. The gratification of senses alone cannot be the only purpose of a human life. That's the way of the animal world. Human life is considered the superb amongst all the 8.4 million species. The philosophical part of the Vedas is known as Vedānt. This is known as 'upaniṣad'. The upaniṣadas throw divine light on enlightenment of human beings in order to see one-self, to know one-self with the sole purpose of liberating one from the endless bondage of a cycle of reincarnation, passing through the harrowing experiences of 8.4 million species. They, therefore, speak repeatedly, for our welfare, in all respects, in order to achieve eternal happiness and eternal peace. As the ultimate Reality, Paramātmā, the Oversoul is 'Sat-Cit-Ānanda' (Existence – Consciousness – Bliss) in unison, inseparable, ONE, eternal, imperishable.

❍ ❍ ❍

ॐयो बह्माणं विदधाति पूर्वं यो वै वेदांश्च प्रहिणोति तस्मै ।
तꣳह देवमात्मबुद्धिप्रकाशं मुमुक्षुर्वै शरणमहं प्रपद्ये ॥
ॐ शान्तिः शान्तिः शान्तिः ॥ १० ॥

[कृष्णयजुर्वेदीय]

oṃyo bahmāṇaṃ vidadhāti pūrvaṃ yo vai vedāṃśca prahiṇoti tasmai |
taꣳha devamātmabuddhiprakāśaṃ mumukṣurvai śaraṇamahaṃ prapadye ||
oṃ śānti: śānti: śānti: || 10 ||

[kṛṣṇayajurvedīya]

This is a Kṛṣṇayajurvedic mantra with a prayer, after making obeisances, seeking the shelter of the Supreme Being. To Him, O Paramātmā (Oversoul)! Who begets Brahmā in the beginning, and who provides for Him (Brahmā) the Vedas, in the shelter of that illuminator of spiritual wisdom, I go with an ardent desire for emancipation from reincarnation.

In the beginning of the creation of the universe, Brahmā emanates from the navel of the Mahā Viṣṇu (The causal

Viṣṇu). And for enlightenment, in order to understand and know the ultimate Reality, the Vedas appear from His (Mahā Viṣṇu) breath, for Brahmā. The spiritual-wisdom cannot blossom and get manifested without the mercy of the Oversoul. His grace alone manifests this, and the seeker, therefore, needs complete devotion and unflinching faith, seeking His shelter.

With a prayer, seeking peace against the three kinds of afflictions, the physical, the natural and the mundane ones, the mantra invokes: Om Peace! Peace!! Peace!!!

Let there be peace, O Lord!

❍ ❍ ❍

Vedic Exhortation

अर्चत प्रार्चत प्रियमेधासो अर्चत ।
अर्चन्तु पुत्रका उत पुरं न धृष्णवर्चत ॥

[ऋक० ८ । ६९ । ८]

arcata prārcata priyamedhāso arcata |
arcantu putrakā uta puraṃ na dhṛṣṇavarcata || 10 ||

[Ṛgo 8|69|8]

O dear wise people! Worship Paramātmā. Worship Him. Worship in a special manner (with firm faith and devotion). Let your children also worship Him. All of you worship Paramātmā, who is like an impenetrable city or a fort.